TAX AND SPEND

Politics and Culture in Modern America

Series Editors: Margot Canaday, Glenda Gilmore, Michael Kazin, and Thomas J. Sugrue

Volumes in the series narrate and analyze political and social change in the broadest dimensions from 1865 to the present, including ideas about the ways people have sought and wielded power in the public sphere and the language and institutions of politics at all levels—local, national, and transnational. The series is motivated by a desire to reverse the fragmentation of modern U.S. history and to encourage synthetic perspectives on social movements and the state, on gender, race, and labor, and on intellectual history and popular culture.

TAX AND SPEND

THE WELFARE STATE, TAX POLITICS, AND THE LIMITS OF AMERICAN LIBERALISM

MOLLY MICHELMORE

PENN

UNIVERSITY OF PENNSYLVANIA PRESS

PHILADELPHIA

Published by
University of Pennsylvania Press
Philadelphia, Pennsylvania 19104-4112
www.upenn.edu/pennpress

Printed in the United States of America on acid-free paper
10 9 8 7 6 5 4 3 2 1

Library of Congress Cataloging-in-Publication Data
ISBN 978-0-8122-4388-8

TAX AND SPEND

THE WELFARE STATE, TAX POLITICS, AND
THE LIMITS OF AMERICAN LIBERALISM

MOLLY MICHELMORE

PENN

UNIVERSITY OF PENNSYLVANIA PRESS

PHILADELPHIA

Published by
University of Pennsylvania Press
Philadelphia, Pennsylvania 19104-4112
www.upenn.edu/pennpress

Printed in the United States of America on acid-free paper
10 9 8 7 6 5 4 3 2 1

Library of Congress Cataloging-in-Publication Data
ISBN 978-0-8122-4388-8

For Mammus and Pappas

CONTENTS

INTRODUCTION

TAX MATTERS

Taxes matter. They matter to every American worker whose paycheck is cut in half by state, local, and federal taxes. They matter to the millions of Americans who file income tax returns each year. They matter to the state, local, and national governments that depend on tax revenue to provide necessary public services. Taxes matter to economists and policymakers who seek to manage the national economy, to control inflation, and to combat unemployment. They matter to the millions of older Americans who rely on Social Security and Medicare, and to the workers whose payroll taxes fund those entitlement programs. Taxes matter to political office seekers—liberal Democrats and conservative Republicans alike—who must balance promises to protect the rights and interests of ordinary taxpayers with other policy priorities. Indeed, taxes and tax talk now dominate domestic policymaking. In 1960, the Democratic Party platform devoted 9 sentences to taxes, and the GOP platform only two. By 2008, the Democrats dedicated 33 sentences and the GOP almost 80 to tax policy.[1] Today's politicians are as likely to speak to Americans as *taxpayers* as they are to address them as citizens or voters.

America's obsession with taxes paralleled the growth of the modern welfare state. Broadly defined to include the myriad ways the federal government protects citizens from what President Franklin D. Roosevelt once described as the "hazards and vicissitudes" of life, the welfare state has grown by leaps and bounds over the last eighty years.[2] At the turn of the twenty-first century, government-sponsored social programs accounted for more than a third of the federal budget; more than 90 percent of Americans relied to some greater or lesser degree on public monies for their social and economic security.[3] Today, as in the past, most of the recipients of federal aid are not the suspect "welfare queens" of the popular imagination, but rather middle-class homeowners, salaried professionals, and retirees. To an extent rarely recognized, much less openly acknowledged, the American middle class is, in fact, the product of almost a century of targeted social and economic policies. Yet, most Americans are far more likely to see themselves as the overburdened victims of the tax code than as the beneficiaries of government programs that have helped to secure economic security and mobility for the vast middle-class majority.

Americans' hostility toward taxes in general, and toward the federal income tax in particular, has marked and fueled the political right turn of the last four decades, as conservative leaders have successfully translated popular frustration over taxes into a broader rejection of the activist state.[4] By the middle of the 1970s, the GOP had developed and popularized a political and policy agenda that attacked federal efforts to redress social and economic inequality as ineffective, counterproductive, and even immoral. "Preoccupied with expanding eligibility and . . . benefits," the Republican National Committee declared in 1978, Democratic liberals had succeeded only in "creating a new caste of Americans . . . free from basic wants, but almost totally dependent on the state, with little or no hope or prospect of breaking free."[5] President Ronald Reagan put it even more succinctly in his First Inaugural Address, insisting that government was "not the solution" to the nation's problems. Government itself *was* the problem.[6]

Yet, the GOP has singularly failed in its efforts to roll back the welfare state. The largest and most expensive parts of the American social safety net—Medicare and Social Security—survived Reagan-era budget cuts. Only two major welfare programs—public service jobs and general revenue sharing—disappeared entirely.[7] What is more, the GOP has not only failed to shrink the state but has actively encouraged its growth. In 2003, for example, President George W. Bush and the Republican Congress added a new, hugely expensive and unpaid-for prescription drug benefit to the existing Medicare program.[8] All told, the U.S. government today spends more money than ever on programs to ensure the economic security and well-being of its citizens.[9] Perhaps even more surprising, the American public continues to support the most basic goals of the welfare state, even as faith in government institutions has been in free fall since the mid-1960s.[10] According to a 2011 Harris Poll, the vast majority of Americans oppose cutting spending on retirement security programs, education, and health care. Indeed, support for specific government programs has actually *increased* in the decades since Reagan took office.[11]

This is the basic paradox of contemporary American politics. Americans

hate government, but demand and expect, almost as a matter of right, the privileges, security, and mobility that government offers.[12] *Tax and Spend* aims to unravel this apparent contradiction by analyzing the development of tax and spending policy from the New Deal of the 1930s through the Reagan revolution of the 1980s. Neither taxes nor spending alone can explain the rightward drift of American politics in the late twentieth and early twenty-first centuries. Only in the context of a politicized struggle between the rights of taxpayers and the claims of what one official in President Lyndon Johnson's White House once called "tax eaters" on the welfare rolls, does this transformation start to make sense.[13] Focusing on two key instruments of economic and social policy—the federal income tax and Aid to Families with Dependent Children (AFDC)—this study provides a new interpretation not only of postwar liberalism—its well-known failures, contradictions, and limitations, as well as its often forgotten successes—but also of the conservative reaction that has both replaced and depended on it.

AFDC—most commonly referred to simply as "welfare"—has played a critical role in Americans' understanding of the state. Created as part of the landmark Social Security Act of 1935, Aid to Dependent Children, AFDC's original name, allowed the federal government to supplement state-run programs providing a bare subsistence income to poor women raising children alone.[14] The program was never large or particularly costly. By 1994, two years before Congress finally abolished it, spending for AFDC amounted to less than 2 percent of the country's entire social welfare budget.[15] Yet, welfare has long held political implications disproportionate to its size or its cost to the average taxpayer. As early as 1949, the national press had raised alarms about "welfare chiselers" stealing the "taxpayer blind" by using public funds to purchase "whiskey, marijuana and tropical fish."[16] By the mid-1950s, lawmakers, the press, and the public had embraced a narrowed definition of the term "welfare," using it almost exclusively to refer to need-based cash assistance to the very poor.[17] The visibility and political vulnerability of welfare stands in stark contrast to the invisibility and relative security of much of what might be called the middle-class welfare state of social insurance entitlements and various forms of tax spending. Indeed, the visibility of AFDC, combined with the suspect racial and moral character of its recipients—by the early 1960s, nonwhite, unmarried mothers made up a disproportionate share of the welfare rolls—have played a critical role not only in obscuring the extent to which government policies have underwritten middle-class prosperity and mobility, but also in diminishing support for the liberal state itself. Conservatives in particular have benefited politically from Americans' truncated definition of welfare. As the economy faltered in the 1970s, the GOP successfully exploited public hostility toward AFDC and AFDC recipients to capture the votes of middle-class homeowners and taxpayers who saw themselves as the casualties of the "tax and spend" liberal state.

That the American right has capitalized on popular antipathy toward taxes and welfare to rebrand itself as the populist defender of taxpayers' rights, of course, is not news. What is more surprising, perhaps, is that in doing so the Republican Party has borrowed a page out of the Democratic Party's playbook. Throughout the postwar period, liberal state builders repeatedly defended low tax rates on ordinary Americans as an essential element of the economic security promised by the liberal state. Liberal antitax logic, apparent even at the birth of the welfare state in the 1930s, at first reflected state builders' assessment of the challenges posed by popular resistance to new taxes, but soon became an essential element of the liberal social compact itself. Even during the supposed Big Bang periods of postwar state building in the 1930s and 1960s, liberal presidents with unprecedented Democratic majorities in both houses of Congress refused to tie new social benefits directly to tax increases on the majority of Americans. President Roosevelt rejected any effort to expand the federal income tax base to pay for the New Deal; Lyndon Johnson likewise simultaneously launched the Great Society and championed a sweeping income tax *cut*. From Roosevelt's pledge to "quit this business of relief," to President Bill Clinton's promise to bring the "era of Big Government" to an end by "ending welfare as we know it," liberal policymakers have combined a marked ambivalence toward welfare with a spirited defense of individual taxpayers' rights.[18] American liberals may have promised to give citizens a Fair Deal, to create a Great Society on the New Frontier, to remedy the poverty of the Other America, and to remove the barriers that have for too long walled some Americans within a "gate-less poverty," but these same liberals consistently coupled these commitments to a policy agenda that promised to protect taxpayers' "rights" to economic security, individual mobility, *and* low taxes.[19] Focusing on the politics of taxation—rather than on the politics of spending alone—illuminates the continuity between the so-called right turn of the late twentieth century and the liberal consensus that preceded it. The supposed conservative backlash of the late twentieth and early twenty-first centuries has deep roots. Reagan's revolution and his promise to slash welfare spending for the poor in the name of ordinary taxpayers did not break radically with the past. Rather it built on and fully realized the antitax logic first articulated by liberal state builders in the New Deal and World War II eras.

Building the Tax and Welfare State

The Great Depression marked a watershed in American state building. As social worker Josephine Brown noted, between 1929 and 1939 more was done in the area of "public welfare than in the [previous] three hundred years."[20] Yet, even at the height of the Depression, liberals' commitment to public welfare was ambivalent at best. The federal government did not provide any direct assistance to individuals until 1933, when President Roosevelt made good on his campaign promise to strike a New Deal with the American people by setting up the Federal Emergency Relief Administration (FERA), which, together with other early New Deal programs, including the Civil Works Administration and the Civilian Conservation Corps, provided much-needed cash and jobs to nearly 28 million people.[21] But, the FERA and other forms of direct relief sat uneasily with some members of the Roosevelt administration and with the president himself. In 1934, worried that "continued dependence on relief" would induce a "spiritual and moral disintegration fundamentally destructive to the national fibre," Roosevelt offered Americans not relief but rather "security of a livelihood," "security against the hazards and vicissitudes of life," and "security of decent homes."[22]

The Social Security Act of 1935, the "cornerstone" of the American welfare state, aimed to realize this commitment to the economic security of the "men, women, and children of the nation."[23] Comprising five major programs—contributory Old Age and Unemployment Insurance (OAI and UI) and federally subsidized but state-run Old Age Assistance (OAA), Aid to Dependent Children (ADC), and Aid to the Blind (AB)—the Social Security Act promised to "promote recovery . . . develop a more stable economic system" and assure "assistance to the victims of insecurity and maladjustment."[24] Contributory social insurance lay at the heart of this new economic security system; most New Dealers saw categorical assistance as a temporary expedient necessary to meet the extreme need created by the Depression itself.[25]

The shape of the New Deal welfare state—and in particular its reliance on regressive, but hidden, payroll taxes to fund its most significant policy innovations—reflected the importance of tax politics to liberal policymaking. New Dealers recognized the need to manage popular opposition to new federal income taxes and to insulate the administration from the kind of tax-payer hostility that had produced a vibrant and powerful grassroots antitax movement in the early 1930s. Rejecting proposals to expand the income tax base to raise new revenues, liberal state builders instead relied on indirect or hidden taxes—including regressive consumption and payroll levies—to off-set the costs of New Deal spending programs. Social Security financing, and the administration's insistence that OAI and UI be financed out of dedicated payroll taxes, also reflected Roosevelt's own preference—shared by many of his key advisors—for a fiscally conservative welfare state.[26] As historian Julian Zelizer has pointed out, the president believed that fiscal conservatism would not only answer the demands of the financial and investment communities, but would also appeal to an electorate who "still saw balanced budgets as a symbol of stable governments" and "shared the traditional American aver-sion to taxation."[27] Indeed, New Deal fiscal conservatives, including Treasury Secretary Henry Morgenthau and Budget Director Lewis Douglas, as well as many members of the new Social Security Board (SSB), argued that con-tributory social insurance alone could provide a secure basis for the kind of economic security promised by the president in his 1935 State of the Union address. Hoping to protect these key economic security policies against anti-tax politics, some of the Social Security program's supporters even went so far as to argue that OAI and UI would ultimately relieve the average taxpayer, not to mention state and local governments, of the "burden of relief."[28]

Of course, the new unemployment and old age insurance programs *did* rely on federal taxes and *did* require a vast expansion of federal responsi-bility for the well-being of large groups of American citizens. But liberal state builders carefully distinguished between social insurance and the wel-fare and relief programs most hoped would disappear once the crisis of the Great Depression had passed. The administration and members of the new SSB usually cast payroll taxes as a kind of insurance premium that entitled contributors to a certain annuity as a matter of right. According to one SSB member, for example, the requirement that "workers and their employers. . . contribute a small portion of their earnings" to cover the "natural risks of life" might best be compared to taking out "insurance against fire and theft."[29] Defended, sold, and understood as more like private insurance than public welfare, OAI—and to a slightly lesser extent UI—have not only escaped the hostility heaped on other forms of public provision, but have often fallen out-side the public's understanding of welfare altogether.

The administration's commitment to this annuity fiction stemmed in part from its need to shore up public support for the Social Security bill and to protect the programs from popular resistance to new or higher taxes. The widespread demand for old age pensions—made most apparent in the groundswell of support for the Townsend Movement's proposal to provide all Americans over age sixty with a $200 monthly pension—did not necessarily translate into public support for new taxes.[30] Indeed, tax revolts and strikes were common throughout the early 1930s, as farmers, real estate agents, and property owners came together to form grassroots taxpayers' leagues to resist state and local property tax laws. These groups wreaked havoc on municipal budgets. By 1932, for example, Chicago taxpayers' refusal to meet their property tax obligations had cost the city $500 million in uncollected tax revenues and forced local policemen, firefighters, and teachers to go without pay.[31] Described by one reporter as the "nearest thing to a political revolution in this country," these tax protests not only inspired local and state officials to sponsor tax limitation laws but also profoundly shaped welfare and social security policy at the national level.[32]

The White House was not alone in designing its economic security programs to minimize taxpayer resistance. The Townsend plan, for example, would have paid for old age pensions with a new federal sales tax—a hugely regressive form of taxation far less visible than either income or property taxes. Even the more radical alternatives to the administration's economic security bill, including Senator Huey P. Long's populist Share Our Wealth scheme and the Workers' Bill sponsored by Minnesota Representative Ernest Lundeen, would have paid for new programs only by taxing the incomes of the wealthy.[33] The administration's reliance on the payroll tax to finance its most significant welfare policy initiatives—and its commitment to the annuity fiction—successfully muted taxpayer resistance to these programs and to the tax dollars used to fund them by distinguishing between social insurance *premiums* and the *taxes* that financed other forms of public welfare.[34]

Other elements of the 1930s taxing state reflect New Dealers' willingness to tailor revenue and spending proposals to meet perceived popular hostility to new and direct federal taxes. The processing, excise, luxury, and other consumer taxes that undergirded the 1930s tax regime, for example, often escaped public notice. Although these hidden taxes generated a considerable amount of revenue, and cost even the poorest taxpayers upward of $100 per year, they did not often register as taxes, nor did they generate any significant degree of tax consciousness.[35] According to one 1939 survey, for example, almost a quarter of those polled believed that they "didn't happen to pay any taxes." Not surprisingly, lower-income taxpayers—who did not pay any federal income tax thanks to high income exemption levels—were least likely to see themselves as taxpayers. While 93 percent of upper-income voters and 81 percent of middle-income voters identified themselves as taxpayers, only 40 percent of lower-income voters did so.[36]

New Dealers' reluctance to risk a taxpayer revolt alone does not explain their commitment to a fiscally conservative welfare state grounded in wage-based social insurance. Equally important were liberals' own understandings of the sources of economic instability and their commitment to an economic security model grounded in the experience of white male industrial workers.[37] The architects of the New Deal welfare state believed that the social insurance programs put in place in 1935 would eventually expand to provide a meaningful degree of economic security for *all* Americans. Most New Dealers, from the president on down, viewed the categorical assistance programs created by the 1935 law as temporary and residual, and predicted that they, like other forms of direct relief, would disappear as the economy recovered and the social insurance system grew. This conviction that a "comprehensive, contributory social insurance system covering all of those economic hazards to which people are exposed" would reduce, if not eliminate the "residual load of public assistance" survived the Great Depression.[38] Even those liberal policymakers most invested in the public assistance programs, including members of the American Public Welfare Association (APWA), favored an insurance-based model. According to the APWA's legislative consultant, Elizabeth Wickenden, the organization always lent its "strongest support to Social Security as a means of preventing the need for assistance."[39] More an article of faith than an empirically tested proposition, the idea that the need for public assistance would soon "wither away" in the face of economic growth and a vibrant, wage-based social safety net only grew stronger in the 1940s as the World War II and postwar economic booms gave lie to Depression-era concerns that the United States had reached a point of "secular stagnation," "sick recoveries," "depressions which feed on themselves," and a "seemingly immovable core of unemployment."[40] By the early 1950s, labor representatives and business groups agreed that a more comprehensive system of social insurances would allow the federal government to "begin an orderly withdrawal from the field of providing assistance to the needy."[41] President Harry Truman gave this idea the presidential seal of approval in 1951, when he announced that the "basic purpose of public assistance" had "always been to supplement our social insurance system."[42]

Although it initially left large numbers of Americans unprotected against economic insecurity, contributory social insurance anchored liberal state builders' plans for the eventual expansion of the social safety net. Social Security advocates in the SSB, and later the Social Security Administration, wary of possible taxpayer resistance to new income taxes, argued that any alternative to contributory financing—whether endorsed by liberal friends of the welfare state or by its conservative opponents—would weaken political incentives to expand this basic economic security system. As SSB Chairman Arthur Altmeyer later admitted, like many Social Security experts he believed that any proposal to supplement contributory social insurance benefits with flat-rate pensions paid for out of general revenues would "weaken the incentive for uncovered groups to be covered under a contributory social insurance system."[43] Altmeyer was, at least in part, prescient in his predictions. Once it began to pay out benefits, this contributory arrangement created new political constituencies interested in not only preserving but improving current benefits. Lawmakers' desire to meet the public demand for higher benefits and their eagerness to keep payroll taxes relatively low created an almost irresistible pressure to expand social insurance coverage to groups— including agricultural and domestic workers—excluded under the original legislation.[44] Indeed, the eventual expansion of OAI did allow OAA—once the largest and most expensive of the programs created by the Social Security Act—to more or less wither away.

This commitment to wage-based social insurance and the widespread acceptance in policymaking circles of the "withering away fallacy" reflected liberal state builders' unacknowledged racial and gendered assumptions and biases.[45] Committed to an economic and family model that viewed women's work as secondary or even deviant, the architects of the Social Security system presumed that the expansion of wage-based social insurance would provide economic security to vulnerable women and children by virtue of their connection to a wage-earning man. Because they understood economic insecurity largely in terms of the Depression-era crisis in male employment, social insurance experts like Abraham Epstein designed both OAI and UI specifically to secure "the worker and his family against the economic emergencies resulting from the temporary or permanent loss of a job through unemployment, sickness, invalidity or old age."[46] That this male-breadwinner model was already becoming obsolete for much of the working class, and had never applied to nonwhite families, did little to dislodge these gendered assumptions from the center of New Deal social policy. As Altmeyer later told the American Federation of Labor—itself deeply committed to the male-breadwinner model and the family-wage system—the expansion of Social Security would "protect *everybody* in the United States who is dependent on his earnings—everybody and *his* family."[47]

Nor did liberal state builders fully consider how the new economic security systems might affect African Americans. Understanding the problem of racial inequality largely in terms of class politics, leading liberals like Harold Ickes insisted that the "Negro problem" be seen primarily in terms of the "greater problem of American citizens generally who are at or below the line in decency or comfort."[48] While many leading black organizations endorsed this color-blind approach to Depression-era policymaking, the strategy failed to open up new economic opportunities to the black community as a whole. White workers determinedly and sometimes violently policed the color line, even laying claim to work previously reviled as "Negro jobs." Unchecked by New Deal labor laws, and in combination with the race-laden occupational exclusions written into the 1935 Social Security Act, persistent labor-market discrimination undermined nonwhite workers' claims to any form of wage-based economic security even as it relegated them to more debased forms of public assistance and set the stage for the racially charged "welfare crisis" of the 1960s and 1970s.[49]

Perhaps even more significantly, the architects of the New Deal welfare state, aware of popular resistance to new taxes on any but the richest Americans, deliberately obscured the relationship between the obligations and the rights of citizenship and never asked ordinary taxpayers to *pay* for the economic security many soon came to expect as a matter of right. In 1932, President Herbert Hoover's treasury secretary Ogden Mills had noted that Americans were "accustomed to high exemptions and very low rates on smaller taxable incomes."[50] The New Deal did little to change this. Despite the unprecedented demand placed on federal coffers by the explosion of New Deal spending programs, and in spite of his own fiscally conservative inclinations, Roosevelt resisted any attempt to include the middle classes in the federal income tax system. Base-broadening tax reform did gain ground among some progressive reformers and liberal economists in the mid-1930s. Championed in Congress by Senator Robert La Follette, a Wisconsin Republican with impeccable progressive credentials, base broadening offered another way to attack the problem of "the maldistribution of wealth and income" and to "rebuild society."[51] Disappointed that the administration lacked the "guts to tax the people," reformers pointed out that higher income taxes on the very

rich and corporations would neither offset the costs of desperately needed social welfare programs nor promote any significant redistribution of economic
power.[52] Efforts to expand the tax base bore little fruit, however, and the public remained hostile to any proposal to tax what Senator Long called the "little
people." According to one 1939 poll, for example, the public overwhelmingly
opposed taxing middle- and lower-income earners.[53] Understandably reluctant to embrace such a "hopelessly unpopular" policy, the Roosevelt administration instead continued to rely on revenues generated by regressive, but
largely hidden consumption and payroll taxes, and to hammer away in public
at the so-called "malefactors of great wealth."[54]

But if liberal state builders had originally eschewed popular taxation for
largely political reasons, by the end of the 1930s leading New Dealers had
begun to incorporate low tax rates on the majority of Americans into the
liberal social compact itself. The recession of 1937, which saw the Dow Jones
Industrial Average drop by 48 percent in only seven months, decimated industrial production and corporate profits and added an additional 4 million
workers to the already swollen unemployment rolls. The so-called Roosevelt
Recession also transformed American liberalism by bringing to the fore a
new economic language that insisted on understanding tax and spending
policy not in terms of distributional consequences or the balance between
revenues and spending, but rather in terms of long-term macroeconomic
consequences.[55] Increasingly convinced that the key to recovery, long-term
stability, and even economic growth lay in stimulating consumer demand,
but constrained by perceived opposition to new, direct spending programs,
liberals made low individual income tax rates on ordinary citizens central to
their promise of economic and social security.[56] World War II, which required
the expansion of the federal income tax base into the ranks of the middle and
working classes even as it gave lie to New Deal era fears about long-term stagnation in the American economy, only reinforced liberals' growing commitment to creating economic growth and stability through low tax rates, hidden
spending, and wage-based social insurance.

Mobilization for World War II completed the transformation of New Deal
liberalism. The Revenue Act of 1942, which together with the Social Security
Act laid the foundations of the modern American taxing and welfare state,
effectively transformed the federal income tax from a class tax to a mass tax
by bringing the majority of Americans into the state as taxpayer-citizens.[57]
To sell this new tax regime, the architects of the 1942 bill depended on the
war and on what historian Mark Leff has termed "the politics of sacrifice."[58]

Almost as soon as the bill was signed, the Treasury Department launched an intensive public relations campaign to encourage all Americans to pay their "taxes to beat the Axis." The administration enlisted popular entertainment figures, including Irving Berlin, Roy Rogers, Danny Kaye, and even Walt Disney's Donald Duck to remind American voters that their income tax money would "keep democracy on the march."[59] Blaming rising taxes on "Hitler and Hirohito" and insisting that the "real authors of our tax burden" could be found in Berlin and Tokyo, the Roosevelt administration sought to capitalize on broad public support for the American war effort.[60]

This campaign was remarkably successful. Even as the tax bite increased, the vast majority of Americans believed that their tax burden was fair. According to the Office of War Information, many saw the income tax as a way for those on the home front to assist in the war effort.[61] But the emphasis on the relationship between World War II and the federal income tax further divorced federal taxes and the burdens they placed on ordinary workers from other public priorities. In fact, the Treasury Department's publicity campaign often deliberately distanced the new tax regime from the administration's previous domestic spending priorities. Just as Roosevelt had declared in 1943 that "Dr. Win-the-War" had replaced "Dr. New Deal," Treasury pamphlets highlighted reductions in nonwar expenditures to counter accusations that the new taxes would be used to fund additional New Deal social programs.[62]

By transforming the majority of American workers into taxpayers whose economic security might be threatened, rather than enhanced, by new tax-and-transfer programs, the 1942 Revenue Act undermined popular support for the kind of cradle-to-grave welfare state liberal policymakers had hoped to build once the Depression and war emergencies had passed. New Deal state builders had gambled that the social insurance programs put in place in 1935 would one day clear the way for a more universal system of social provision and provide a genuine guarantee of economic security for all Americans. Throughout the late 1930s and early 1940s, liberal activists and policymakers had hoped and planned to transform the existing Social Security system into a universal and national welfare state that would protect "everybody in the United States who is dependent on his earnings" against "loss or interruption of earning power."[63] Well aware of the limitations of the existing patchwork of social insurance and categorical public assistance programs that left "thousands of needy persons . . . without any public help at all," policymakers like the SSB's Ewan Clague hoped to close the sizeable holes in the New Deal social safety net.[64] In Congress, Democratic Senators James Murray of Montana and Robert Wagner of New York, working with Michigan Democratic Congressman John Dingell, introduced legislation in both 1943 and 1945 to create a cradle-to-grave welfare state that would "complete the framework of protection against economic insecurity."[65]

This Third New Deal never happened, as conservatives in Congress joined with a resurgent business lobby to beat back these efforts. Neither the 1943 version of the Wagner-Murray-Dingell bill, nor its 1945 iteration even made it out of committee. Although most analyses of these bills focus on the American Medical Association's successful campaign against socialized medicine, tax politics were equally important in undermining congressional and popular support for a "cradle-to-grave" welfare state.[66] Opponents routinely argued that expanding the Social Security program would only layer new taxes on top of existing obligations and hamper reconversion efforts in the postwar period by putting a "penalty" on any employer who wished to hire "a new man."[67] Rejecting the insurance imagery so carefully constructed by liberal state builders in the 1930s and early 1940s, critics of new welfare programs called attention to their potential costs, arguing that the taxes required to pay for the programs would stifle American economic output, impose unprecedented tax burdens on ordinary workers, and jeopardize Americans' newfound expectations of economic security and prosperity. Liberals' emerging commitment to the politics of growth, and the absence of any political tradition linking the obligations of citizenship to its benefits, made it difficult to counter these arguments successfully.

Indeed, in more ways than one, conservative opposition to the Wagner-Murray-Dingell bills and other comprehensive economic and social security proposals depended on both the institutional structure and ideological framing of the New Deal welfare state itself. Throughout the 1930s and early 1940s, Social Security experts carefully and repeatedly cast both OAI and UI as distinct from and superior to other forms of public welfare. SSB members often favorably compared the independence engendered by contributory social insurance entitlements to the degradation that allegedly stemmed from welfare "dependency." While social insurance would allow a "spinster lady and a self-respecting man" to receive an income as a "matter of right," only the very "down and out" could lay claim to welfare benefits.[68] Such language, mobilized to protect and expand the social insurance heart of the New Deal welfare state, ultimately called into question the legitimacy of other forms of public spending. The annuity fiction likewise proved a double-edged sword. Social Security advocates' success in packaging the payroll tax as a kind of premium helped, as Roosevelt had predicted in 1941, to give recipients a kind of "legal, moral and political right" to collect benefits and to insulate both the retirement and unemployment programs against retrenchment.[69] But, while the payroll tax did allow, and even require, lawmakers to improve on *existing* benefits it did not generate much support for new kinds of entitlements or for the activist state in general.[70]

The policy choices made in the crisis years of the Great Depression and World War II effectively hid the public welfare aspects of liberals' most impressive policy achievements and decoupled the obligations of citizenship, made most apparent in the federal income tax, from its benefits. By the end of the 1940s, most liberals had abandoned any hope of creating a cradle-to-grave welfare state, instead settling on a political and policy strategy that relied on earmarked payroll taxes, automatic revenues generated by economic growth, and a system of "hidden" tax spending to pay for new programs or to expand existing ones. While this strategy allowed policymakers to overcome both ideological opposition and institutional barriers to new forms of social welfare, such hidden forms of economic assistance did not generate popular support for the welfare state or for the political actors who had helped to build it.[71] In fact, the very success of these stealth programs in expanding economic security and opportunity to a wide swath of Americans, in combination with a bipartisan defense of low tax rates has, for more than sixty years, undermined support for the activist state by allowing the middle-class to see itself as the victim, rather than the beneficiary, of liberal tax and welfare policies.

Outline of the Book

Moving in roughly chronological order, *Tax and Spend* traces the development of what I have called the American tax and welfare state from its origins in the Great Depression through the end of the Reagan revolution of the 1980s. New Deal and World War II tax and welfare policy at once acknowledged the federal government's responsibility to provide Americans with a certain degree of economic security and incorporated the majority of citizens into the state as *taxpayers*. Committed to a welfare state grounded in wage-based social insurance, constrained by popular opposition to new income taxes, and optimistic about the possibility and effects of economic growth, New Dealers laid the institutional foundations of a liberal social compact that pledged both economic security *and* low individual tax rates. As I show in

Chapter 1, the return of prosperity after the war gave conservatives in the GOP and the business community an opportunity to take advantage of certain contradictions embedded in the New Deal and World War II social compact to roll back the liberal tax and welfare state by appealing to the self-interest of newly empowered taxpayers. Liberal state builders met these challenges to existing tax and welfare policies by eschewing the defense of direct forms of welfare provision in favor of hidden tax subsidies and managed economic growth. This strategic choice, while more than understandable in the context of Cold War-era hostility toward statist politics, and liberals' genuine faith in Keynesian economics, nonetheless undermined the liberal project as a whole by weakening the link between the taxes paid by the majority of Americans and the benefits they received from the state.

The policy institutions and ideological commitments formed in the New Deal, World War II, and immediate postwar periods informed and constrained liberal politics over the following decades. Liberal tax and spending policy in the 1960s reflected policymakers' faith in the free market's ability to guarantee the social and economic security of all Americans. Focusing on the Revenue Act of 1964—better known as the Kennedy-Johnson tax cut—and the War on Poverty, Chapter 2 shows how liberals' commitment to the market limited their ability to respond to changes in the domestic and international political economy and further undercut popular support for the activist state. The collapse of the American economy in the late 1960s and 1970s illuminated all too clearly the limits of mainstream American liberalism. Chapters 3 and 4 examine the collapse of the New Deal order, liberals' failure to reconstruct an ideologically coherent political majority, and the GOP's transformation into what supply-side enthusiast Jude Wanniski once called the "Santa Claus of tax reduction."[72] The brand of tax politics embraced by Republican leaders in the mid-1970s nationalized earlier popular opposition to taxation and resonated powerfully with members of a silent majority buffeted by the era's relative economic decline.

The book concludes with an examination of the tax and spending policies that animated the Reagan revolution of the 1980s and helped popularize conservative politics in the United States. Close examination of GOP tax and spending policies and politics before, during, and after President Ronald Reagan's tenure shows how this conservative revival depended on, and reproduced, a great deal of the social compact negotiated between the state and its citizens in the 1940s, 1950s, and 1960s. Dependent as it was on both the ideology and the institutions of postwar liberalism, the Reagan administration failed—with few exceptions—to dismantle or even significantly reduce the size of the federal state. Tax and welfare politics, which had sustained the postwar liberal consensus and justified its replacement by a more conservative policy settlement, reached its limit during the first years of the 1980s. The exhaustion of this politics has helped produce the contemporary political stalemate, as neither liberals nor conservatives have managed to construct a lasting, and ideologically coherent, electoral majority.

Understanding the development of the tax and welfare state—and the politics it engendered—reveals the relationship between the two major political transformations of the past seventy years: the rise of the activist state and the emergence of a powerful and invigorated conservative movement, capable of generating popular support (at least at election time), and concerned to confront, and, in some cases, roll back, the institutions of the liberal state.[73] The tax cut agenda of the early 1970s that helped to drive the Reagan revolution drew much of its force from liberals' success in hiding the state in plain view and in decoupling the burden of taxes from the benefits it purchased for the majority of American citizens. That conservatives have been able to co-opt liberal commitments to individual rights, low tax rates, and the preservation of the American Dream guaranteed by the postwar social compact speaks to both the strengths and the weaknesses of postwar liberalism itself.

CHAPTER 1

DEFENDING THE WELFARE
AND TAXING STATE

I n January 1947, Thomas Waxter, chief of the Baltimore Department of
Welfare (BDW) announced cutbacks in the city's public assistance programs and called on a local, nongovernmental group to investigate his
department and recommend measures to "remedy any defects" in the existing system.[1] Only weeks later, the city's largest daily newspaper, the *Baltimore
Sun*, premiered the first in a seven-part series of front-page articles expos-
ing how fraud, inexperience, and lax administration in the BDW had already
taken considerable sums "out of the taxpayer's pocket."[2] That same year, in
New York City, the local press's discovery of a few families living in apparent
luxury at public expense set off a chain reaction that ultimately resulted in
two separate probes into the city's public relief system by local and state officials and cost the city's welfare director his job.[3] Similar contests over public assistance cropped up in cities and states across the country. By the early
1950s, public assistance programs had "returned to page one" as state and
local politicians from Maine to California attacked Aid to Dependent Children (ADC) and General Assistance.[4] The federal government also got into
the act, approving legislation to make public the identity of ADC and Old Age
Assistance (OAA) recipients and to assist states in tracking down dependent
children's "runaway poppas."[5] These innovations, and the public's approval of
them, reflected the widely held opinion, first articulated by the authors of the
Baltimore probe, that the "public treasury" could not and should not provide
a "dependable substitute for frugality, prudence and self denial."[6]

These postwar welfare crises paralleled a contemporary effort to limit the
taxing powers of the federal government. At the national level, Republican
legislators, temporarily returned to power after the 1946 midterm elections,
promised to slash federal tax rates, roll back federal spending, and "cast out

a great many chapters of the New Deal."[7] At the grass roots, antitax groups revived a Depression-era campaign to cap federal income, estate, and gift tax rates. By 1953, tax limitation advocates had convinced the National Bar Association, the American Legion, the National Association of Manufacturers and some twenty-five state legislatures to endorse a constitutional amendment limiting federal tax rates to 25 percent. Two years later, one national poll found that almost 70 percent of Americans across all socioeconomic categories favored a 25 percent ceiling on federal taxes.

The apparently robust support for tax limitation and hostility toward all but the most minimal forms of direct public assistance masked a widespread acceptance of other important, though largely unacknowledged, government-supported economic and social security programs. While politicians, the press, and the public expressed outrage at "welfare queens" and "welfare kings" whose unwholesome dependence on government subsidy threatened the nation's social and economic future, more expensive and extensive forms of public provision, including veterans' programs, social insurance for the aged and the unemployed, farm subsidies, and mortgage tax subsidies for middle-class homeowners, enjoyed broad support.[8] As David Lawrence, editor of the frankly pro-business *U.S. News and World Report*, wrote in 1950, federal intervention "in the economic life of business and the individual" was "no longer vulnerable as a principle." Only the "scope and degree and quality thereof" remained in question.[9]

Indeed, despite the public's professed distaste for government spending, the state grew by leaps and bounds in the postwar years. Federal spending, which had crested at 10.5 percent of Gross Domestic Product (GDP) at the height of the New Deal, averaged 17.3 percent of GDP over the 1947–1960 period.[10] Most of the liberal social programs of the 1930s and early 1940s survived the brief conservative resurgence of the immediate postwar period. Lawmakers—with the support of the public—showered new and ever more generous benefits on veterans and their families, increasing the value of education benefits and making it even easier for veterans to buy a home.[11] Social Security likewise expanded. To be sure, some continued to attack the program as an un-American form of state "charity received by virtue of a token payment by the worker and his employer."[12] But by the early 1950s, even such conservative stalwarts as Ohio Republican Senator Robert Taft and the National Chambers of Commerce had come to accept, if not embrace, the program as a fact of political life. The Social Security Amendments of 1950, passed by large and bipartisan margins in both houses of Congress, set the program on a course of long-term expansion, secured its place at the center of the American welfare state, and helped to transform the once vulnerable program into the "third rail" of American politics. Efforts to undo the World War II taxing state also failed. The World War II tax regime survived and even thrived, as policymakers on both sides of the aisle came to depend on the federal income tax as a critical tool in creating and managing economic growth, delivering concrete tax benefits to certain groups, individuals, and businesses, and assuring individual and national prosperity. In 1954, Congress rejected alternative revenue schemes and instead voted, again on a bipartisan basis, to affirm the revenue system put in place in 1942.[13]

The taxing and welfare states thus survived the immediate challenge of the postwar return to prosperity. Liberal state builders quickly integrated the promise of national affluence and individual prosperity into their vision for the postwar world, grafting new commitments to national economic growth and individual economic mobility onto the New Deal's promise of economic security.[14] These visions of abundance grew out of the war itself, as full employment, labor shortages, and unrealized consumer power replaced the widespread unemployment and deprivation of the previous decade. The postwar period promised more of the same, a world in which a "rising standard of living coupled with real security for all" would become the "accepted pattern of American life."[15] At the same time, liberal state builders molded their defense of social policies enacted during the Depression to the nation's newfound affluence and to the postwar growth imperative. As one liberal policymaker explained, economic security programs would not only protect "against the loss of income due to unemployment, old age, disability, etc.," but would also contribute to the prosperity of the nation as a whole by leaving "every employer and every worker free to make any adjustments necessary to meet industrial or market changes."[16]

The political contests over the shape and future of the U.S. tax and welfare state in the early postwar period, and the ways in which liberal state builders responded to them, helped to determine the nature and content of the postwar social compact by establishing policy institutions and ways of thinking about government that influenced policy and politics for the rest of the century. The public's taste for certain public spending programs, combined with elites' faith in their own ability to use tax and spending policy to manage economic growth, effectively protected the taxing and welfare systems put in place during the New Deal and World War II. However, their survival required a refashioning of both conservative and liberal ideology and politics to meet the challenges and opportunities of what publisher Henry Luce called the "American Century." For their part, the mainstream of the GOP and organized business jettisoned prior commitments to annually balanced budgets, opposition to the progressive income tax, and determination to block any and all forms of government intervention in the economy in favor of a limited form of "commercial Keynesianism" that relied on public resources—provided largely through the federal income tax code—to underwrite and stimulate the growth of private sector market activity.[17]

Liberals too adjusted their sights. The postwar survival of the welfare and taxing states was far from assured. Both had been created and approved in the context of serious national emergencies that had since disappeared. Challenges to both the taxing and welfare states had begun before the war ended. In 1942, even as it approved the watershed Revenue Act to finance the war, Congress froze scheduled Social Security tax increases, closed down Depression-era relief organizations like the Works Progress Administration, and refused even to consider proposals to expand the existing regime of social protection, effectively serving notice to liberal state builders who had once hoped to launch a "third New Deal." Efforts to contain and roll back the liberal state mounted in the postwar years, as conservative policy elites rushed to slash taxes, eliminate New Deal social programs, and contain the growth of the state. At the grassroots level, state and local investigations into and purges of ADC and General Assistance rolls and mounting popular frustration with rising tax burdens threatened to undo the successes of the last two decades.

In the end, liberals managed to protect the basic institutions of the welfare and taxing states only by mortgaging the liberal political project as a whole. Their fears that antitax sentiment might endanger existing social and economic programs—in concert with early Cold War antipathy toward statist policies and the centrality of Keynesian growth economics to postwar liberal policymaking—led lawmakers to embrace ever more complicated and obscure ways of financing key economic and social programs. Policy decisions made in the immediate postwar years—decisions that compounded the limitations of the taxing and welfare states established in the 1930s and early 1940s—set the stage for the decline of the New Deal order in the late 1960s and early 1970s. By hiding the state in plain view, liberal postwar state builders effectively divorced the welfare state benefits enjoyed and expected by the nonpoor majority from the taxes that paid for them, the government that provided them, and the more direct forms of public assistance they resembled.

Contesting the Welfare State at the Grass Roots

In late 1947, the Commission on Governmental Efficiency and Economy released its long-awaited survey of Baltimore's public assistance programs. Finding "much in need of correction" and concerned about the long-term cost to the "average citizen," the Commission recommended fundamental changes in the practices and principles of public welfare.[18] The Commission report attracted "more public notice than any similar document in American public welfare history" and helped to shape welfare politics not only in Baltimore but in cities and towns across the country.[19] The New York State Department of Social Welfare, which conducted its own audit of public assistance programs in 1947 and 1948, pointed out the "striking" parallels between the "results of [its] own investigation" and the findings of the Baltimore study.[20] Echoed by welfare authorities in other states and cities, the conclusions and recommendations reached by the Baltimore and New York investigating committees encapsulated and shaped what would become the dominant view of welfare for the remainder of the twentieth century. Focusing on only a discrete section of the larger American welfare state and insisting that the "individual" owed, both to himself and to "society" at large, "the obligation to work out his own security," state and local welfare authorities helped to ratify a narrowed definition of welfare that comprised only cash assistance programs for the very poor and obscured the state's growing role in other areas of the economy and society.[21]

The welfare politics of the late 1940s and early 1950s drew on long-standing prejudices against providing public assistance to the undeserving poor, rehearsed familiar paeans to individualism, and paid deference to the nation's antistatist rhetorical tradition. Ambitious politicians had long campaigned on promises to purge public relief rolls of undeserving chiselers and malingerers. Even during the depths of the Great Depression, local officials routinely reexamined relief histories to check abuse and reduce assistance costs.[22] But, these postwar welfare crises and the public attention paid to the apparent costs of public welfare can be fully understood only in light of the fundamental changes in the American state and in Americans' relationship to that state wrought by almost two decades of depression and war. The postwar purges in Baltimore, New York City, Detroit and elsewhere reflected political and economic pressures unique to the postwar period as well as the dilemmas posed by the vast expansion of the taxing and welfare state over the previous decades. For one thing, the size and costs of public assistance programs were unprecedented. Although unemployment virtually disappeared during and after the war, costs for ADC and General Assistance spiraled. In Baltimore, to take but one example, ADC caseloads grew by 122 percent between 1945 and 1947; the General Assistance population grew by 60 percent.[23] Costs spiked accordingly. In 1946, the city's welfare budget was $3.9 million. A year later, the BDW spent $6.6 million on public welfare, with the largest cost increases in its ADC and General Assistance programs.[24] Fearful of the public's reaction to these rising costs, BDW officials worried about how they could "explain to the public why such large additional funds were needed in a time of full employment?"[25]

The popular press asked the same question. Even before the Efficiency and Economy Commission issued its report, the *Baltimore Sun* did its part to draw attention to fraud and abuse in the city's welfare system.[26] Despite the editorial board's stated commitment to public programs "to succor the needy," the *Sun*'s seven-part series, written by Howard Norton, characterized the city's welfare system as rife with inefficiency, mismanagement, and possibly criminal abuse. The first article of the series set the tone for the rest, stressing the cost of the city's assistance programs—by which Norton meant only ADC and General Assistance—and pointing to the "paradox" of more than "23,000 people living on relief" in spite of "virtually full employment."[27] As welfare costs rose, and imposed a heavier burden on the taxpayer, Norton and the paper's editorial board insisted, the conduct of the assistance program had become undeniably a "public affair."[28]

Rising costs helped to produce a similar welfare crisis in postwar New York City. The New York welfare system, the largest in the nation, witnessed an explosion in its caseload after the war; annual costs for the city's welfare department rose from $75 million in 1946 to $122 million a year later.[29] Given the postwar boom, such increases seemed difficult to account for, until the chance discovery of a few "luxury relief" cases by the city's press provided a simple—if erroneous—explanation. A routine check of local welfare practice by state officials found that city welfare officials had, on occasion, housed public assistance recipients in local hotels. That these cases were relatively rare—only thirty-seven families lived in hotels—and that the hotels involved could scarcely be described as deluxe accommodations hardly mattered. Nor did the fact that the city acted quickly to address these so-called luxury relief cases. By 26 May, two weeks after the press first got hold of the story, only one family remained in a hotel; thirty-six others had been relocated. Nonetheless, the headlines were sensational and the city's press relished describing how the city had lodged a "family on relief" in a hotel at a cost of $500 per month at a time when the quip "two families for every garage" described all too well the housing shortage faced by many Americans.[30] For more than a month, local newspapers applied public pressure, highlighting the "shameless prodigality" of the city's welfare department and attacking those welfare workers whose "poor judgment" had "made the city a laughing stock for the nation."[31] Not surprisingly, the public shared this hostility toward apparently "able-bodied" welfare "cheats, bums, prostitutes, irresponsible parents, and well-heeled sons and daughters of the aged" who used taxpayer dollars to help themselves to luxuries such as "liquor and soft drinks, pre-season melons, candy . . . [and] use of taxicabs."[32]

This widespread public hostility toward public welfare programs speaks both to the limits of the welfare state inherited from the New Deal and the unsettled and frankly anxious political and economic character of the immediate postwar period. Though most Americans looked hopefully toward a future of peace and prosperity after decades of depression and war, they also entertained doubts that such a future was possible. The explosion of atomic bombs at Hiroshima and Nagasaki cast a long shadow. Souring relations with the Soviet Union and the emerging Cold War raised the specter of another and perhaps final global conflict. In March 1946, only six months after the end of the Pacific War, 70 percent of Americans believed that the United States would find itself "in another war within 25 years."[33] Few doubted that this next conflict would be a nuclear war. According to a 1946 survey, 80 percent of Americans believed that other nations either had nuclear technology or would have it within five years. More than 60 percent of those surveyed believed that there was a very "real danger" that atomic bombs would someday be used against the United States.[34] The successful explosion of a nuclear weapon by the Soviet Union in 1948, followed quickly by the "loss" of China to Mao Zedong's communist forces, only heightened the public's nuclear anxiety.

Postwar economic growth produced its own problems. The boom itself was disorienting, a confusion of "luxuries and shortages," where the "list of shortages" was "endless . . . the demand . . . fantastic," a world where even though "everyone seems to have money" and "no one seems to go broke," the future seemed insecure.[35] Many doubted that prosperity could last, anticipating another "serious business depression within the next ten years."[36] Inflation and the frightening prospect of a wage and price spiral that would "destroy the value of savings deposits, bonds and insurance policies" and jeopardize the economic security of "pensioners, disabled veterans, people living on annuities . . . [and] white collar workers" posed a more immediate problem.[37] Inflation, the liberal Union for Democratic Action reported in 1945, could intrude its "shadows into the homes of every family" and jeopardize the "health and welfare of every worker, salaried person, and small businessman."[38] While liberals argued that only federal action through the wartime Office of Price Administration (OPA) could protect ordinary consumers against spiraling prices, business groups, led by the National Association of Manufacturers, countered that government intervention, and the OPA in particular, bore responsibility for the postwar price spiral. If the government removed price controls, business groups and their congressional allies argued, individual corporations would respond by introducing more supply into the market, thus driving down prices.[39]

Whatever its causes, inflation wreaked havoc on the lives of ordinary Americans and helped to politicize tax and spending policy in the immediate postwar period. Widespread anxiety about the rising cost of living certainly helps explain the public's fixation on the apparently irresponsible spending habits of "relief chiselers" who used "public charity" to buy "cars, television sets, radio phonographs, furs, and jewelry" and generally managed to "live better" than their neighbors.[40] Public frustration at federal income taxation rose in tandem with the rising cost of living. In 1944, 90 percent of those polled felt their tax burdens to be fair; three years later, almost 60 percent believed their taxes to be too high.[41] Average tax burdens did, in fact, rise sharply after the war. Between 1948 and 1953, the percentage of income the average American owed in tax to the federal government increased by almost 25 percent; total federal, state, and local tax burdens rose from about 27 percent of personal income to about 31 percent. Rising tax liabilities in concert with the rapidly rising cost of living affected the politics of spending. As political journalist Samuel Lubell noted in 1950, "once the bite of taxes was felt . . . the welfare state took on a new aspect."[42]

Lubell took it for granted that the "welfare state" meant government expenditures for the poor or near poor. Official and public condemnations of welfare programs for encouraging "dependence upon the government, idleness, pauperism, desertion, illegitimacy, dishonesty and irresponsibility" drew a clear and inviolable distinction between direct assistance programs for the poor and all other forms of government intervention in the economy.[43] This narrowed definition was one critical consequence of the state and local battles over welfare finance and fraud—and one that fundamentally mischaracterized the nature, purpose, and extent of federal spending and the forces behind rising tax burdens. Despite hysterical headlines accusing "relief chiselers" of stealing the taxpaying public blind, public assistance was by no means the cause of rising tax bills, nor did it account for a particularly large percentage of public spending. In 1946, local, state, and federal expenditures on public assistance totaled about $1.44 billion; by 1956, the total had reached $3.2 billion—an increase of 122 percent over a ten-year period. Although this was certainly a significant increase, it must be seen in perspective. Over the same period, the costs of the U.S. Postal Service grew from about $1.4 billion to almost $2.9 billion, an increase of 110 percent. Not surprisingly, defense dwarfed all other categories of spending. In 1948, three years after the end of the war, the United States spent $16 billion—almost 30 percent of the national budget—on military and other international commitments. At $2.1 billion, public welfare spending that same year accounted for only 3.9 percent of the national budget (see Figure 1).

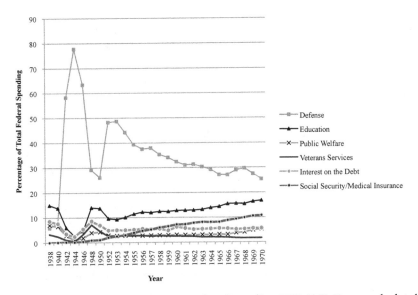

Figure 1. Select spending as percentage of total spending, 1936–1960. Figures calculated using data in John J. Wallis, "Total Government Expenditure, by Function, 1902–1995," table Ea61-124, in *Historical Statistics of the United States, Earliest Times to the Present: Millennial Edition*, ed. Susan B. Carter, Scott Sigmund Gartner, Michael R. Haines, Alan L. Olmstead, Richard Sutch, and Gavin Wright (New York: Cambridge University Press, 2006).

Public welfare was far from the country's most expensive domestic policy commitment. Between 1952 and 1960, the United States spent $107 billion for education and less than $27 billion on public welfare. Nor did the poor, or the near poor, receive the majority of even *direct* public subventions. By 1960, Americans with incomes above the median claimed a slim majority (51 percent) of direct transfer payments from the federal government. Middle-class taxpayers benefited especially from veterans and farm payments, but even those programs that most benefited the poor provided some aid to the middle and upper income brackets. By 1960, for example, more than 30 percent of social insurance payments went to those with incomes above the national median.[44] But the language of federal fiscal policy continued to disguise and even erase the vast majority of this domestic spending, allowing members of the middle classes—newly self-conscious and entertaining dreams of an abundant future—to ignore the links between their newfound affluence and security and direct and indirect government spending.

Policy choices reinforced these rhetorical divisions. Liberal policymakers, in particular Social Security experts and advocates, responded to congressional and popular hostility toward public spending and rising taxes by redoubling their efforts to protect existing institutions—namely Old Age and Survivors' Insurance (OASI). Worried that Social Security, now the more common name for OASI, would fall victim to the same tax and antistate rhetoric that drove the era's campaigns against ADC and General Assistance, experts in the Social Security Administration stepped up their efforts to distance their program from failed welfare policies and to put its financing beyond the reach of the annual budgetary process. Insisting that OASI was nothing more than a "kind of government insurance company" designed to "cover the social risk[s] faced by all American families," Social Security advocates favorably compared their program for "organized and intelligent thrift" to welfare programs that supposedly encouraged unwholesome dependency on the state at great cost to hardworking taxpayers.[45] Social Security experts won an important victory when overwhelming majorities of both the House (333–14) and Senate (81–2) approved the Social Security Amendments of 1950, which put the program on a course of steady expansion and ensured the system's long-term political viability and financial security.[46] These changes to the Social Security program also marked a turning point in the relationship between the social insurance and public assistance streams of the American welfare state. The bill expanded OASI eligibility by removing many of the occupational exclusions—including those for most domestic and agricultural workers—written into the 1935 bill and increased benefit amounts available to present and future retirees. As a result of these changes, OASI overtook OAA—once the most expensive form of direct government grants to individuals—in 1951[47] (see Figure 2).

The 1950 amendments tightened the link between payroll taxes and OASI benefits and foreclosed any possibility of using general revenues to supplement benefits, particularly for poorer retirees. These changes further distinguished Social Security "contributions" and "annuities" from the taxes used to pay for other economic security programs, and erased the public and redistributive nature of what would soon become the most expensive part of the nation's social safety net. Although the architects of the 1950 amendments certainly understood that Social Security bore little resemblance to a private pension plan, but was rather a government program that effected an intergenerational transfer of money from current wage-earners to current retirees, they nonetheless insisted that Social Security offered the best of both worlds: long-term financial security for the nation's retired workers without a welfare state. Ways and Means Chairman Wilbur Mills, the Arkansas Democrat who steered the Social Security bill through Congress, even went so far as to "challenge the statement that the creation of machinery providing security against need in old age constitutes a welfare state, or is in the direction of a welfare state." Rather, Mills insisted, Social Security simply allowed an "individual during his productive years to lay aside . . . an amount of money which will

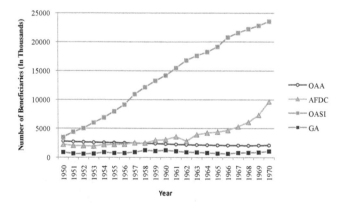

Figure 2. Public "welfare" caseloads by program, 1950–1970. Blanche Coll, *Safety Net: Welfare and Social Security,* 1929–1979 (New Brunswick, N.J.: Rutgers University Press, 1995), table 7.1.

enable an agency of the Government to provide him with benefits after he becomes 65."[48]

If changes to Social Security and its financing helped to disguise the long-term costs and distributive consequences of that program, changes to the way that the federal government paid for ADC compounded the program's already significant political liabilities. After the failure of comprehensive welfare reform in 1943 and 1945, and in the context of rising state and local concerns about the cost of public assistance, welfare experts, both inside and outside the federal government, concentrated their energies on increasing the federal share of public assistance spending and varying those payments with individual states' fiscal capacities. Between 1946 and 1958, Congress experimented with variable financing formulas designed to provide greater federal subventions to poorer states, where need was greatest but where governments were least able to care for their welfare populations because of limited fiscal capacity.[49] These changes drove federal welfare costs up from $1.3 billion in 1953 to $2.06 billion in 1960 without producing any real improvements in ADC payment levels.[50] Instead of increasing individual ADC benefits, variable financing effectively nationalized the costs of the program and convinced local and state welfare officials to shift their welfare populations into ADC and away from unsubsidized General Assistance programs that provided support to both men and women.[51] The resultant stagnation in General Assistance programs, even during times of relatively high unemployment, not only reinforced public perceptions that welfare "dependency" afflicted only unwed mothers and their children but also highlighted the apparent link between rising federal tax burdens and rising ADC costs, setting the stage for a national welfare crisis that pitted the rights of taxpayers against the suspect rights claims of tax eaters. As Robert Ball of the Social Security Administration later pointed out, in "public assistance, the community is divided. Only the 'poor' receive benefits. The others pay for it."[52]

Folded into the federal taxing state created by the Revenue Act of 1942 and expecting to enjoy the prosperity and abundance the war's end seemed to promise, middle- and working-class Americans increasingly saw welfare—and the taxes that paid for it—as a threat to their own American dream. The Revenue Act of 1942 had democratized fiscal citizenship in the United States, but it had also allowed conservative critics of the liberal state to appeal to middle- and lower-income Americans who benefited from and supported many of the Social Security programs inherited from the New Deal as potentially overburdened taxpayers. As one former Democrat explained his decision to cast his vote, for the first time for the GOP candidate in 1950, "We're being taxed to death!"[53]

Good-Bye to the New Deal?

The end of the Second World War and Franklin Roosevelt's death in 1944 presented American conservatives with an opportunity to challenge the political drift of the 1930s and early 1940s. Even before the war ended, the political right had begun to coalesce around opposition to the extension of the New Deal state. In 1945 and 1946, the GOP, with critical assistance from conservative Southern Democrats eager to maintain the region's racial status quo, had gutted the Full Employment Bill and disbanded the OPA—two key elements of liberals' postwar domestic agenda. Right-leaning politicians drew some support from a business community that, empowered economically and politically by the war and aroused to action by union activity and the massive strike waves of 1945 and 1946, was anxious to roll back some of the New Deal era laws that they believed constrained free enterprise and reduced corporate influence. The results of the 1946 midterm elections—in which a Republican Party led by its more conservative members gained control of both houses of Congress for the first time in almost two decades— seemed to signal a rightward shift in the nation's politics. Average Americans, reported the *Washington Post*, were "fed up on government controls, angry over strikes, and irritated by shortages" when they had "expected abundance." As voters became "ever more gripped by heavy taxes," the "pendulum" would only continue its "mighty swing" to the right.[54]

Republicans welcomed their return from the political wilderness and predicted a new era in American politics. The new Speaker of the House, Joe Martin of Massachusetts, looked forward to the further "revival of the Republican Party" and interpreted the 1946 election results as proof that his party had "survived the ordeal of the thirties."[55] Across the country, GOP legislators eagerly announced plans to root out "New Deal incompetence, waste, graft, extravagance and bureaucracy."[56] The GOP, crowed Senator Taft, had been sent to Washington to restore freedom and eliminate the "constantly increasing interference with family life and with business by autocratic government bureaucrats and autocratic labor leaders."[57] A renewed conservative era in American governance, predicted one House Republican, would mean nothing less than the end of the "New Deal parasitic philosophy of the Government supporting the people."[58]

The Republican campaign against New Deal spending included a commitment to tax reduction. Slashing taxes, party insiders explained, would indirectly contain the New Deal by cutting off "much of the government's income" and compelling it to retrench.[59] The GOP's defense of a tax cut drew on a variety of political and economic arguments. Many Republican legislators sincerely believed that a tax reduction would provide the surest route to new investment, more jobs, more production, and a better standard of living for all Americans. Reducing individual and corporate income tax rates, the GOP argued, would not only help individual taxpayers by giving them a "reduction . . . equivalent to a rise in pay," it would also provide a "stimulus to investment and managerial initiative."[60] According to Speaker Martin, for example, only by reducing taxes, balancing the budget, and reducing spending could the country look forward to "more production, lower prices" and increases in "real income" for everyone.[61] Newly elected Nevada Republican Senator George Malone concurred, reminding his Senate colleagues that the "high rate of taxation now in effect" would "surely shut off at the source the flow of money necessary to continue our gradual economic expansion."[62] The GOP's new congressional majority signaled its commitment to tax reduction by designating the party's 1947 proposal to cut personal and business income tax rates as HR 1—the first order of business for the Eightieth Congress.[63]

The GOP also recognized the political appeal of tax reduction. Tax cuts, asserted one party activist in 1947, would be critical not only to the "welfare of the country" but to the "success of the Republican Party in 1948" and beyond.[64] The total tax burden borne by the average citizen had increased noticeably both during and after the war (see Figure 3). The first tax bracket—that is the percentage of taxable income owed to the federal government by the poorest wage earners—had stood at 4 percent in 1939; the high personal exemption of $5,000 for married couples meant that very few paid even this nominal tax. By 1948, the lowest tax rate had reached 20 percent, and the $1,000 exemption for a married couple pushed far more lower-income earners onto the federal tax rolls.[65] As incomes rose after the war, so too did the percentage of each paycheck owed to the federal government. In 1948, the federal income tax claimed an average of 8.65 percent of personal income. Five years later, that number had risen to 10.77 percent, an increase of almost 25 percent.[66]

State and local taxes followed a similar pattern. In 1944, states and cities

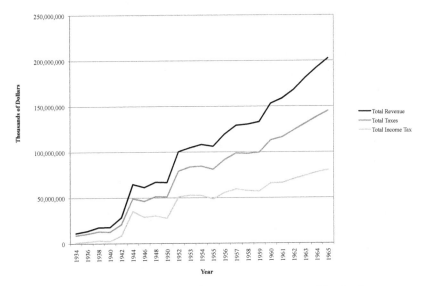

Figure 3. Total revenue, tax revenue, and income tax revenue at all levels of government, 1935–1965. Wallis, "Total Government Revenue, by Source, 1902–1995," table Ea24-512, in *Historical Statistics of the United States,* ed. Carter et al.

raised only $2.8 billion in income and sales taxes; by 1953, state and local sales and income tax collections had grown to almost $8 billion.[67] Rising tax loads, combined with the rising cost of living, produced mounting voter frustration at the grass roots that seemed to offer the GOP a golden opportunity to lure voters away from their home in the Democratic Party.

Changes in the national economy helped to transform taxes into a pressing political issue. Inflation drove up the cost of living, and wages, while rising, failed to keep up with rapidly mounting costs. As inflation made ordinary Americans more and more tax conscious, the political appeal of tax cuts increased. Moreover, tax reduction offered the GOP a way to broaden its electoral appeal without violating core principles or alienating its base in the business community. The shadow cast by Herbert Hoover and Republican inaction in the face of the Great Depression continued to hang over the party. According to a 1945 survey, most voters still identified the Republican Party with the interests of "business and white collar groups." The creation of a mass income tax during the war offered the GOP an opportunity to reach and appeal to a majority of voters *as taxpayers* and to give the party, in the

words of one political consultant, a "sense of idealism and devotion to the
good life."[68] The "heavy burden of taxation," one GOP heavyweight pointed
out in a 1947 radio address, required the average worker to work "three days
out of ten for the government."[69] Taxes, party leaders and strategists advised,
might allow the GOP to broaden its support among the ranks of the emerging American middle class, those people who "own things, or who aspire to
ownership" and who "dislike regimentation." Middle-class men and women
who had invested in a "home, a life insurance policy," or a "savings account"
could be appealed to as taxpayers who bore the burden of supporting liberal social experiments. Whereas in the 1930s the "majority of the 'have-nots'
got the benefits of public spending and the minority of the 'haves' worried
about the costs," the return of prosperity and the expansion of the taxing state
had brought the 'haves' into the majority" as "taxpayers and the holders of E
bonds."[70] Tax politics might allow the GOP to co-opt the Democratic Party's
promise of a future of both security and unlimited prosperity and cast liberal
social and economic policies as anathema to the latter and increasingly more
important goal.

The 1948 tax cut, introduced in early 1947, passed into law just months
before the 1948 election over President Truman's third and final veto of the
bill, aimed to capitalize on and exacerbate the American public's growing
anxiety about and antipathy toward federal taxation. Most of the pressure for
tax relief came not from ordinary voters but from organized business groups
that mobilized quickly after the war to roll back what they viewed as oner-
ous and unfair excess-profits taxes and to lower corporate and individual
income tax rates across the board. These groups also revived a Depression-
era campaign to place a constitutional cap on federal estate, gift, and income
tax rates.[71] Unable to generate any "substantial enthusiasm" for the proposal
on Capitol Hill, tax limitation advocates took their campaign to the states,
lobbying state legislatures to petition Congress to call a constitutional convention on the question of tax limitation.[72] The shift in strategy paid off almost immediately. In 1939, Wyoming became the first state to endorse tax
limitation. Over the next five years, sixteen additional states approved similar resolutions.[73] Not surprisingly, tax limitation proved particularly successful in 1943, the year the Revenue Act of 1942 took effect, when eight states
approved tax limitation resolutions. The movement slowed between 1945
and 1950—with several states withdrawing earlier support of the limitation
measures—but picked up again with the outbreak of the Korean conflict,
and corresponding tax increases. By 1954, twenty-six state legislatures in

all regions of the country had voted in favor of a constitutional cap on the federal taxing power.[74]

Tax limitation supporters often claimed theirs was a spontaneous, "unprompted" and "voluntary" grassroots movement.[75] New York Republican Representative Ralph Gwinn, for example, claimed publicly that the movement had grown out of ordinary workers' demands for lower tax rates. Speaking before the New Jersey Association of Real Estate Boards in 1949, Gwinn lent his support to the Realtors' efforts to cap federal income taxes in the name of the "working man" who now "carried the major part of the income tax burden."[76] But the drive to limit federal taxes had elite rather than popular origins. The leadership of the Western Tax Council, a Chicago-based organization described as a "prime mover" in the state-level campaign for tax reduction, for example, included representatives from Standard Oil, Eli Lilly, Borg Warner, National Automotive Fibers, and the Shaeffer Pen Company.[77] And as a rule, the national organizations that came out in favor of tax limitation—including the American Bar Association, the United States Chamber of Commerce, and the National Association of Manufacturers— represented tax-sensitive businesses, professionals, and wealthier individuals.

Large corporations also helped to bankroll the nationwide lobbying effort against the federal income tax through the Committee for Constitutional Government (CCG), a conservative advocacy group whose founder, the anti-New Deal newspaper publisher Frank Gannett, once claimed that President Roosevelt and the "Communist-Left Wing Axis" had plans to move the United States into the "jaws of the Moloch of all-out Federal and anti-American control of our private interests."[78] Formed in 1937, in response to Roosevelt's ill-conceived proposal to pack the Supreme Court, by the late '40s and early '50s, the CCG had become a formidable political force. In 1950, the House Select Committee on Lobbying Activities reported that the group had spent $750,000 in 1949 alone, enough to make it the "second largest spender" among all registered lobbying groups that year.[79] Although the Committee refused to release the names of its financial backers, even under the threat of a citation for contempt of Congress, newspaper reports linked the organization to the "Mellon interests, the duPonts, Republic Steel, Standard Oil of New Jersey, Texas Oil, and the Joe Pew Sun Oil interests."[80]

Much of the CCG's time and money went toward stirring up "public sentiment."[81] According to its executive director, Edward Rumely, the group took a "grassroots approach to lobbying" and dedicated its efforts to "informing people and letting the people talk to their Members of Congress."[82] The CCG's most important function, the Select Committee found, was the "distribution of pamphlets in order to influence legislation directly and indirectly . . . by influencing public opinion."[83] Between 1937 and 1944, the group distributed 82 million pamphlets, books, and other materials designed to influence legislation. This pace of activity continued after the war. According to some estimates, by the late 1940s, the CCG had "disseminated millions of letters and documents to educators, civic bodies, and other molders of public opinion, including members of Congress." On the issue of tax limitation alone, the organization claimed to have reached over 650,000 people.[84]

Lobbying and educational efforts by these elite groups impressed state lawmakers, helped to sway public opinion, and transformed tax limitation into a question of national political importance. In 1951, *U.S. News and World Report* noted a "growing" but largely unacknowledged "movement . . . underway . . . to force a drastic reduction in federal income, estate and gift taxes."[85] The next year, the American Taxpayers Association, a leader in the fourteen-year fight for a constitutional amendment to limit federal taxation, predicted that it would soon have enough state support to force congressional action.[86] In July of that same year, a Gallup Poll found that 68 percent of those surveyed approved of proposals to establish a federal tax ceiling of 25 percent. Support for the measure was strong across demographic groups: 64 percent of business and professional respondents expressed support; the level rose to 68 percent among manual workers and farmers and 69 percent among white-collar workers.[87]

Few of these taxpayers would have benefited from the proposed tax limitation. Opponents of the measure correctly identified tax limitation as a way to shift the burden of taxation away from corporations and the wealthy and onto middle- and lower-income taxpayers.[88] In 1952, the median annual income in the United States was $2,890. That same year, according to a study made by the professional staffs of the Joint Committee on the Economic Report and the House Select Committee on Small Business, a single taxpayer would have had to earn more than $8,000 per year, and a married couple with two children more than $20,000, to benefit materially from the 25 percent tax ceiling.[89] Indeed, only about 1 percent of individual taxpayers would have received a direct benefit from tax limitation.[90] For these lucky few, the size of that benefit would have increased directly with the size of their income. While a family of four living on $25,000 a year could expect a tax cut of about $750, a similar couple with $1,000,000 per year in income could expect a tax windfall of more than $620,000.[91] Large corporations would fare even better.

In the early 1950s, all corporations faced a 30 percent tax on business income, as well as a 22 percent tax surcharge on taxable corporate income over $25,000. Tax limitation proposals would have eliminated the surtax completely, providing massive benefits to the nation's largest and richest corporations. The biggest companies—those with net income in excess of one million dollars—would see their taxes cut by more than 50 percent.[92]

Sensing an opportunity for grandstanding, if not policymaking, several members of Congress took up the cause of tax limitation in the late 1940s and early 1950s. In 1951 and again in 1953, Senator Everett Dirksen and his fellow Illinois Republican Representative Chauncy Reed introduced legislation calling for a constitutional convention to repeal the Sixteenth Amendment and place a 25 percent cap on federal tax rates. Other approaches to the question of the federal government's taxing and spending power also gained a hearing in the early 1950s. New York Republican Representative Frederic Coudert, for example, introduced legislation stipulating that federal expenditures not exceed federal revenues, except in time of national emergency. Robert Taft and his fellow Republican Senator Homer Ferguson of Michigan proposed to limit federal expenditures, except for military or defense purposes, to 5 percent of national income. Taxpayers' associations from around the country called for what one such group described as the "orderly reduction in the overall tax burden."[93]

These campaigns to limit the federal taxing power represented an indirect attack on liberal spending programs, and aimed to roll back the New Deal state. Representative Gwinn, a New York conservative with close ties to the CCG, argued that a tax cap would limit the federal government's functions to those "traditional" ones "performed from the beginning of our country" and insulate Congress from popular demands for more and more services from government. Only by depriving Congress of "any money" to "satisfy any group" could one expect to roll back the size of government.[94] Gwinn's comments suggest the uneasy populism of most early tax limitation advocates. Although they were quick to claim popular support for the movement, many of the most outspoken spokesmen for tax limitation also expressed considerable suspicion about democratic politics, particularly when questions of taxing and spending were involved. The progressive income tax, argued one Indiana lawyer in the pages of the *American Bar Association Journal*, was nothing less than a weapon in the "war of the poor against the rich" that permitted the "confiscation of the wealth of the few by the votes of the many."[95]

The supporters of some kind of constitutional limitation on the federal government's taxing power yearned for a fundamental revision of the nation's fiscal structure and posed a significant challenge to the World War II tax regime. Although advocates sometimes contended that the government could recoup much of the $16 billion revenue loss produced by a 25 percent tax cap through spending cuts, or—in a precursor to the supply-side economics of the 1970s and 1980s—that the stimulative effect of the cut would ultimately result in "even greater revenue than that produced by higher rates," most experts believed that capping taxes at 25 or even 35 percent would require the government to enact a national sales tax or some other kind of consumption-based tax regime. Some groups, most notably the National Association of Manufacturers, had been pushing just such a solution since 1942. The threat of a national sales tax that would put what many viewed as an "undue or disproportionate tax burden on those least able to pay" survived into the postwar years.[96] In 1953, the liberal Americans for Democratic Action (ADA) listed proposals for both a national sales tax and a federal tax ceiling as significant threats to progressive taxation.[97] Indeed, tax limitation may be seen as a kind of stealth campaign to replace the existing income-based revenue system with one that relied more substantially on consumption levies. As one limitation supporter lamented, because so much "sentiment" had been "built up . . . for the idea of progressive taxation," it had become politically necessary to "accept it in practice."[98] A 25 percent ceiling on corporate and individual tax rates, concluded Harvard Law School dean Erwin Griswold, who opposed tax limitation, might ultimately require the adoption of a substantial sales tax that in other circumstances voters would not "consciously adopt."[99]

Congress had the chance to consider such far-reaching proposals as a universal sales tax, the abolition of the corporate income tax, a flat ceiling on personal income tax rates, and the scrapping of excise taxes in 1953 and 1954 when the Ways and Means Committee and Treasury Department, at the request of President Dwight D. Eisenhower, initiated a major study of the Internal Revenue Code.[100] For more than three months, staff members from the Treasury, Internal Revenue Service, and House Legislative Counsel spent over 300,000 man-hours poring over the tax code and preparing policy recommendations. The product of this review—the Revenue Act of 1954—rejected calls to revamp the revenue system, and instead institutionalized the existing system of steeply progressive marginal tax rates offset by a series of tax breaks for specific forms of nonwage income and supplemented by the Social Security payroll tax.

The 1954 law provided for marginal tax rates that ranged from 20 percent on taxable income under $2,000 to 91 percent on taxable income over $200,000. This progressivity, however, was more apparent than real, thanks to the proliferation of special tax exemptions, deductions, and other tax preferences that reduced the tax burdens on both individuals and corporations. The Revenue Act of 1954 affirmed the importance of these special tax preferences to the overall structure of the American taxing state and offered something for everyone. For lower- and middle-income Americans, the recodification liberalized the definition of dependent children, increased the deductions available for medical expenses, and allowed for the deduction of childcare costs. For wealthier taxpayers, the bill increased the amount of income that could be deducted as charitable donations and created both a credit and an exclusion for certain kinds of dividend income. Corporations benefited from the law's treatment of depreciation costs and operating losses. Congress also chose to exempt employers' contributions to employee health plans in the all-important definition of taxable income.[101]

The Revenue Act of 1954 was the last significant tax bill for eight years. The legislation confirmed the tax regime put in place in 1942, and, perhaps more importantly, reflected a bipartisan agreement among policy elites about the purpose of income taxation. Where debates about tax rates had once concerned balancing revenues and expenditures, raising additional funds, or effecting some kinds of economic redistribution, by the mid-1950s—with the mass income tax now a permanent part of the American state—Congress focused more and more on the larger, macroeconomic consequences of tax legislation. The federal tax structure reaffirmed by the 1954 tax law reflected and reinforced American policymakers' central commitment to economic growth through a kind of domesticated Keynesianism that relied largely on taxation rather than spending to create stable economic growth.[102]

Liberals' success in defending the progressive income tax, like their success in ensuring the survival and expansion of the New Deal welfare state, came at a price. The progressive income tax favored by social democrats and liberals as best embodying the "ability to pay" standard central to good tax policy ultimately fueled popular rejection, not only of welfare, but of liberalism itself by making visible the "costs" of the liberal state.[103] Some GOP insiders had recognized this potential check on the liberal state even before the end of the war. Admitting that consumption and other indirect taxes would be "less equitable" than a progressive income tax, and that the income tax alone could provide the "necessary revenues" to meet national needs, members of the Republican National Advisory Committee also identified a politically powerful and ideologically conservative argument in favor of the World War II tax regime: "Direct taxes on the majority of income earners," the Republican group correctly predicted in 1944, would effectively check the growth of the national state by making "the majority of citizens conscious of their participation in government activities."[104]

Taxpayers, Tax Eaters, and the Politics of Growth

The push to place a constitutional cap on federal income, estate, and gift taxes and the campaign waged against welfare, welfare cheats, and welfare officials suggest the hurdles faced by liberal state builders in the immediate postwar period. Liberal policymakers inherited many of these problems from the New Deal itself—a watershed in American state building that nonetheless failed to clarify the relationship between the taxes paid by individual taxpayers and the benefits they could expect to receive from newly enacted economic and social security institutions.[105] New Deal tax rhetoric, at least after 1935, tended to focus on the tax obligation of "economic royalists" while absolving ordinary taxpayers of their moral and political obligations to contribute much by the way of direct federal taxes.[106] The Revenue Act of 1942 expanded the reach of the federal income tax into the ranks of the middle and working classes and democratized taxpaying citizenship. But by choosing to defend the new income tax as necessary to pay for the war abroad and to control inflationary threats at home, the architects and advocates of the World War II tax regime, like their New Deal predecessors, failed to link these new tax burdens to a coherent theory about the mutual obligations of the state and its citizens. What was more, that tax regime built on prewar precedent by carving out special privileges for special *kinds* of taxpayers—from middle-class homeowners and relatively wealthy holders of state and local bonds, to large oil companies—that not only offset the income tax's apparent progressivity but also obscured the federal government's role in subsidizing individual and corporate well-being through the Internal Revenue Code. Crafted largely without public input by the powerful House Ways and Means Committee, these tax exemptions, deductions, and special rates functioned as a hidden system of federal benefits that rarely attracted public attention.[107]

Postwar state builders succeeded in institutionalizing much of the taxing and welfare states put in place by the previous generation, and codified the federal government's responsibility to ensure both national affluence and

individual security for the majority of Americans only by hiding their signal social policy achievements. The federal government exercised its considerable power not through direct spending but rather through indirect incentives and subsidies—often referred to as tax expenditures to highlight their functional equivalence to direct spending—to private individuals and enterprises. Because these incentives and subsidies were provided only indirectly they were not often recognized as emanating from government at all. Postwar policies like the GI Bill of Rights and employment-based health and pension programs, which earned the support of major labor unions and were underwritten by the federal tax code, likewise contributed to the well-being of a growing middle class at the same time as they enhanced macroeconomic growth. Social insurance programs, nurtured and protected by a small group of policy insiders since their inception in the 1930s, supplemented this "hidden welfare state." Although programs like Social Security provided direct monetary assistance to individuals, they escaped the scorn and hostility heaped on other welfare programs. That they did so was thanks largely to the success of policy advocates in the Social Security community in distinguishing the "annuity" earned by Social Security beneficiaries thanks to their contributions to a "national pension plan" from the suspect public charity enjoyed by welfare recipients dependent on taxes paid by working citizens.

The emergence of economic growthmanship as the central preoccupation of postwar policymakers, economists, and state builders grew out of and compounded the contradictions of the New Deal and World War II taxing and welfare state. The pursuit and management of economic growth shaped economic policy and politics throughout the late 1940s, 1950s, and 1960s. The economic decline and stagnation predicted by so many in the 1930s did not materialize. Instead, the American economy boomed. World War II defense spending transformed quickly into the military-industrial complex of the Cold War, which in turn stimulated domestic production and underwrote postwar economic prosperity.[108] Rising GNP held out the promise of an abundant future, an age characterized by a "richer measure" of "freedom, security and adventure" than "ever before in history."[109] "Economic growth and broader opportunity for all," President Truman promised in 1950, would flow naturally from the American economy's "perpetual will to move ahead."[110] For labor leaders and ordinary American workers, economic growth held out the promise of a rising standard of living, a society which, in the words of labor leader Walter Reuther, had "achieved economic democracy . . . full production . . . full employment, [and] full distribution," all within the "framework of political democracy."[111] Business leaders shared these dreams of abundance. "Widening job opportunities, a dynamic and expanding economy," and "higher standards of living," General Motors chairman Alfred P. Sloan announced in 1943, must be the objective of every "individual in the country."[112] Full employment, high production, and a rising GNP would raise the American standard of living for workers and owners alike. This "People's Capitalism," as General Electric called it in 1956, would provide everyone, including "consumers, employees, shareowners, all businesses large and small," with "continued progress."[113]

During and immediately after the war, many businessmen and their representatives feared that the federal government would crowd out private interests. Were business to fail in providing adequate employment, Sloan warned the nation's corporate elite two years into World War II, the federal government would soon be required to "compete directly with private enterprise in the production of goods and services."[114] The GM chief need not have worried. Rather than supplanting the private sector, as many had feared, the federal government instead underwrote it.[115] Growth economics did indeed require an active federal state to use its resources to "promote maximum employment, production, and purchasing power."[116] But the state acted behind the scenes, funneling public resources into private hands. As President Truman announced in a January 1946 radio address, reconversion, economic growth, and the nation's prosperity would depend on the combined efforts of private enterprise and the state to lay the "foundation of our economic structure" and achieve both "full production and full employment." Private enterprise would play the lead role, with the hidden "encouragement and assistance" of the public sector.[117]

As Truman's comments suggest, most liberals fully embraced the politics of growth and cooperated enthusiastically in obscuring the role played by federal policy and federal revenues in securing for the majority of Americans a rising standard of living and a basic economic security net. In part, liberals' embrace of economic growthmanship and their increased reliance on invisible spending reflected the political realities of an era marked by ideological and military conflicts with statist regimes. As the Cold War between the United States and the Soviet Union intensified in the late 1940s, many liberals rushed to dissociate themselves from any political program that could be described as statist. The collapse of the Henry Wallace insurgency in 1948 seemed to signal the impotence of the American left and to confirm what Arthur Schlesinger termed the "vital center" liberalism of the Truman administration. The resurgence of the business community during and after the war and the rise of Wisconsin Senator Joe McCarthy and his campaign against communists in government further raised the political risks of advocating direct government intervention.[118]

Many businesses were indeed quick to invoke the specter of state socialism to undercut popular support for any number of government programs. No company was more committed to warning the magazine-reading public of such dangers than the Warner and Swasey Company of Cleveland, Ohio. Throughout the 1950s, the precision-machine-parts manufacturer took out a full-page advertisement in *U.S. News and World Report* almost weekly to remind the magazine's readers of the dangers posed by the welfare state and excessive taxation. In one 1959 example, the company compared "federal aid" to "Santa Claus or Easter Rabbits." In another, it equated federal aid with "Robin Hood . . . the original socialist." Yet another warned that Americans' taste for security would ultimately result in "the only permanent security there is . . . slavery." Warner and Swasey was unusual only in the frequency with which it took out ad space. Other companies and industry-wide organizations also placed advertisements in popular news magazines to warn against a powerful cabal and urge all Americans to protect their "rights and freedoms" against those welfare state "Sirens" who "plan and work for a socialistic U.S.A." (Electric Power and Light Companies); to highlight the threat posed by those "prophets of something-for-nothing" whose "Share the Wealth" plans would saddle the next generation with "State Socialism," a "gradual loss of individual freedoms," and a "lower standard of living" (Republic Steel); or simply to suggest that government spending was part of a Soviet plot to "force the United States to spend itself to destruction" (Timken Roller Bearing Company).[119]

According to some conservatives, almost any form of direct spending or federal taxation might be seen as part of Karl Marx's master plan. The nation had reached a "crossroads," one speaker told the National Retail Dry Goods Association in early 1944, where good citizens must "choose between powerful socialized paternalistic control of Federal Government" and "preserving the traditional American way of opportunity for employment and success of those who work."[120] A group of GOP elected officials likewise claimed that "American freedom for the individual under just laws fairly administered for all" and the "protection of the American way of life against either fascist or communist trends" could be maintained only by resisting the "radicalism, regimentation, all-powerful bureaucracy, class exploitation, deficit spending and machine politics" of Democratic liberalism.[121] Defenders of the era's tax limitation amendments routinely pointed out that the Communist platform included a "heavy or progressive income tax."[122] Senator Taft, in a 1948 speech meant to further his presidential ambitions, warned that high tax rates "must lead directly to socialism."[123] It was a "matter of historical fact," Pennsylvania Representative Leon Gavin reminded his House colleagues in 1950, that "socialism and high taxes" were "synonymous" and that their combination had "always meant the loss of freedom, liberty and opportunities for the people, and a complete domination by the state over the lives of all."[124] The federal income tax, claimed the National Association of Manufacturers in 1954, had not only been "conceived by Karl Marx to liquidate the middle class," but also bore responsibility for 95 percent of the nation's troubles.[125]

Anticommunist rhetoric suffused the era's spending politics as well. During the late 1940s crackdown on welfare abuse, New York City's prolific tabloid press routinely claimed to have found communists embedded in the city's social service bureaucracy. The *New York Journal-American* was particularly interested in ferreting out communists or fellow travelers in the city's welfare department. Two days after the second luxury relief case was reported in the press, the Hearst-owned and virulently anticommunist paper ran the strident headline: "Reds Linked to Relief!" A day later, in a front-page editorial, the *Journal-American* lamented that Stalin and Lenin had been shown to have "500 followers . . . in the city's Department of Welfare" well positioned to "dictate to whom relief grants shall be made—to buy political loyalty with cold cash."[126] Under the foreign and dangerous influence of communists and communist sympathizers, the "red tinged NYC Welfare Department" had served up the city taxpayers' money to the welfare relief recipient (see Figure 4).[127]

Of course, the Cold War itself dramatically expanded the power and reach of the national state.[128] Between 1952 and 1959, the federal government spent almost $38.3 billion on the military and other Cold War-related programs. Defense and defense-related spending transformed the regional geography of the United States, funneling federal tax dollars to the South and Southwest and accelerating the decline of what would soon be known as the Rust Belt. The Federal Highway Act, itself a product of Cold War politics, facilitated the development of the American suburb and the decentralization of the American metropolis. Federal defense contracts underwrote the expansion of companies like General Electric, Westinghouse, Chrysler, and Goodyear, who plowed that money into both defense and consumer production.[129] De-

Figure 4. Burris Jenkins, Jr., "What? No Caviar?" Editorial cartoon, *New York Journal-American,* 23 May 1947, 20.

fense spending also helped sustain the postwar boom and keep the economy close to full employment.

Military and other defense-related spending escaped the red-baiting routinely aimed at other, less costly forms of public expenditure. So too did more indirect forms of federal subsidy. During a 1950 debate on a housing bill proposed by the Truman administration, GOP lawmakers attacked any form of public housing as "nothing but another brick in the structure of socialism." The same policymakers who violently attacked direct subsidies for public housing, however, embraced, perhaps even unknowingly, more indirect forms of public support. For example, even as he declared his unalloyed opposition to the "cooperative housing features" of the administration's housing bill, one New York Republican heaped praise on the success of "private industry" in building low-cost homes—construction made possible only by the easy availability of federally-backed mortgages.[130] Spending programs that relied on earmarked taxes—often referred to as contributions—also evaded the socialist label. A 1950 pamphlet distributed by the National Economic Council, for example, simultaneously promised to tell the "truth about the Socialistic 'Fair Deal'" and warned seniors that their "social security payments" would be endangered unless the "Welfare State Socialists were stopped!"[131]

But it would be a mistake to understand liberal growthmanship as merely a reaction to the Cold War or to the political challenges posed by the resurgent postwar right. Indeed, liberals warmed to economic growth as both a political and an economic goal in the late 1930s. Beginning with the recession of 1937, American liberals abandoned an economic agenda concerned with the structural reform of the American economy and the redistribution of economic power in favor of an agenda that relied on macroeconomic policies to create a mixed economy of abundance, rising living standards, and economic security.[132] Whereas the Depression had created a political context in which average citizens were both more amenable to government programs and more hostile to business in general and concentrations of wealth and economic power in particular, the return to prosperity militated against openly redistributive tax-and-transfer programs.[133] The performance of the U.S. economy during the war put to rest concerns that the U.S. economy had reached a point of secular stagnation that would require constant and direct federal intervention in and direction of the national economy. The attraction of a politics grounded in the promise of uninterrupted growth lay in its ability to moderate the kinds of class warfare politics that had characterized the 1930s and had reemerged in the strike-torn years immediately after the war by allowing "various economic groups" to "prosper and progress together instead of engaging in bitter, hopeless conflicts."[134] As liberal economist Walter Heller, who advised both President John F. Kennedy and his successor, noted, when the "social pie grows bigger, there is less reason to quarrel over who gets the biggest slices."[135] According to the gospel of growth, prosperity and social justice would progress together; the market properly guided and stimulated by wise tax and spending policy, would ultimately democratize prosperity and make the American dream available to ordinary line workers and corporate executives alike.

Growthmanship at once protected and limited the federal income tax and the liberalism that depended on it. On the one hand, federal tax policy, and the federal income tax in particular, became the central policymaking tool available to policymakers interested in managing the growth of the national economy and providing broader opportunity for all American citizens.[136] By the mid-1950s both Republicans and Democrats had come to accept the federal government's responsibility to use its power to stabilize the economy and maintain high, if not full, employment. The tax limitation movement failed to make a real impact at the national level in large part because the mainstream of both the Republican Party and the business community accepted and even welcomed this limited form of government intervention as providing relative stability without infringing on corporate managerial prerogatives.[137] Constitutional tax limitation threatened to impair the flexibility of the tax system and to limit the government's ability to sustain and manage high rates of growth. Given the centrality of the Internal Revenue Code to the economic policies of both the Democratic Party and the GOP, it is hardly surprising that Dwight Eisenhower publicly expressed opposition to any tax ceiling during his 1952 campaign, and that once in office his administration continued to oppose it. Tax limitation, Treasury Secretary George Humphrey warned in 1954, would require a "fundamental reconstruction" of the entire system that might "easily result" in a "financial breakdown."[138]

If the midcentury emphasis on growth helped to institutionalize the World War II taxing state and to provide a relatively stable revenue system that would enable the growth of the modern American state, the politics of economic growth ultimately produced a limited and truncated form of liberalism. By defending the taxing state primarily in macroeconomic terms as a critical tool in preventing inflation, in curbing unemployment, and in stimulating general economic growth, liberal policymakers abandoned alternative ways of thinking about and defending both tax *and* spending policy. The liberal state's increasing reliance on indirect expenditures and on contributory social insurance programs as key forms of social assistance only widened the gap between the obligations of citizenship and its benefits and helped to instill in the rising white middle class a sense of uncomplicated and individual entitlement to the fruits of postwar prosperity. Liberals' success in protecting the progressive income tax against conservative assault and in hiding the most successful parts of the American welfare state in plain view created the institutional and political architecture for a political sea change that not only "ended welfare as we know it" but also shattered the New Deal coalition.

The language of economic growthmanship could also be turned against the state in the name of the beleaguered taxpayer. The "welfare crises" of the late 1940s and early 1950s captured this dynamic, and right-leaning politicians experimented, throughout the decade, with ways to use the taxing state to build a new, majoritarian coalition to counterbalance the New Deal order. High taxes on both personal and corporate income, the argument went, both directly and indirectly imposed costs on consumers and threatened the American standard of living. Not only did income taxes take money directly out of taxpayers' pockets, they also threatened economic growth, jobs, and the standard of living many Americans now viewed as an essential part of the postwar social compact. The federal income tax, Senator Taft warned voters in 1950, "reduces the standard of living of the people," and would one day "kill the goose that lays the golden egg and prevent the operation of the free economy."[139] Tax cutters had only limited success with this kind of rhetoric in the decade and a half after the war, but this line of argument would ultimately bear fruit in the late 1960s, when healthy growth gave way to stagnation, unemployment, and inflation.

Taxes and welfare both slipped off the public radar in the late 1950s. Policy elites and professional lobbying organizations continued to work together behind closed doors to expand and secure the taxing and welfare states. OASI continued to grow, as Congress gradually eliminated existing occupational exclusions, imposed scheduled contribution increases, and raised benefits. ADC too expanded, thanks in part to the migration of poor African Americans from the rural South to the urban—but rapidly deindustrializing—North and Midwest, where benefits were higher and eligibility restrictions less draconian. Welfare experts, exiled during the Eisenhower administration to universities and other nongovernmental institutions, worked behind the scenes to transform public welfare from an income support program to a program designed to rehabilitate the dependent poor and provide them with the social and economic skills needed to enter the mainstream of American life.

This quiet period ended suddenly in the early 1960s, when a well-publicized welfare crisis in the small town of Newburgh, New York, again thrust welfare into the national political spotlight. Taxes too became a political issue as Democratic liberals in the Kennedy administration pushed through Congress a massive cut in individual and corporate tax rates meant to stimulate economic growth and make good on postwar liberalism's promise of economic security, national abundance, and individual economic mobility. As it had in the early postwar period, the politics of taxing and spending would define liberalism in the 1960s.

CHAPTER 2

MARKET FAILURE

I n 1960, few Americans could have found Newburgh, New York, on a map, much less have been able to identify its local politicians. A year later, thanks to the well-publicized campaign by the city's town manager, Joseph Mitchell, to rid the city of welfare "chiselers, loafers and social parasites," Newburgh had become a household name.[1] Mitchell's controversial "13-point plan" to reform the city's welfare system—a plan that included a daily military-style muster of public assistance recipients in front of the New-burgh City Hall—made the small-town politician into a minor celebrity and transformed welfare into what *Los Angeles Times* reporter John Averill called a "smoldering political issue that [could] roar into flames at any minute."[2] Blaming welfare for everything from the "loss of assessed valuations . . . [and] the wreckage of an entire business district" to "sanitation hazards," rising violence, and spiraling rates of out-of-wedlock births, Mitchell repeatedly and publicly challenged welfare recipients' "right . . . to loaf by state or federal edict" and to "quit jobs and go on relief like spoiled children."[3] His campaign attracted front-page publicity in newspapers all over the country, raised welfare's national profile, and sharpened "calls for reform, or even an overhaul of the public assistance program generally."[4] According to one observer, it was in Newburgh that public welfare "really became public."[5]

The so-called Battle of Newburgh captured the difficulties facing liberal policymakers in the early 1960s. For one, the Newburgh crisis suggested the outlines of a racially charged politics that would, by the end of the decade, fracture the already tenuous New Deal coalition of white Southerners, African Americans, white urban workers, and political progressives. Throughout the crisis, Mitchell made little attempt to hide the racial politics at the heart of his welfare crackdown, repeatedly blaming "southern migrants" for the city's economic and social problems.[6] The town manager's chief ally on the City Council, George McKenally, agreed that the "deterioration began when the

migration from the South got underway about ten years ago."[7] But understanding Newburgh exclusively in racial terms is to miss an important part
of the story. Throughout the crisis, the town manager presented himself as
the self-appointed defender of Newburgh's "responsible taxpaying citizens"
whose rights and interests were threatened by "outsiders . . . the state and
federal governments" and "social theorists and philosophers."[8] Others echoed
Mitchell's language, casting the debate over welfare as a significant struggle
between the rights of taxpayers and the rights claims of tax recipients. In a
public letter expressing his support for the Newburgh program, Arizona Senator Barry Goldwater, the standard bearer for American conservatism, wrote
that he was "tired" of seeing "his taxes paid for children born out of wedlock."
Later, the Arizona Republican told reporters that he respected Mitchell for
his determination to "protect my taxes."[9] Much like the conservative backlash
politics of the late 1960s and early 1970s, the broad antiwelfare sentiment revealed by Mitchell's welfare reform program stemmed as much from the fear
that liberal social interventions and redistributive politics would jeopardize
the social and economic privileges, including low tax rates, that the middle
and working classes had come to expect as a matter of right, as from simple
racial hostility.

The Newburgh crisis grew out of the compromises that liberal state builders had made in the immediate postwar period and was the direct result of
a political discourse and policy apparatus that linked an increasingly narrow
definition of welfare to the rising tax burdens of ordinary Americans. The tax
and spending politics that animated Mitchell's war against the welfare state
also informed the key domestic policy initiatives of Presidents John F. Kennedy and Lyndon B. Johnson. Anxious to shore up the increasingly fragile
Democratic electoral coalition, and keenly aware of both public and congressional hostility to new or higher taxes, both Kennedy and Johnson relied on
the spoils of economic growth to underwrite their domestic and international
policy commitments and promised to protect the low taxes, social security,
and economic mobility promised by the postwar social compact.

Tax cuts anchored the liberal reform agenda of the 1960s. The Revenue
Act of 1964—better known as the Kennedy-Johnson tax cut—slashed taxes
across the board and promised to benefit all Americans, "taxpayers and non-
taxpayers" alike, by "releasing tax savings into the private economy."[10] According to its architects, the tax cut would "provide for much needed jobs
for . . . [the] economy," release the "fuller power of consumers to buy the
things they want and need," and increase the "incentive for producers to pro-

duce them."[11] This economic growth, spokesmen for both Kennedy and Johnson promised, would ultimately reduce or even eliminate the need for direct welfare spending. By loosing the "economic energy" of the private enterprise system, the tax cut promised to relieve pressure on state and local governments to provide certain "public services" and reduce demand for welfare and other public assistance programs.[12] President Kennedy expressed this trade-off between tax cuts and new spending programs in a public letter to Ways and Means Chairman Wilbur Mills, in which the president pledged to take steps to "improve governmental efficiency . . . promote economy [and] . . . prune expenditures."[13]

The same political calculations and economic theories that drove Kennedy's tax cut animated his successor's key policy commitments. On the international front, Johnson counted on the "growth dividend" promised by the 1964 tax bill to pay for the rapidly expanding war in Vietnam. At home, Johnson championed policies that would have little impact on the federal budget. The Civil Rights Act of 1964 and the Voting Rights Act of 1965, for example, effected a fundamental revolution in American social policy at very little direct cost to the Treasury or to the taxpayer.[14] Even the War on Poverty—which President Johnson described in 1964 as an "all-out" assault on "human poverty and unemployment"—promised to cost very little and to maintain the low tax rates enjoyed by most Americans. Economic growth, stimulated by the 1964 tax law, provided the rationale and the means for this antipoverty agenda. "As long as the economy was growing rapidly," economist Arthur Okun later recalled, the president believed he could shift the "distribution of public services toward the disadvantaged without having anybody feel it very much."[15] Rejecting expensive income transfer programs, and offering a hand-up, rather than a handout, 1960s poverty warriors promised to transform the "indigent . . . from tax eaters to taxpayers."[16] Like the 1964 Revenue Act, the War on Poverty looked to the free market—managed, but not directed, by wise federal policy—to ensure economic growth, guarantee individual mobility, *and* deliver social and economic justice.

Liberal arguments in favor of both the tax cut and the War on Poverty reinforced and depended on the negative perceptions of welfare and its relationship to rising tax burdens. The policy and political decisions made by liberals in the 1960s with regard to both taxing and spending policy reproduced the limited definitions of taxpaying citizenship and welfare inherited from the New Deal and World War II taxing and welfare state. Indeed, the Kennedy and Johnson administrations sold the 1964 tax cut and the War on

Poverty as a way to avoid welfare dependency, privileging the rights and interests of taxpayers over those of tax eaters dependent on federal assistance. This defense of both the tax cut and the poverty programs ignored the vast federal subsidies—in the form of social insurance programs, hidden tax expenditures, and federal loan guarantees—that underwrote middle-class prosperity and economic security. By failing to defend welfare as a broad-based set of policies that benefited a majority of citizens, liberal policymakers not only left poor women and their children to the vagaries of the market, but also undercut important ideological defenses of the activist state and limited liberals' ability to respond to changes in the domestic and international political economy.

These changes included the political and moral challenges posed by the Civil Rights revolution. While leading liberals in the Kennedy and Johnson administrations counted on the supposedly race-neutral mechanisms of the market to generate growth and ensure equal economic opportunity, some Civil Rights leaders, as well as members of the nascent welfare rights movement, challenged the narrowed definitions of welfare and taxpaying citizenship that drove and limited the mainstream liberal reform agenda. Proposals like the National Urban League's Domestic Marshall Plan and A. Philip Randolph's multibillion dollar Freedom Budget envisioned an active and visible role for the federal government in ensuring and securing racial and economic justice. Ironically, the liberal state's success in transforming the majority of the white middle class from workers to homeowners and taxpayers undercut the potential coalitional politics required to implement this far-reaching agenda. The civil and welfare rights movements' challenge to the institutional and ideological legacies of postwar liberalism remained unanswered.

By the end of the 1960s, American liberalism faced a crisis largely of its own making. Promising simultaneously to open the American dream up to all citizens, to protect the low tax rates that every taxpaying citizen "surely deserved" and to ensure the progress of the free enterprise economy, the Revenue Act of 1964 and the War on Poverty together crystallized the contradictions of postwar liberalism. The tax cut implicitly recognized federal responsibility for both national economic growth and individual economic security; the War on Poverty reaffirmed liberal state builders' commitment to providing all citizens with at least a modicum of economic security. But the role of the liberal state in providing these rights to the nonpoor majority was ever more hidden from view, buried deep within the federal corporate and individual tax codes or tied to paid labor in the private market. These policies, designed to minimize congressional and popular resistance to the expansion of the state and to protect a liberal social compact whose terms included low individual tax rates, effectively decoupled the federal income tax from the benefits delivered to the majority of Americans, rendering increased tax burdens on ordinary Americans largely inexplicable, except as the result of either spiraling welfare loads or the mismanagement of taxpayer dollars.[17]

Cutting Taxes the Liberal Way: The Revenue Act of 1964

The 1964 tax cut was an inside job. Although the public no doubt welcomed the rate cuts, and business groups certainly lobbied hard for reductions in corporate taxes and for new investment incentives, it was the White House itself that put tax reduction on the political agenda. Kennedy's economic team, which included academic heavyweights like John Kenneth Galbraith, Seymour Harris, Paul Samuelson, James Tobin, and Walter Heller, had been foot soldiers in the Keynesian revolution of the 1930s and 1940s. They believed that any economic policy should have as its goal high and rapidly rising total output. This emphasis on macroeconomic growth was hardly unique. By the early 1960s, labor and business groups had acknowledged the federal government's responsibility to use tax and spending policy to stimulate and manage economic growth, even at the expense of annually balanced budgets.[18] The use of compensatory fiscal policy—in which public tax or spending policy aimed to offset unhealthy expansions or contractions in the private market, to produce full employment, and to increase the size of the economy—had likewise been accepted by the majority of professional economists. As Heller, chief of Kennedy's Council of Economic Advisors (CEA) and head cheerleader for the 1964 Revenue Act later recalled, "the rationale of the 1964 tax-cut proposal came straight out of the country's . . . economic textbooks."[19]

Kennedy and his advisors believed that the U.S. economy had underperformed in the 1950s. Slow growth and a "blight of chronic unemployment"— which had risen to 6.7 percent by the time Kennedy took office—had led to "idle workers, idle capital and idle machines."[20] What was needed, the president claimed, was a program to expand "American productive capacity at a rate that shows the world the vigor and vitality of a free economy."[21] Tax reductions were not the only way to achieve economic growth, or to rouse the nation from what the Kennedy campaign had deemed the "drugged and fitful sleep" of the Eisenhower era.[22] Economic expansion could also be achieved through new or expanded expenditures. Indeed, the Kennedy administration initially counted on public "investments in physical and human resources" to pull the economy out of recession. Wise public spending policies, Kennedy insisted in a March 1961 address to Congress, would not only fulfill the nation's "responsibility to alleviate distress . . . through benefits directly available to needy persons" but would also speed recovery by sustaining consumer spending and increasing aggregate demand.[23] Several weeks after first introducing his "program for economic recovery and growth," the president proposed $2.3 billion in nondefense spending increases for education, scientific research, health care, area redevelopment, urban renewal, and veterans' and farm programs.[24] A few months later, in the wake of the Berlin crisis, the president asked for an additional increase of $3 billion for defense spending.[25]

New and direct spending was a tough sell. Although the president's proposals were relatively modest, Congress felt little inclination to increase spending on domestic programs. Congressional conservatives, including Southern Democrats, most Republicans, and deficit hawks in both parties, blocked Kennedy's 1961 stimulus package and warned that future spending programs would meet a similar fate. CEA member James Tobin later recalled that he and his colleagues quickly realized that an economic recovery plan that depended on " 'more spending, more spending, more spending' by everyone" would not succeed in the existing political climate.[26] The national uproar over welfare sparked by Joseph Mitchell's war on Newburgh's welfare poor demonstrated even more dramatically the public's resistance to direct social and economic programs. Given public and congressional hostility to tax increases, and the widespread belief that such tax increases were driven by liberal welfare policies aimed at the poor, it is hardly surprising that the economic planners in the Kennedy White House turned quickly to tax policy rather than spending policy to provide the economy with the fiscal stimulus they believed necessary to avoid a recession that might damage the president's chances for reelection in 1964.

The Kennedy White House began to push for a significant, stimulative tax cut to kick-start the economy in the early summer of 1962. In a 7 June press conference, the president made the economic case for cutting taxes, arguing that some adjustment to the present tax structure would be necessary to ensure a prosperous economy and to prevent another recession.[27] Six months later, in his 1963 State of the Union Address, Kennedy laid out the details of the tax cut, calling for a reduction of individual income tax rates—then set between 20 and 91 percent at the margins—to a "more sensible range" of 14 to 65 percent over a three-year period. Yielding to congressional hostility to new spending programs, the president insisted that he preferred to use tax reductions rather than spending increases to stimulate the economy, noting that the desired growth might be achieved through a "massive increase in federal spending" but that he would rather give "private consumers, employers and investors" the first opportunity.[28] As he had a month before, speaking to the economic elite of the New York Economic Club, Kennedy argued that the federal government's role in economic management should not be to rush into a program of "excessive increases in public expenditures," but rather to expand incentives and opportunities for private investment and spending.[29]

A little more than a week after the State of the Union, the White House sent a formal tax cut and reform package to the House Ways and Means Committee. The proposed legislation contained $11 billion in individual rate cuts and about $2.6 billion in corporate rate reductions, only partially offset by $3.4 billion in revenue-raising structural reforms. Congressional response was mixed and reactions to the proposal cut across party lines. Conservatives in both parties tended to focus on the irresponsibility of the tax cut in the face of large deficits and spending increases in the president's budget. Rep. Clarence Cannon, the Missouri Democrat who chaired the House Appropriations Committee, complained that the president's budget was "loaded with waste" and accused the administration of "spending money that we do not have for things we could get along without." Democratic Senator Clinton Anderson of New Mexico, a member of the Finance Committee, admitted that it was a "little discouraging to have a Budget with an $11.9 billion deficit and face a huge tax cut." While Chairman Mills refused to comment publicly on the proposal, his Republican counterpart, Ways and Means ranking member Rep. John Byrnes of Wisconsin, told reporters that the tax package would not pass unless "Congress does more to bring spending under control."[30] On the left, critics claimed that the across-the-board cut would provide too little relief to those at the bottom of the income scale, while providing corporations and the wealthy with a large windfall. Liberal economist and former Truman CEA chief Leon Keyserling criticized the program as "very small, but sent out to do a giant's job."[31] A flier, distributed by the AFL-CIO in July 1963, likewise expressed the union's concern that the tax bill did too little for "moderate and low income families."[32] As George Meany, the labor organization's president, argued repeatedly, tax cuts targeted at lower- and middle-income workers were most likely to "release . . . money" into the economy and improve the "purchasing power stream" needed to "meet this problem of unemployment."[33]

Although both parties scrambled to associate themselves with the cause of tax relief, the GOP attacked the president's specific proposals as a risky economic gamble and a crass attempt to "buy" votes through tax reduction (see Figure 5). Representative Byrnes accused the White House of irresponsibly promising that the tax cut would cure all the nation's ills, noting caustically that the "great majority of the American people and the Congress" had been "somewhat aghast when we asked the New Frontier what we can do for our country" and were "told we must buck up and accept both $100 billion in federal spending and a tax cut as the price of good citizens."[34] While agreeing that "high and steeply progressive tax rates" had created a "drag on our private enterprise economy," the Ways and Means Republican questioned the wisdom of providing tax relief while federal spending continued to rise. According to Byrnes, the Kennedy tax cut was nothing more than a dangerous game of "Russian roulette" that promised only an "unending parade of deficits" and an "inflationary binge."[35] In return for his support of the bill, Byrnes proposed that the administration put spending in a "deep freeze."[36] The Joint Senate-House Republican leadership likewise called the combination of increased expenditures and decreased tax revenues the "biggest economic gamble in the history of nations."[37] The White House, GOP spokesmen insisted, was engaged in a "desperate kind of economics" because it had no real "solution to the unemployment problem."[38]

In response, the White House signaled its commitment to "holding down expenditures to the maximum extent feasible over the coming years."[39] Treasury Secretary C. Douglas Dillon repeated again and again during his Ways and Means testimony that the administration was committed to a policy of "strict control of expenditures."[40] Budget Director Kermit Gordon likewise reiterated the administration's preference for tax reductions over spending increases as the best way to stimulate the economy. Admitting that the White House's commitment to addressing "unsolved domestic problems" would likely require "some increase in Federal expenditures," he promised that the tax cut would "require that the size of those increases be sharply restrained."[41]

Gordon was not alone in making this argument. Administration spokesmen repeatedly warned that if the tax cut were not enacted, Congress and the White House would be left with only one option in the event of a likely recession—increased expenditures. As Dillon told Ways and Means members, "if we do not [enact the tax cut] . . .the pressures to increase expenditures, if only to take care of the large number of unemployed and areas of

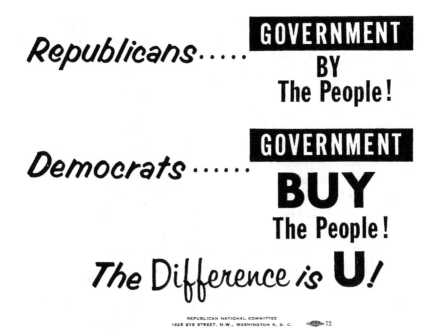

Republicans.....GOVERNMENT BY The People!

Democrats......GOVERNMENT BUY The People!

The Difference is U!

REPUBLICAN NATIONAL COMMITTEE
1625 EYE STREET, N.W., WASHINGTON 6, D. C.   72

Figure 5. GOP campaign flier, circa 1960, accusing Democratic Party of "buying" votes with both spending programs and tax cuts. Courtesy of Division of Political History, National Museum of American History, Smithsonian Institution, Washington D.C.

distress, will be much larger than otherwise and we will continue to have high expenditures."[42] Dillon pressed this point with the nation's business community, warning the blue-chip Business Council that failure to enact the tax cut would create new pressures to enact permanent increases in federal spending, "thus increasing the size and economic influence of Government."[43] Commerce Secretary Luther Hodges made a similar argument, claiming that the tax cut would not only set free the nation's productive capacities but would also lead to "fewer claims on welfare and other public assistance."[44] The administration and its supporters in Congress thus defended the tax cut as a way to *prevent* the further growth of the national state. According to Louisiana Democratic Representative Hale Boggs, for example, the tax cut proposal was nothing less than "good free enterprise economics" that would allow individuals and businesses to "make their own individual determinations on how they are going to use these funds rather than having these . . . determinations made at the Government level."[45]

The Ways and Means Committee finished its mark-up of the tax bill on 14 August 1963. The committee bill rejected most of the administration's proposed revenue-raising structural reforms, and provided about $11 billion in tax cuts for individuals and corporations.[46] Although the Ways and Means bill differed significantly from the original White House proposal, Kennedy signaled his support for the committee's version and pledged to work with Mills for final passage. On 19 August, President Kennedy sent the chairman a letter, later released to the White House press corps, praising the committee for its "long and constructive labors in formulating a new tax bill." The legislation, the president predicted, would "provide much needed jobs for our economy, increase our rate of economic growth, promote balance in our international trade and benefit the individual and corporate taxpayer."[47] The president also took advantage of the occasion to assure both the chairman and the public of his resolution to cut, or at least contain, federal spending. In a September speech to a group of leading businessmen, Kennedy repeated his pledge to exercise more control over federal spending and touted his administration's record of slowing the growth of the national debt, shifting certain programs from the public to the private economy, and reducing federal civilian employment.[48]

Most of the discussion about the merits and liabilities of the tax program took place inside the D.C. beltway; the general public seemed less than interested in income tax cuts. "We haven't felt much heat yet" from the "grassroots," admitted one Ways and Means Democrat in early 1963.[49] Even those "special interests" that favored the bill expressed only "moderate enthusiasm" about its provisions.[50] The "tax cut fever" *Wall Street Journal* reporter Robert Novak had predicted early in the year had failed to materialize.[51] By mid-March, nearly three months after the president had announced the tax cut, the White House reported that it had received fewer than 2,000 telephone calls or letters about the tax proposals.[52] According to a September *New York Times* report, few small taxpayers seemed to be "eagerly awaiting more money in their pockets."[53] The White House actually had to *sell* the proposal to voters. According to Assistant Treasury Secretary Stanley Surrey and White House staffer Lawrence O'Brien, the administration needed to do everything possible to "convince people that something personally helpful is good for the country."[54] To drum up public support, the Treasury published a pamphlet explaining that the proposal promised "virtually every taxpayer in the country" a significant tax cut. Structured as a question and answer session, the pamphlet responded to both liberal and conservative critiques of the

tax plan. In answer to conservative concerns about potential deficits, for example, the Treasury brochure claimed that the tax cut would actually "reduce
the likelihood of continuing budget deficits" because it would "increase economic activity." To the left's critique of the administration's abandonment of
targeted social spending programs, the department responded that a "tax cut
now" would enable the "nation to meet . . . educational and other needs better in the future." Although spending "more money on education and other
programs . . .might be desirable," it would not cure the nation's economic
problems. Instead, the Treasury Department put its full faith in the market,
predicting that the tax cut would produce "faster economic growth, full employment, and rising incomes," and would "generate more ample revenues in
the long run to support . . . important programs."[55]

To generate public and congressional enthusiasm for the tax measure, the
administration enlisted the help of the nation's corporate leaders as well as
representatives from the small-business community, organized labor, agriculture, and certain social service groups. Two groups—the Business Committee
for Tax Reduction in 1963 and the Citizens' Committee for Tax Reduction and
Revision in 1963—were particularly important to the administration's effort
to secure popular support for the tax cut. Neither the Business Committee
nor the Citizens' Committee had any direct connection to government agen-
cies; nonetheless, the White House played a critical role in their formation,
and the goals of both groups dovetailed neatly with the administration's own
priorities.[56] After all, both committees had been formed in the late spring of
1963 with the "urgent blessing" of the Kennedy White House and its "leading
inspirer of committees," Treasury Undersecretary Henry Fowler.[57]

The Business Committee was far more influential—and well funded—
than its citizen counterpart.[58] The group claimed 2,767 members drawn from
the ranks of the country's largest corporations; it issued at least twenty-four
press releases advocating tax reduction and had a budget of about $150,000 to
spend on its lobbying and public relations campaign. Formed on the recommendation of Undersecretary Fowler, the Committee's leadership included
many of the country's top corporate executives, including representatives
from Ford Motor Company, General Motors, Chase Manhattan Bank, and
AT&T. In April 1963, the Committee released a statement of principles calling for a "strong stimulus to the economy" in the form of a "substantial reduction in all individual tax rates" and a "reduction in the rate of corporate
income tax." Insisting on the immediate necessity of a tax cut, the Business
Committee recommended that the administration drop politically contro-

versial tax reform proposals, most of which would have increased the tax burdens of higher-income taxpayers, so as not to "delay tax reduction."[59]

The Citizens' Committee for Tax Reduction and Revision might be seen as a public interest analog to the Business Committee, one that aimed to "arouse public opinion in support of a single, comprehensive, [tax reform and revision] bill." Comprising forty-five "prominent leaders of small business, labor, agriculture, housing, aging and welfare, and education," the Citizens' Committee provided a "point of coordination among the various constituent organizations" in order to "promote widespread public understanding and acceptance of the national need for prompt and effective action on the tax bill."[60] The new committee's purpose was frankly political; it provided the Kennedy administration with cover on its left flank. Shortly after the Business Committee had announced its recommendations, several liberal advocacy groups, including the Americans for Democratic Action and the Industrial Union Department of the AFL-CIO, publicly criticized the administration for "turning . . . the tax decisions over to a . . . business group . . . [un] representative of the whole economic community . . . [or] the public interest."[61] Accusing the Business Group of trying to "redesign the President's tax program" to favor high-income taxpayers and corporations, these liberal groups organized themselves into the short-lived Committee for Full Employment and pushed for a tax reduction concentrated more squarely "in the lower brackets."[62] The Citizens' Committee—formed at the behest of the White House—aimed to defuse these kinds of criticisms. According to one White House insider, the committee was useful largely as a "symbol of the support of the tax bill from the sectors of our economy *not* identified with large or medium sized business" and as an indication of "mass interest and support."[63]

Like the Business Committee, the Citizens' Committee worked closely with the White House to rally support for the administration's tax proposals. From within the administration, Walter Heller played a critical role in forming the Citizens' Committee and in facilitating communication between the group and the White House and the Treasury Department. Throughout the spring and summer of 1963, the CEA chief reached out to his contacts and friends in academia, contacting the chancellor of Indiana University and the presidents of the University of Wisconsin and the University of California at Berkeley to ask them to join the group and support its efforts.[64] Heller even offered to let the Committee chair, Grinnell College president Howard Bowen, use his membership to stay at Washington's elite Cosmos Club while the group met.[65]

According to the organization's "statement of principles," the Citizens' Committee hoped to drum up public and congressional support for "meaningful revision in Federal income tax laws" as well as a $10 billion "net tax reduction of individual and corporate taxes . . . to take effect as early as possible in 1963."[66] For the most part, however, the committee's efforts to create a groundswell of support for the tax cut failed. In August, the group reported "considerable public apathy concerning the vital tax legislation" and pledged to redouble its efforts to promote "widespread public understanding and acceptance of the national need for prompt and effective congressional action."[67] Noting that Congress had received little mail concerning the tax program, the Committee urged its members to demonstrate to voters how the tax cut would benefit individual taxpayers by creating "Fact Sheets concerning specific proposals."[68]

Even absent a strong public demand for tax cuts, the Ways and Means Committee formally reported the tax bill in the second week of September. Approval was largely along party lines. Nine of ten Committee Republicans signed onto a minority report that accused the Democratic Party and the Kennedy White House of irresponsibly risking "inflation and the cheapening of the dollar" for a tax cut that would provide the average taxpayer with little more than a "week's cigarette money."[69] The committee's Democratic majority approved the plan and rejected a GOP proposal to formally tie the second stage of the tax cut to specific spending reduction targets. The majority, however, did make clear that the tax cut should be seen as a distinct *alternative* to new social spending. The main purpose of the tax bill, the Ways and Means Committee insisted, was to "remove from the private sector its present high tax straitjacket" and to "lessen restraints which prevent . . . necessary growth" in the market economy. "Top priority," the Democratic majority concluded, "cannot be given to both tax reductions and to spending at the same time."[70]

Chairman Mills made this point abundantly clear on the House floor when he insisted that the country faced two paths to economic growth and a more prosperous America—the "tax reduction road or the government expenditure increase road." While admitting that increases in government expenditures might produce a "higher level of economic activity," Mills argued that it would do so only if "larger and larger shares of that activity" were initiated by government. The "tax cut reduction road," on the other hand, would produce a "higher level of economic activity . . . with a larger and larger share of that enlarged activity initiating in the private sector of the economy.[71] The revenue bill drafted by the Ways and Means Committee, he insisted, signaled a "firm, positive assertion of the preference for the tax reduction road" and marked a "turning point" in the country's history.[72] If Congress failed to cut tax rates, as the administration had asked, others would try to solve the nation's economic problems by "more and more government spending."[73] Swayed by the chairman's arguments, and over the opposition of the GOP minority, the House passed the tax package by 271–155 on 25 September. The final bill provided for over $11 billion in individual and corporate tax cuts.

The Senate Finance Committee, which received the bill after the House had passed it, had not yet completed its work when President Kennedy was shot and Vice President Lyndon Johnson was sworn in as the new president of the United States.

Although Johnson had not been intimately involved in the tax cut fight, he kept Kennedy's economic team in place, and his administration continued to push for the economic stimulus package. Unfortunately, the Finance Committee was reluctant to report the bill and send it to the full Senate for a vote. Most of the opposition to the tax cut came, as it had in the House, from fiscal conservatives, who insisted on the "important connection between tax reduction and expenditure control."[74] But, some committee liberals raised serious questions about the bill's basic premises. Democratic Senator Albert Gore, who made opposition to the tax cut bill a key part of his reelection campaign efforts in Tennessee, was particularly persistent in his opposition.[75] Forcing attention to the long-range implications of the tax cut for certain discretionary spending programs, the Tennessee liberal accused the administration of placing the nation in a "fiscal straitjacket" that would produce a "drastic reduction in federal revenue" and reduce the administration's "ability, except at greater deficits, to stimulate the public sector of our economy."[76] Gore recognized more clearly than the Johnson or Kennedy administrations the long-term consequences of the tax cut for the liberal project. Although such a view might be "unsophisticated" or "erroneous," the senator counseled, most people tend to judge the question of federal spending "in the simple terms of the family budget." "A reduction in revenue," he continued, "will set up a howling campaign for a reduction in expenditures," with the ax falling "heaviest on foreign aid and on programs that may be needed to stimulate the economy, such as public works."[77]

Though prescient, Gore's protests fell on deaf ears. By early 1964, most of the resistance to the tax bill had crumbled. Not only did the Johnson administration successfully package the deal as a key commitment of the late president, but the new administration's budget proposals, submitted in late

January, also reduced federal spending to under $100 billion and thus seemed to make good on earlier promises to "keep a tight rein" on spending. The tax bill, Johnson argued in his 1964 State of the Union Address, was necessary to keep the "country moving." Cuts made in the budget, he claimed "clearly allow it" and the "economy strongly demands it." But, perhaps more importantly, the taxpayers "surely deserve it."[78] The final bill, which included about $10 billion in across-the-board rate reductions, sailed through Congress in February 1964. On signing the legislation, President Johnson called the tax cut the "single most important step . . . taken to strengthen [the] national economy since World War II." The president also reiterated his faith in the American economy as the best guarantor of liberty. By reducing the amount citizens owed in federal taxes and "releasing millions of dollars into the private economy," the tax cut would ensure that the "Federal Government will not have to do for the economy what the economy should do for itself."[79]

A Plea for Equity: The War on Poverty

In the short term, the tax cut worked, helping to launch what Treasury Secretary Dillon later called a "brilliant new chapter in the economic history of the United States."[80] Walter Heller favorably compared the "vigorous Democratic" economy to the "sluggish Republican one," and credited the tax cut with boosting employment, increasing economic output, and improving business productivity.[81] The tax cut also had an apparently salutary effect on the budget. Despite severe cuts in income tax rates, federal revenues rose by about $1.2 billion between 1963 and 1965 and the federal deficit declined from $4.8 billion in 1963 to $1.4 billion in 1965. Individual citizens benefited both from improvements in the general economy and from the individual rate reductions. According to Gardner Ackley, who had recently taken over for Heller at the CEA, the 1964 tax cuts, together with a 1962 measure geared toward creating investment incentives, had reduced the tax liabilities of all Americans by about $21 billion between 1962 and 1966.[82] Publicly touting the Revenue Act's success in producing economic growth and creating new jobs, the Johnson administration predicted a $700 "growth dividend" for the average American household by the end of the decade.[83] If not a cure-all, the Johnson administration, like the Kennedy administration before it, saw the tax cut, and its positive effects on the rate of economic growth as a way to solve any number of social ills—from unemployment to welfare dependence.

GNP growth, Ackley promised President Johnson, would "do much . . . to promote the escape from poverty." "Americans at all rungs of the income ladder," he concluded, "have an important stake in the pace of overall economic advance."[84]

Others were less sure that the benefits of the tax cut could be sustained, or that GNP growth alone would secure economic justice for all Americans. Suspicious of the Kennedy and Johnson administrations' reliance on private market mechanisms to eliminate poverty, some labor movement and civil rights leaders, as well as members of the new welfare rights movement, tried to convince the Johnson administration to use the power of the federal government directly to eliminate the last vestiges of "second class citizenship" in an "otherwise affluent society."[85] However, if some on the left championed an activist state dedicated to securing economic and social rights for all citizens, the Johnson administration embraced a far more limited role for itself in enabling "every American citizen to fulfill his basic hopes."[86] Announced in January 1964, the War on Poverty amounted to little more than a skirmish, fought at little or no cost to the nonpoor majority. What is more, the administration's promise to turn tax eaters into taxpayers by replacing a government "hand out" with a "hand-up" implicitly condemned more direct forms of government interventionism, and set the stage for a backlash against both liberalism and the activist state.

Plans for a national antipoverty initiative began in 1963. Inspired by Michael Harrington's description of the desperate poverty of the "Other America," and prodded into action by an increasingly powerful and impatient Civil Rights movement, President Kennedy directed Heller and the CEA to "pull together . . . a set of measures which might be woven into a basic attack on the problems of poverty and waste of human resources."[87] The poverty program, Kennedy and his advisors believed, would complement the Revenue Act and the larger growth agenda; Heller, for example, insisted that a more robust economic expansion would automatically increase the number of Americans able to rise above the poverty line.[88] CEA staff economist Robert Lampman likewise claimed that a "good deal" of the poverty problem would "yield to a successful tax cut, full employment and faster growth."[89] The Kennedy administration thus conceived of the antipoverty programs as one part of a larger political agenda in which economic growth, provided by the private market and stimulated by the invisible hand of the federal government, would allow for the cost-free expansion of the national state. Together with the tax cut, the public welfare laws of 1961 and 1962 and the Civil Rights Act of 1964, the poverty program would provide access and opportunity to those Americans left behind in the "wake of progress"—and all at relatively little cost to the Treasury or to individual taxpayers. Equally important, the elimination of poverty would improve the overall health of the nation by creating "additional national product," reducing "market barriers" and protecting against "crime and delinquency."[90]

After Kennedy's assassination, an enthusiastic Lyndon Johnson embraced the poverty program as his own.[91] And like Kennedy before him, Johnson was careful to distance himself and the poverty programs from any hint of income redistribution. Very early on, Lampman had counseled the president that a "politically acceptable program" would "avoid completely the use of the term 'inequality' or the term 'redistribution' of income or wealth."[92] White House aide Adam Yarmolinsky even advised the president to avoid discussing the poor whenever possible in favor of talking about "targets of opportunity."[93] The president's advisors also counseled their boss to frame the poverty program as a "long-run" and "meaningful" attack on poverty that would add only a "small increment to the budget."[94] Sargent Shriver, the head of the new Office of Economic Opportunity (OEO), similarly assured Congress that the poverty program would not "raise the national budget by a single dollar."[95] And indeed, Johnson asked Congress for only $500 million in new appropriations to pay for the poverty program, and then publicly asked his Cabinet to undertake "hard-hitting, tough-minded reforms in existing programs" to ensure that the government was "spending only where [it] legitimately need[ed] to spend."[96] When Johnson unthinkingly discussed the new programs in terms of "redistribution" from "those who have it to those who don't," the White House was quick to clarify that the president had meant only that the poverty program would take funds from existing "have" *government programs*—not from individuals.[97] Indeed the Johnson administration explicitly and repeatedly rejected income transfers as a solution to the poverty problem, choosing instead to focus on long-term solutions to integrate the poor into the mainstream of economic life.

This emphasis built on an existing consensus among welfare experts and social workers developed over the course of the 1950s. Convinced that a "cradle-to-grave" welfare state was a political nonstarter, and concerned about the changing character of the nation's public assistance population—which included increasing numbers of single-mother and minority families—welfare experts abandoned income maintenance in favor of social and personal rehabilitation.[98] Arguing that welfare spending, without accompanying rehabilitative services might actually increase dependency, these policy entrepreneurs, who had been largely exiled to academia and private foundations during the Eisenhower years, worked tirelessly throughout the decade to formalize the place of social services within the welfare system.[99] Congress signed off on this rehabilitative approach in 1962 when it approved legislation to increase the federal money available to states to provide social services to "strengthen or broaden the rehabilitation and preventative services . . . offered to persons who are dependent or who might become dependent" on government assistance.[100] Rehabilitation's promise to help "welfare recipients move off the rolls by becoming self-supporting," *Congressional Quarterly* noted approvingly a week after the passage of the Public Welfare Amendments of 1962, was understandably "appealing to conservative and liberal congressmen alike."[101] The welfare experts and social workers behind the rehabilitative consensus promised that this approach would not only alleviate dependency but would actually prevent it.[102] Likewise, at their most grandiose, poverty warriors in the Kennedy and Johnson administrations claimed that wise policy could eliminate poverty within a generation and "bind together those who are now comfortable and those who feel set apart."[103]

Like an earlier generation of social insurance advocates who sought to protect their favored program by demeaning the "dole," poverty warriors often went to great lengths to distinguish their programs from the failed public assistance programs and redistributive politics of an earlier era. As one federal report later pointed out, the War on Poverty represented an attempt on the part of a Democratic administration to "institute a poverty policy that would be separate from the public assistance programs."[104] The Johnson White House explicitly rejected income transfer programs as a lasting solution to the problem of poverty and avoided policies that merely enriched the poor, instead favoring those that would allow the poor to contribute to and fully share in the promise of economic growth.[105] As the president himself noted, the War on Poverty was not a "struggle simply to support people, to make them dependent on others," but was rather a comprehensive plan to "give people a chance" to "develop and use their capacities . . . so that they can share as others share in the promise of the nation."[106]

The administration even claimed that antipoverty programs would eventually save taxpayer dollars by eliminating poverty and the need for costly welfare programs. Heller's draft of Johnson's first poverty message claimed that the programs would "in the end bring important savings in the $4 billion annual cost of public assistance."[107] At Shriver's swearing-in ceremony, the president described the philosophy of the new programs as one that "rejects growing relief rolls."[108] With their focus on manpower training programs and education, Johnson-era antipoverty programs offered a market-driven alternative to a "federal hand-out or national dole."[109] Taking shape within a political economy deeply inflected by the Cold War, these policies both reflected and reproduced the suspicion of statist policies, putting their "faith in the dignity and the capacity of the individual to grow, to bloom, through education."[110] Eliminating poverty, Johnson claimed in his 1964 State of the Union address, would allow the United States to vindicate the free market system and "disprove those cynics and critics" both at home and abroad "who question our purpose and competence."[111] Even the Community Action Programs, later a much reviled policy, aimed first to integrate the poor into the political and economic mainstream by allowing them "to develop sufficient strength and skill to maneuver themselves . . . out of where they are and into something better."[112]

The architects and defenders of the New Frontier, the Great Society, and the War on Poverty promised that the poor minority could be brought into the mainstream of American life at little or no cost to the nonpoor majority. As a political strategy, this certainly made sense, allowing the Johnson administration to launch an unprecedented and very public attack on poverty, despite the reticence of many conservative Democrats and the opposition of most Republicans. But the limited appropriations provided for antipoverty programs exacerbated both class and racial tensions by pitting various needy groups and individuals against one another in a pitched battle for limited resources.[113] Equally important, by fighting a war on poverty on the terms established by the existing taxing and welfare state—terms that promised low taxes, delivered economic security to the broad middle class through private intermediaries, and identified as government spending only a narrow band of welfare programs aimed at the very poor—liberal policymakers ultimately undercut support for the activist state and liberalism in general. The racial politics of the War on Poverty and the subsequent backlash against government spending derived not so much from racial animus—although that certainly played a part—but from the ways in which the taxing and welfare state, erected in the 1930s and 1940s and reinforced in the 1950s and 1960s, delivered benefits (visible and invisible) and distributed costs (visible and invisible) in a racially stratified way. That the War on Poverty would soon come to embody a redistributive program that taxed the white majority to shower benefits on the black minority was a fiction, but it was a fiction that made sense given the institutional and ideological legacies of the American taxing and welfare state.

The conceptual and practical limitations of the War on Poverty are especially apparent in comparison with more radical proposals to reshape the nation's political economy by comprehensively addressing the "deep structural inequalities in American life."[114] These proposals, advocated by some labor unions, many Civil Rights leaders, and members of the new welfare rights movement, challenged head-on the narrowed definitions of taxpaying citizenship and welfare that constrained official poverty policy and envisioned a real and enduring role for the activist state in ensuring economic justice and racial equality.

Challenges to the market-based approach to poverty policy pursued by both the Kennedy and Johnson administrations came largely from the African American freedom movements, whose leaders understood all too well the relationship between public policy and racial and class inequalities. Civil Rights activists knew that the civil and political rights guaranteed by the Civil Rights and Voting Rights Acts of 1964 and 1965 would mean little without positive policies to ensure black Americans' economic security. Only federal investment, comparable in scope and scale to the 1945 Servicemen's Readjustment Act—or GI Bill of Rights—could tear down the "walls of the black ghetto" by providing "all persons with a decent level of income."[115] In September 1964, three months after President Johnson had signed the Civil Rights Act, the Rev. Martin Luther King, Jr., told the annual convention of the Southern Christian Leadership Conference (SCLC) that although the Civil Rights bill had brought African Americans to the "threshold of becoming . . . first class participant[s] in our society," until the black community was "released from economic privation" it could "not fully be deemed liberated."[116] "Giving a pair of shoes to a man who has not learned to walk," King reminded the Convention, was little more than a "cruel jest."[117]

Any program to secure full economic and social citizenship for all would depend on substantial government investment. In 1961, Whitney Young, the new president of the National Urban League, proposed what he called a Domestic Marshall Plan to rebuild the nation's cities and rural areas. Named after the popular and successful postwar reconstruction of Western Europe, and short on policy details, Young's plan called on the federal government to underwrite a similar kind of reconstruction at home. This "massive, crash effort on the part of all governmental bodies, private institutions, foundations and settlement houses," Young argued in 1965, would help "Negro citizens qualify themselves for the new opportunities opening before them."[118] Defending his proposal, Young, like many other Civil Rights leaders, sought to broaden the definition of welfare and to link public efforts to assist the "oppressed, the sick, the handicapped and deprived" to the nation's "political and economic credo."[119] This approach challenged the distinction between taxpayers and tax eaters endorsed by the Kennedy and Johnson administrations by pointing out and even celebrating the extent to which federal largesse enabled the apparent independence of the American taxpayer. As Young noted in a 1963 piece for the *New York Times* Sunday magazine, the GI Bill of Rights was a welfare program created in "recognition of the special need of our discharged veterans for education, housing, employment and other benefits." Dismissing claims that his Domestic Marshall Plan amounted to "special consideration" or "preferential treatment" for black Americans, Young instead cast the recommendations as "necessary and just corrective measures" to give meaning to the phrase "equal opportunity."[120]

The Freedom Budget, written under the direction of Bayard Rustin and released in 1966 by the A. Phillip Randolph Institute, represented a more developed policy program than the Domestic Marshall Plan. The Freedom Budget embraced a "vision of social justice and equality . . . rapidly and forthrightly achieved," and called on the federal government to work toward abolishing poverty within a decade through a combination of full employment policies and federal income maintenance programs.[121] Envisioning a distinct role for the federal government in raising the living standards of all Americans, the proposal called for the creation of a total of 16.6 million new jobs by 1973, as well as a "federally initiated and supported guaranteed annual income" for those "who cannot achieve adequacy [sic] incomes through the employment process."[122]

Randolph, a Civil Rights leader and long-time union activist, first laid out the parameters of the Freedom Budget in his opening address to the November planning session for the 1965 White House Conference on Civil Rights.[123] In the following months, Randolph and Rustin worked with religious groups, labor unions and other Civil Rights leaders to develop a multibillion dollar statement of domestic priorities. Endorsed by more than two hundred independent advocacy groups, the $185 billion, ten-year, Freedom Budget included proposals to raise the minimum wage, create millions of new jobs over the next decade, use federal money—in the form of publicly subsidized private construction—to build 500,000 new low-income housing units to "wipe out slum ghettoes," and provide a "federally-initiated and supported guaranteed annual income to supplement . . . a sustained full-employment policy at decent pay."[124] Claiming that "poverty, ignorance and despair" lay at the "real root of all America's domestic problems," and pledging to move beyond the "haphazard and piecemeal efforts" of the War on Poverty, the Freedom Budget promised a "coordinated mobilization" of "national resources" to "provide the schools . . . the jobs . . . the homes . . . the health care" to those left behind by postwar affluence.[125] Reflecting growing cynicism about War on Poverty programs that sought to "fix people" rather than institutions, Randolph and Rustin insisted that their Freedom Budget would move beyond the "personal characteristics of the poor" to address the inequitable distribution of material, social, and cultural resources embedded in the national economy.[126]

The Freedom Budget, like the Rev. Martin Luther King's GI Bill of Rights for Disadvantaged Americans or the Domestic Marshall Plan, represented an attempt to forge a biracial alliance in support of a remedial Civil Rights agenda by appealing to the shared material interests of the white and black working classes. The "economically deprived condition" of African Americans, King told the SCLC, would "remain unless the Negro revolution builds and maintains alliances with the majority of the white community."[127] Such an alliance was not simply a question of practical coalition politics. Rather, the Freedom Budget and similar programs represented an explicitly class-conscious call for the expansion of economic and social citizenship that promised to transcend the divisions of race. Writing to John Lewis of the Student Nonviolent Coordinating Committee, Randolph insisted that the Freedom Budget was not "limited to the plight of the Negro or other minority groups."[128] The "legitimate aspirations" of African Americans could not be "fulfilled in isolation." Only through the "abolition of poverty (almost three-quarters of whose victims are whites)" could the country reaffirm its historical commitment to "human freedom and democracy."[129] Dorothy DiMascio, a white welfare recipient testifying before the Senate Finance Committee, likewise insisted, "it [welfare] is not so much of a racial issue any more. . . . It has become very quickly an economical issue, where black people, white people, poor people are finally realizing that their problems are much the same and they are banding together all over the nation."[130]

In linking increased social spending to the fate of "human freedom" and "democracy," and insisting on the equivalence between economic security and civil and political rights, the architects of the Freedom Budget and similar proposals hoped to tie these policy prescriptions to the successful and popular postwar programs that had guaranteed economic security and citizenship to the white majority. As such, their political appeals directly challenged the narrowed definition of welfare and government spending that had emerged in the 1940s and 1950s. Testifying before the Ways and Means Committee, Young compared the Freedom Budget to the GI Bill of Rights. Calling the proposal a long-term "investment," the Urban League president told the committee that the country stood at a historic turning point: "We will either decide in this generation," he argued, "that we are going to rehabilitate the victims of our society and make them self sufficient," or we will perpetuate "the social disorganization that we find in many communities."[131] Aware of the hidden nature of the middle-class welfare state, Young urged the committee to "help . . . society to understand that it isn't just Congressmen and welfare clients who get their salaries paid by the government, who are subsidized by Government." After all, he concluded, "there is hardly a business today whose chief executive cannot trace some of his own salary right back to the federal government."[132]

Young's plea, as well as the recommendation of President Johnson's own Income Maintenance Task Force (IMTF) for a comprehensive "public reeducation" project, sought to erase the fictive distinction between taxpayers and tax consumers by making visible the role that the federal government had played in securing and defending the rights and privileges of the white middle-class majority.[133] Welfare recipients too challenged what they viewed as an artificial and arbitrary distinction between taxpayers and tax eaters. "You say we are not taxpayers," welfare mother Alice Nixon told one Senate panel, but "every time we buy a can of beans, we keep the bean farmer in business, the aluminum companies in business, and if we decide we would not buy a can tomorrow, how many steelworkers would be out of work?"[134] Like the architects of the Freedom Budget, welfare rights advocates located their defense of a right to welfare within a historical analysis of the patterns of disadvantage and advantage written into the structures of the postwar state, and rejected the traditional distinction between the public sphere of government policy and the private sphere of economic decision making. Echoing the conclusions of the *1968 Report* of the National Advisory Commission on Civil Disorders—better known as the Kerner Commission—that "white society" and "white institutions" had created and maintained the ghetto, welfare rights spokesman Edward Sparer asserted that postwar social and economic policy had "enrich[ed] one group of citizens" by stripping "other citizens . . . of the means of survival." Federal agricultural policy had materially disadvantaged tenant farmers; federal inflation policy, predicated on the assumption that some degree of unemployment was necessary to contain inflationary pressures, had cost workers their jobs. Indeed, Sparer demanded rhetorically, "cannot a substantial case be made that there is a direct, causal link between affirmative government policy on behalf of the middle class and the rich and the substandard condition of the poor?"[135]

The growth of the national state, many welfare rights advocates argued, had rendered the line between the state and the market irrelevant. In an influential 1964 article in the *Yale Law Journal*, law professor Charles Reich suggested that the postwar expansion of government had created what he termed "a new property." The "wealth of more and more Americans," Reich noted, "depends upon a relationship to the government." The postwar expansion of the federal state on a "vast and imperial scale" had effectively broken "down the distinctions between public and private" and "blurred" or "fused" the "public and private spheres."[136] Given the interconnectedness of the state and the market, Reich concluded, all Americans had a "right—not a mere privilege—to a minimal share in the commonwealth."[137]

Demanding both political empowerment and economic security, Civil Rights leaders and welfare rights advocates launched a historically informed challenge to the false dichotomy between taxpayers and tax eaters that increasingly guided both Democratic and GOP politics. This strategy was largely unsuccessful. Although welfare and Civil Rights leaders correctly pointed out that federal policy actively created and secured new social and economic rights for many white Americans, the form the American welfare state had taken in the 1930s, 1940s, and 1950s—its reliance on indirect tax expenditures, economic growth, and certain social insurance programs—ensured that the federal subsidy under the white middle class could be easily denied and largely ignored. Once the majority of Americans had, with the critical but hidden help of the federal government, secured for themselves a certain degree of economic security and mobility, the prospects for a broad coalition in support of the extension of those same privileges to the poor and to African Americans dimmed considerably.[138] The simultaneous transformation of the federal income tax from a class tax to a mass tax created the institutional material for a majoritarian, class-based politics that pitted the rights of taxpayers against the needs of the poor.[139] As general economic growth drew more and more Americans into the federal income tax system, the policies of the taxing state visibly connected their fortunes to those of the poor minority in tangible and immediate ways. The Internal Revenue Code helped to fashion a new political identity of taxpayer, providing, as Andrea

Louise Campbell has argued with respect to Social Security, a "basis for mobilization by political parties, interest groups and policy entrepreneurs."[140]

The success of a multibillion dollar Freedom Budget or a Domestic Marshall Plan designed to extend social and economic citizenship to the poor minority depended on the support of a broad coalition of interests. By the late 1960s, thanks in large part to the institutional and ideological legacies of the postwar welfare and taxing state that divided the taxpaying majority from the tax-eating minority, that coalition did not exist. In fact, the opposite had occurred. According to a 1969 *Newsweek* poll, many white Americans even believed that African Americans had a better chance than they did to get "well-paying jobs," "a good education for their children," "good housing," and "financial help from the government."[141] Convinced that black Americans were actually better off than they were, many working- and middle-class whites had no interest in an expanded welfare state and, identifying as taxpayers, claimed a vested interest in containing the size and cost of the U.S. welfare state. Determined to protect their prerogatives, these voters threatened to oppose not only the further expansion of welfare or the War on Poverty, but also the entire liberal project that supported and sustained the activist state.

CHAPTER 3

THINGS FALL APART

Early in 1967, public opinion expert Ben Wattenberg issued President Lyndon Johnson a simple warning: the administration's focus on the War on Poverty and the war in Vietnam threatened to cost the Democratic Party the affection and votes of the "middle-class working man in America." Although it had been only a few years earlier that "union men had looked to the federal government for the same things that today the persons in poverty look for," the landscape of middle- and working-class America had changed. Where American workers could once be found in slums they were now more likely to be found in suburbia. With little interest in poverty programs or even the minimum wage, the unionized worker had become "quite properly, quite naturally, more interested in getting his children into college than . . . [in] a welfare program designed to provide more aid for fatherless, poor children." All too often, Wattenberg concluded, the working man and the union man wanted to know of the federal government, "What have you done for me lately?"[1]

Wattenberg's memorandum summarized the dilemma facing the Johnson administration and its liberal allies at the end of the 1960s. By decade's end America's middle-class majority had grown frustrated, angry, and disillusioned by policymakers' apparent "obsession" with the nation's "alienated minorities—the incendiary black militant and the welfare mothers, the hedonistic hippie and the campus revolutionary."[2] Indeed, many Americans, particularly the white middle- and working-class voters of what President Richard Nixon would soon dub the Silent Majority, did feel both alienated from the government and victimized by the War on Poverty and the Civil Rights revolution. "Isn't it about time," demanded one group of white homeowners in 1967, that "Congress takes some action on behalf of the vast majority, the law abiding society, in the United States?"[3] Targeting Civil Rights and poverty programs, these voters expressed their outrage at "continued giveaways" to "all these damn welfare loafers and rioters," and demanded that their elected officials "do something to help those average Americans who pay most of the taxes that support this country."[4]

Although historians have correctly called attention to the racial dimensions of the backlash against Democratic liberalism in the late 1960s, they have all but ignored the importance of taxpaying citizenship to the Silent Majority's frustrations with the liberal state. In the late 1960s, public discussions surrounding two pieces of legislation—the Social Security Amendments of 1967 and the Revenue and Expenditure Control Act of 1968—are particularly illuminating in this regard.[5] During debate on these two laws, lawmakers repeatedly invoked the interests of taxpayers to justify reductions in both welfare and the War on Poverty. Reproducing the arguments made by state and local politicians in the 1940s, 1950s, and early 1960s, congressional conservatives targeted Aid to Families with Dependent Children (AFDC) and the poverty programs as responsible for the "always increasing tax burdens" of the "conscientious, middle-class taxpayers."[6] This discourse, which nurtured the Silent Majority's sense of victimization at the hands of "ultra-liberals who overlook the well-being of the masses and accede to the demands of well organized minorities," depended on hiding the federal subsidy underwriting middle- and working-class economic security.[7] Indeed, congressional conservatives' decision to frame their attack on both AFDC and the poverty programs as necessary to protect and defend the system of social protections that the majority of Americans had come to expect grew directly out of the institutions and ideological commitments of the postwar liberal state and left untouched the vast majority of liberal spending programs.[8] Even in a season of retrenchment, the New Deal social compact proved difficult to break.

The divergent fates of Social Security on the one hand and AFDC and the poverty programs on the other illustrate the paradoxical consequences of a liberal reform agenda and political discourse that enabled and encouraged the majority of citizens to define themselves as taxpayers with legitimate claims on the state not shared by tax eaters on the welfare rolls. The expansion of both the taxing and the welfare states, despite persistent popular hostility to federal taxation and *direct* spending programs, was a remarkable achievement that not only enabled the economic security enjoyed by the majority of Americans, but also empowered citizens to make new and powerful claims to governmental protection. This expansion and empowerment, however, came at a steep cost. Liberals' success in constructing a hidden welfare state comprising social insurance entitlements and invisible tax spending made it difficult for the Johnson administration to demonstrate just how federal spending had responded to the "new needs of a more affluent working class."[9] With the benefits of liberalism attributed largely to the market economy, only its costs remained visible. As one Detroit resident complained, by 1968 it seemed like the only thing the "poor working people" got from government was more taxes.[10] As healthy economic growth gave way to an inflationary spiral that seemed to threaten the American dream, congressional conservatives successfully turned liberals' traditional commitments to economic growth, individual rights, and low taxes, not only against AFDC and the poverty programs but against liberalism itself.

AFDC Under Attack

By the end of 1966 the political consensus that allowed President Johnson to secure historic Civil Rights legislation, to enact the country's first national health insurance system, to increase the federal government's commitment to and investment in education, and to launch the War on Poverty in the search for the Great Society had all but fallen apart. Inflation and the increasingly unpopular war in Vietnam had depleted the administration's political capital. Encouraged by their gains in the 1966 midterm elections, Republican members of Congress, assisted by conservative Southern Democrats, launched high profile hearings into waste and abuse in the poverty programs and threatened to derail the president's legislative agenda.[11] A wave of riots that began in the Los Angeles neighborhood of Watts in 1965 and spread to urban areas throughout the nation the following summer raised serious questions about the capacity of existing political institutions to redress the alienation and deprivation of the black and urban poor. The economy, too, had soured for the administration. The healthy growth attributed to the Revenue Act of 1964 threatened to spiral into dangerous inflation. The outlook for 1967 was dismal. The previous year, 1966, had been a bad year for the Johnson administration, but for all the headaches it caused, it was a "mere seasonal inclemency" compared to the "raging storm at sea" of 1967.[12]

The economy played a key role in the administration's undoing. Despite sustained and unprecedented economic growth, and a high profile, if underfunded, antipoverty initiative, poverty had not disappeared. As budget director and presidential advisor Charles Schultze noted in a 1966 memorandum to the president, the "great expectations" of the War on Poverty and Great

Society had given way to frustration and disappointment.[13] To make matters worse, inflation now threatened to raise the cost of living for many Americans who only recently had broken into the ranks of the middle class. Within his own party, the president faced a revolt from the left – peace activists unhappy with the war in Vietnam and Civil Rights leaders frustrated with the slow progress in the struggle for full citizenship and equal rights. The conservative wing of the Democratic Party, too, had grown disillusioned with the administration, and, in coalition with congressional Republicans, controlled enough votes to block many of the president's legislative priorities, particularly in the area of civil rights and antipoverty policy.

Faced with a hostile Congress and an uncertain economy, Johnson struck a conciliatory note in his 1967 State of the Union address. Recognizing a "time of testing" for the nation, the president challenged members of the opposition to engage in a "creative debate that offers choices and reasonable alternatives."[14] As always, the budget constrained the administration's policy options. "Until we catch up with existing programs," Shultze advised the president in November 1966, "we should *concentrate our scarce funds*, digest what *we have* and be *very selective* in asking for new programs."[15] The president's domestic agenda reflected these political and economic realities. Eschewing the "soaring rhetoric, vivid slogans, and glowing promises of his first State of the Union addresses," Johnson focused on three relatively modest domestic policy priorities for 1967: a tax increase to restrain inflation and pay for the war in Vietnam, the preservation, if not expansion of the War on Poverty and Great Society, and liberalizations to existing Social Security and welfare programs.[16]

The administration expected little trouble over its welfare and Social Security proposals. The Social Security package, which included a 15 percent across-the-board benefit increase for all beneficiaries, drew bipartisan approval from Congress and enthusiastic support from the public. The outlook for the administration's modest welfare reforms also looked good. Despite rhetorical attacks on the nation's public assistance programs, Congress historically had been willing to increase federal spending on AFDC, if only as a disguised way to funnel federal revenues to individual states.[17] The Social Security and welfare bill, acting Health, Education, and Welfare Secretary Wilbur Cohen predicted in mid-July, was one the president would "want to take credit for" in the 1968 presidential contest.[18]

Cohen was wrong. Rather than underwriting a new consensus, the Social Security Amendments of 1967 further fragmented the already tenuous

Democratic coalition. Led by Chairman Wilbur Mills, the House Ways and Means Committee delayed consideration of the bill for nearly six months. Then, in the summer of 1967, in the immediate aftermath of urban uprisings in Newark and Detroit, and just weeks after Johnson formally requested an across-the-board temporary tax increase of 10 percent, the Ways and Means Committee rewrote the administration's welfare proposals.[19] Formulated without the input of the White House or welfare experts, the House bill set the stage for a direct confrontation between the advocates of an expanded welfare state on the one hand and the defenders of taxpayer rights on the other.

The ease with which the Ways and Means Committee targeted AFDC reflected the program's isolation and the vulnerability of its recipients. Few stepped forward to defend the system, to challenge widely shared assumptions about the social and economic costs of the program, or to defend the character of its beneficiaries. "The welfare system," Johnson admitted in January 1968, "pleases no one. It is criticized by liberals and by conservatives, by the poor and the wealthy, by social workers and politicians, by whites and Negroes in every area of the nation."[20] The President's Advisory Council on Public Welfare likewise condemned AFDC for sinking "people into a poverty from which there is no escape."[21] Conservatives echoed liberal condemnations of the existing welfare system but drew quite different policy conclusions. The system needed to be reformed, not to provide more effective assistance to the welfare poor, but rather to protect taxpayers' interests and paychecks. Defending its changes to the administration's welfare reform package, the House Ways and Means Committee expressed its concern that the "growth in the number of families receiving Aid to Families with Dependent Children" had resulted in "rapidly increasing costs to the taxpayers."[22] The Republican Coordinating Committee similarly warned that the nation faced an "ugly crisis of failure" in its "social welfare system. . . . A crisis of confidence—of fear and alarm among taxpayers, of mounting frustration, ill feeling and disorder in smoldering urban ghettoes, of widening disillusion among men of good will."[23] According to Ronald Reagan, California's newly elected Republican governor, the welfare system was an abject failure that had shifted resources from "people who earned their own way to those who could not earn theirs."[24]

Indeed, there was little disagreement that AFDC had failed to bring its recipients out of poverty or to rehabilitate them sufficiently to participate in the mainstream of the American economy or society. And there was no denying that the program had grown significantly since the end of the Second World

War. Even more troubling were signs that program growth had accelerated quickly over the previous decade. Between 1961 and 1967, annual spending on public welfare programs had almost doubled, from $2.1 billion to $4.1 billion. The total number of public welfare recipients had increased from 5.8 million to 8.1 million. Increased AFDC enrollment accounted for most (2.1 million) of this increase.[25] As one government commission pointed out two decades later, by the "early 1960s, even Congress was beginning to question the basic tenet of welfare—it simply wasn't withering away."[26]

Despite growing dissatisfaction with the system and mounting awareness of its deficiencies, the administration's welfare proposals did little to alter the basic structure of the AFDC program, seeking rather to "increase the adequacy of the public assistance payment" and create new incentives to move welfare recipients into the paid labor force.[27] Far more concerned about the fate of its proposed Social Security increase, the White House fully expected Congress to approve the relatively modest changes to AFDC. As late as 14 July, Cohen advised the president to "expect a good bill" that would "strengthen the welfare programs to give further thrust to rehabilitation and to work incentives."[28] But, on 5 August, James Lyday, an official with the Office of Economic Opportunity (OEO), reported with alarm that Mills had "gutted" the administration bill.[29] Containing none of the moderately liberalizing features proposed by the administration, the committee bill created new, mandatory workfare programs for all AFDC recipients, and threatened to cut off aid to illegitimate children. Where the administration had proposed minimum benefit standards, the House substituted a freeze on federal aid to nonmarital children. Where the White House had called for more aid to the children of unemployed parents, the Ways and Means Committee created new work requirements even for the mothers of very young children. The committee's changes, Lyday concluded, would be nothing short of disastrous for the nation's welfare poor.[30]

There is little doubt that the wave of urban violence that started in Newark on 12 July and spread to Detroit two weeks later informed the Ways and Means Committee's decision to take AFDC policy in a "new direction." The Mills bill, which took shape during this "tense and frightening period," sought at once to address the social pathologies that had allegedly produced the riot mentality, to reorient social policy away from failed War on Poverty programs, and to capitalize on growing discontent and frustration among the white majority with liberal social-engineering programs largely seen as benefiting the African American poor. On 17 July, the same day that President Johnson announced the formation of the Kerner Commission, the *Wall Street Journal* reported that the Ways and Means Committee intended to "kill a major proposal to liberalize welfare."[31] Although welfare had little to do with the larger War on Poverty, and poverty warriors had taken great pains to distinguish their programs from discredited welfare policies, conservatives often conflated the two and even used the growth of the AFDC rolls in the 1960s as evidence of the War on Poverty's abject failure.[32]

Tax politics played a critical if underappreciated role in the Ways and Means Committee's decision to gut the administration's welfare package. The Committee reported its revised bill only weeks after the administration formally requested a 10 percent corporate and individual income tax surcharge to control inflation, reduce budget deficits, and offset the cost of the war in Vietnam.[33] With a request for a substantial tax increase on the table, Mills and his colleagues justified the shift in welfare policy as necessary to protect the interests of taxpayers fed up with the ever-escalating costs of liberal social and economic programs. With little control over other areas of the budget, Mills targeted the one poverty program within his committee's jurisdiction—AFDC. Warning of a possible "revolution" over taxes, the chairman reminded his colleagues that taxpayers wanted to be sure that "giveaway programs and programs that can be pared to the bone are pared to the bone."[34] The growth in the number of families receiving AFDC, the committee reported, required a fundamental change in the way the program worked. For more than thirty years, welfare had failed to enable families to achieve independence and self-support at the same time as it imposed rapidly increasing costs on taxpayers.[35] Only drastic action could "reverse the trend toward higher and higher federal financial commitments" by reducing AFDC rolls and restore "more families to employment and self reliance."[36]

The Mills bill promised both to bring welfare families into the "mainstream of economic life" and to keep "federal financial participation in the . . . program within reasonable bounds."[37] "Taxpayers," Mills told his House colleagues, "want us to be rough" with AFDC recipients.[38] His Republican counterpart, Representative John Byrnes of Wisconsin concurred, adding that a "continuation of present policies" would only "perpetuate the abysmal conditions affecting families who live on welfare" and impose a "growing burden on taxpayers."[39] From the other side of Capitol Hill, Senate Finance Committee Chairman Russell Long of Louisiana defended the Ways and Means bill as an "investment" to help "qualify people for the future so that they will not be tax consumers but taxpayers."[40] Much like the discourse surrounding the earlier state and local welfare crises, policymakers' defense of taxpayers, and the policy substance of the committee bill, strongly suggested that rising tax burdens could be attributed largely to ballooning welfare rolls and rising social spending for the poor minority.[41]

The Ways and Means Committee identified two "basic causes of . . . anticipated growth" in the AFDC programs: the failure of AFDC recipients to work outside the home and the incidence of "family break-up and illegitimacy" among welfare dependents. Although conservatives' diagnosis of the "welfare problem" echoed the conclusions that the program's liberal defenders had drawn in the 1950s and early 1960s, Mills and his colleagues rejected the rehabilitative approach endorsed by most welfare experts and social work professionals. To address the problem of nonwork, the Ways and Means Committee balanced work incentives, including a new rule that allowed AFDC recipients to add some earned income to their welfare benefits, with a system of mandatory work requirements. Reminding his colleagues that the public interest would not be served if welfare became a "way of life," Mills insisted that AFDC recipients should "submit themselves . . . to a test of their ability to learn a job . . . [to] draw public funds."[42] According to the Committee, a "great many mothers," as well as "virtually all unemployed fathers," could be "trained for and placed in productive employment."[43] The Finance Committee placed an even heavier emphasis on work requirements, creating a new Work Incentive, or WIN, Program, designed to ensure that welfare recipients would no longer receive a welfare check from the government, but rather a "payment from an employer for services."[44]

The work provisions of the 1967 law reflected the widespread, though factually inaccurate, idea that welfare recipients chose not to work.[45] This discourse not only erased the work that welfare recipients performed inside the home, but also ignored the substantial numbers of women who already combined wage work with welfare.[46] Lawmakers' insistence on the dysfunctional dependency of lazy "brood mares" certainly revealed deep-seated racial hostility and reflected long-standing and pernicious myths about black women's sexuality.[47] Equally important, this kind of discourse depended on and reinforced fictive and politically motivated distinctions between the dependent poor minority and the independent taxpaying majority. As such, these attacks on welfare and on welfare recipients served both to undermine poor families' claims to governmental protection and to reaffirm the government's obligation to protect the legitimate interests of taxpaying citizens.

In addition to enforcing work requirements, the Ways and Means Committee's welfare bill also promised to address the problems of family breakup and illegitimacy. By the end of the 1960s, policymakers and the public had come to identify unwed motherhood, particularly within the African American community, as a fundamental cause of welfare dependency. Liberals had helped to create this association by calling attention to the "premium" AFDC placed on desertion and unwed motherhood by denying aid to intact families. In 1966, for example, the Southern Christian Leadership Conference accused AFDC of contributing to "the breakdown of family life by making it more difficult to obtain money if the father is in the household."[48] Although liberal welfare experts saw illegitimate children on the welfare rolls as a reason to expand existing income maintenance programs to two-parent families, more conservative opponents of welfare spending easily co-opted this discourse to cast moral aspersions on welfare recipients and justify reductions in welfare spending. Casting illegitimacy as "a social disease . . . passed on from one generation to the next" that threatened not only the individual or family unit but society at large, conservative lawmakers believed they had an obligation to defend taxpayers against the "almost daily . . . flagrant and wanton abuses" of welfare laws and public mores by AFDC recipients.[49]

The House bill represented the logical culmination of a public discourse that assumed illegitimacy created welfare dependency and that took the "the steady expansion of this welfare program [AFDC] . . . as a measure of the steady disintegration of the [black] family," and proposed to deal with the problem of broken families in two ways.[50] First, the Ways and Means Committee proposed to freeze AFDC funds for children born out of wedlock at 1967 levels.[51] Designed explicitly to discipline high-benefit states and to reduce *federal* welfare expenditures, the freeze provision would have required some states and localities "to either trim welfare rolls or pick up the tab" using state and local money. "If they do the latter," warned one member of New York Senator Robert Kennedy's staff, "the result will be a tremendous burden on local taxes, and real estate taxes will shoot up all over the country."[52] New York City Mayor John Lindsay blasted the bill as "disastrous" and estimated that it would cost his city's taxpayers between $50 million and $70 million in the next year and a half. Like many state and local politicians, Lindsay feared that the bill might exacerbate the already tense relationship between the poor and the nonpoor. "The choices," the liberal Republican warned, "will be whether to place further heavy financial burdens on the already hard-pressed local taxpayers or to turn our backs on the pledges made to the poorest of our citizens."[53]

A similar concern to protect the interests of taxpayers by enforcing the obligations of tax eaters animated congressional attempts to collect child support payments for AFDC children. During the Finance Committee's mark-up of the House bill, Chairman Long inserted a requirement that states establish programs to determine the "paternity of illegitimate children receiving assistance" and to establish procedures for "securing support for these children as well as those who have been abandoned by their parents."[54] Over the next several years, congressional welfare reformers tried several times to "clarify congressional intent" with regard to child support enforcement and AFDC eligibility.[55] In doing so, they articulated a strong defense of an aggressive child support regime rooted not only in traditional notions of familial responsibility but also in an ideology of taxpayers' rights. For example, in 1971, Chairman Long complained that it was "brutally unfair" that "American taxpayers who are living up to their own responsibilities, supporting their own children," also be required to "support the children of the deadbeats who abandon them to welfare."[56] New Mexico Republican Senator Pete Domenici agreed, promising his colleagues that if "more support money [was] obtained from the deserting parent, fewer taxpayer dollars [would] be spent on the program for aid to dependent children."[57]

According to the dominant language of welfare reform, AFDC recipients' pathological dependence on government subsidies jeopardized both individual taxpayers' wallets *and* the social and economic well-being of the nation as a whole. Moving AFDC recipients into the paid labor force and reducing the incidence of family breakup and illegitimacy would both control welfare costs and do "some public good."[58] Moreover, because conservative attacks on welfare drew on many of the critiques leveled by liberal defenders of the program in the 1950s and early 1960s, neither the Johnson administration nor the community of welfare experts were well prepared to answer this unexpected onslaught.[59] Equally important, the president's major legislative priority—the income tax surcharge—depended on Mills's support. Rather than attacking the House-passed welfare reform proposals, the White House publicly complimented the chairman on his "wonderful success in getting the bill passed with only three dissenting votes."[60] In their testimony to the Finance Committee, administration officials likewise refused to attack the bill directly and consistently expressed support for the chairman's "general approach."[61]

The administration's tepid response to the crisis created by the Mills bill opened up space for more radical challenges to the welfare status quo. On 19

September 1967, representatives of the National Welfare Rights Organization (NWRO), a grassroots organization of AFDC recipients founded only two years earlier, staged a three-hour "wait-in" in the Finance Committee hearing room.[62] Believing that their testimony had not been given the proper attention and respect, NWRO witnesses refused to leave the hearing room until the Capitol Police forcibly removed them and barred them from the Senate office buildings.[63] Chairman Long was unimpressed. "If they can find the time to march the streets, and if they can find time to picket congressional committees," the Finance Committee chairman complained the following day, they "should have time to do some work."[64] Most observers agreed that the demonstration hurt the welfare mothers' cause. New York Welfare Commissioner George Wyman criticized the protesters for kicking their "friends in the teeth" and worried that the protest might "adversely affect the attitude of the Committee." Democratic Representative Phillip Burton, a California liberal who opposed the welfare provisions of the Mills bill, nevertheless distanced himself from the NWRO protest and came to Long's defense, citing the chairman's long history of helping "poor people receive some measure of economic security."[65]

Like the authors of the Freedom Budget and the Domestic Marshall Plan, welfare rights advocates challenged many of the basic tenets of the liberal social compact. NWRO members rejected what they viewed as an artificial and arbitrary distinction between taxpayers and tax eaters, and defended their own productive and reproductive labor. In their testimony to the Finance Committee, NWRO witnesses borrowed heavily from the Progressive-era "maternalist" tradition, basing their claims for public assistance in their roles as "mother-citizens" and mothers of citizens. The organization's president, George Wiley, for example, pointed out that "welfare mothers already have more than a full time job—raising their children on inadequate welfare grants."[66] Adequate public assistance, NWRO member Etta Horn argued, would make the children of welfare recipients "fit for service to fight for this country." Another welfare rights spokeswoman, Marion Kidd, likewise reminded the committee that poor children were required to register for the draft. "They are not asked," she argued, "are you on welfare, but they are taken into service to fight."[67]

The women who staged the Finance Committee wait-in insisted that welfare mothers simply wanted their "children to have the same rights as any other equal citizen in this country."[68] Motherhood, some welfare rights activists insisted, was a "full time job," and welfare mothers, like all other mothers, had a "right to raise their children to the best of their ability."[69] A few years later, Lillian Baines, vice chairman of a Kansas welfare rights organization, editorialized that motherhood, like agriculture, should be subsidized. Children were the nation's "most important national produce," and mothers, like farmers, should be "given subsidies for raising good children."[70] This gendered defense of welfare rights was not a novel approach. Rather, NWRO mothers tapped into the family wage assumptions that had guided the development of social welfare systems in the first half of the twentieth century.[71] By the end of the 1960s, however, the family wage system itself had become increasingly tenuous, thanks to the increased labor-force participation of women and the emerging feminist movement. In this political and economic context, the NWRO's gender-conscious maternalism seemed irrelevant to both political debate and policy formation. Unsympathetic policymakers easily answered the welfare mothers' arguments with a facially gender-neutral defense of taxpayers' rights.[72] Defending a requirement that the mothers of young children be required to participate in the new mandatory workfare programs created by the 1967 bill, for example, Chairman Long reasoned that it was unfair to ask working mothers to "pay taxes . . . which are used to pay for the cost of public assistance." "There is no reason," he concluded, "why the taxes paid by ten million American mothers who work should be used to support those few mothers on assistance who refuse" to do so.[73] This argument appealed particularly to the working- and lower middle-class men and women buffeted by the massive and destabilizing structural changes in the American economy that required more and more women to work for wages simply to make ends meet. As Felicia Kornbluh has pointed out, the "gradual but dramatic decline" in the number and stability of well-paying blue-collar jobs meant that many married women could no longer enjoy the privilege of "being able to withdraw from the waged workforce to raise children if they so desired."[74] As more and more white, married women moved into the workforce, the NWRO's claim to "paid motherhood" lost much of its political force.[75]

The 1967 welfare reform bill put the Johnson administration in an impossible political position and jeopardized both its domestic and foreign priorities. Throughout the fall of 1967, administration officials had worked closely with Chairman Long and the rest of the Senate Finance Committee to delete the most offensive aspects of the House-passed bill. Facing considerable pressure on its left flank from liberal senators determined to "filibuster the bill to death if necessary," and genuinely concerned about the negative effects of the freeze provision and of the requirement that mothers of young children work outside the home or risk losing AFDC benefits, the administration hoped that the Finance Committee would produce a less punitive bill. When the Conference Committee, under the direction of Long and Mills, reported a version of the bill that included both the freeze and the work requirement, some administration insiders urged the president to veto the bill in order to shore up his support among liberals.[76] The president's domestic position, HEW Secretary John Gardner concluded, rested on his opposition to the conference report.[77] But others within the Johnson White House doubted the political wisdom and practical value of such counsel. Joseph Califano, Johnson's senior domestic policy advisor, warned his boss that public opposition to the conference report would not satisfy the "liberals and labor people" and would simply enrage "those who favor the Mills provisions."[78] Senator Ed Muskie of Maine and Majority Leader Mike Mansfield of Montana warned that the threatened filibuster would damage the Democratic Party and injure the president and those Democrats running the next year.[79] Backed into a corner, and convinced that the administration had "better take what [it] could get," Johnson signed the welfare reform bill into law on 23 December 1967.[80]

Guns or Butter

The debate over the welfare provisions of the 1967 bill provided a kind of dress rehearsal for the final showdown between congressional conservatives and the Johnson administration over tax and spending issues. The Revenue and Expenditure Control Act of 1968 marked the end of President Johnson's eighteen-month struggle to convince Congress to enact a temporary tax increase to reduce inflationary pressures and pay for the war in Vietnam. The 1968 law pitted congressional conservatives led by Chairman Mills against the Johnson administration in a battle for control over the nation's tax and spending priorities. Although Johnson finally got his tax increase in June 1968, he paid dearly for it, sacrificing the War on Poverty to budget cutters in Congress who insisted he choose between guns and butter. The struggle over the tax and spending bill further alienated the progressive wing of the Democratic Party from the Johnson White House, exacerbated already existing divisions within the party over Vietnam and Civil Rights and helped set the stage for Richard Nixon's victory in the 1968 presidential contest.

The Johnson administration began to consider a tax increase as early as 1965, when Defense Secretary Robert McNamara's request for a doubling of troop commitments in Vietnam threatened to dangerously overheat the economy. Although the administration publicly downplayed the inflationary threat and tried to hide the costs of the war from both Congress and the public, by year's end many in the White House believed that a tax increase would be needed to control the deficit and prevent a disastrous price spiral.[81] The Revenue Act of 1964 had perhaps stimulated the economy too well. As Walter Heller pointed out, the "logic of the tax cut" was a "two-way street": the same economic theory that had justified the tax cut in 1964 might point toward a tax hike in 1966 or 1967.[82] The rising cost of the Vietnam War threatened the healthy economic growth that Johnson had counted on to underwrite both his domestic and military priorities. Between 1964 and 1967, spending for defense and other international programs had grown from $5.58 billion to $7.46 billion.[83] These larger-than-expected defense outlays, the Council of Economic Advisors (CEA) advised the president in late 1965, would likely require him to propose and pass "a significant tax increase . . . to prevent an intolerable degree of inflationary pressure."[84] Aware of the potentially disastrous political consequences of a tax increase, and convinced that Congress would demand that he choose between the War on Poverty and the Vietnam War, Johnson instructed his advisors to tread carefully and to work up tax increase proposals on only the "most discreet basis."[85] Although the president included a vague call for a tax increase in his 1966 State of the Union address, he continued to insist that the country was "mighty" and "healthy" enough to afford both the Vietnam War and the Great Society, and steadfastly refused to put his weight behind an across-the-board tax increase.[86]

The president's reluctance to propose a general tax increase had more to do with politics than economic theory. Tax hikes appealed to no one. Antiwar Democrats were likely to see any tax increase as a way to fund "another ill-advised escalation of the war."[87] More concerned about unemployment than possible increases in prices, organized labor too expressed considerable doubts about the economic and political advisability of a tax increase.[88] The president faced an even graver threat from the right. Congressional conservatives, Johnson knew, would try to exact reductions in domestic expenditures in return for a tax increase. Opponents of the War on Poverty had already used the debate over the administration's 1966 excise tax bill to send a message to the White House about its "failure to face up to the financial realities of fighting a war in Viet Nam . . .while still attempting to carry out 'world-saving programs'" at home.[89] Sensing the president's weakness, the GOP ramped up its opposition to his domestic program. The party had long criticized the War on Poverty as a wasteful and extravagant effort to drag the poor up the "economic and social ladder" by the "green rope of dollar bills."[90] The administration successfully dodged these attacks in 1964 and most of 1965, when the economy appeared to be improving and the GNP was rising steadily. As inflation began to creep upward in 1965 and 1966, however, these attacks hit their mark, and the GOP immediately blamed Democratic spending policies for rising inflation. The "Great Society," claimed House Minority Leader Gerald Ford of Michigan and Senate Minority Leader Everett Dirksen of Illinois, had become the "High society" with "high taxes, high prices, high spending, high deficits."[91] "Great society funny money," the Republican National Committee claimed, had cut into the purchasing power of the average, nonpoor American, whose hard-earned dollar bought him and "his family less of everything than ever before"[92] (see Figure 6).

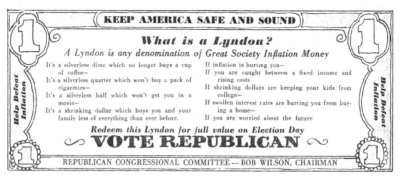

Figure 6. *Great Society Funny Money*, produced by the Republican Congressional Committee in 1964, attacking Lyndon Johnson and the Great Society for inflation that threatened the "future" of average Americans. Courtesy of Division of Political History, National Museum of American History, Smithsonian Institution, Washington, D.C.

A brief improvement in economic conditions in the third and fourth quarters of 1966 allowed the president to temporarily put the "tax increase on the shelf."[93] But the White House could only delay, not avoid, asking Congress for a tax hike. The rising cost of living had already become a political liability. On the eve of the 1966 congressional midterm elections that cost the White House forty-five allies in the House of Representatives alone, inflation and the war in Vietnam topped the list of the public's concerns.[94] In early 1967, the president's cabinet advised him to propose a temporary 6 percent income tax surcharge to defray the extraordinary costs of military operations in Vietnam.[95] Federal Reserve Chairman William McChesney Martin optimistically assured the president that "congressional and public understanding of the need to demonstrate the fiscal responsibility of the United States and the willingness of its citizens to share in the burdens of the war in Vietnam" would assure prompt enactment.[96] A few weeks later, in his annual State of the Union Address, Johnson urged Congress to consider a 6 percent temporary tax surcharge on corporate and personal income taxes in order to bring inflation under control and to offset the "unusual expenditures associated" with American military operations in Vietnam.[97] Nine months later, the administration formally submitted a request for a larger—10 percent—surcharge, arguing that an "unacceptable deficit . . . rising interest rates and inflationary pressures" made such a tax necessary to prevent economic disaster.[98] Failure to act, Johnson warned, would lead to more "inflation, tight money, and shortages that would tax the American people cruelly and capriciously."[99]

Rather than defending it as a "war tax," the administration usually justified its request for a tax increase as necessary to stem inflationary pressures created by an excess of consumer demand over supply. Johnson's economic advisors had long worried that the economy was growing too quickly, as "consumers, business and government together" sought to *buy more than our economy can produce*." By reducing private purchasing power, a "tax increase now" would prevent the "painful and prolonged" increases in "prices, wages and costs" likely to accompany such "demand-pull" inflation.[100] Heller, who served as a kind of informal economic advisor to the president from his post at the University of Wisconsin, agreed, arguing that a "6 to 10 percent surtax" would help to "avoid a new round of inflation," bring down the previous year's "brutally high interest rates," tame the deficit, and "spread the home-front burdens of the war more fairly."[101] Tax restraint, Treasury Secretary Henry Fowler counseled, would ultimately help the working- and middle-class backbone of the Democratic coalition by preventing serious

inflation—the "'cruelest form of taxation'"—that would impose "grossly inequitable sacrifices . . . [on] those least able to bear them."[102] Over the course
of 1967, the administration's predictions about the costs of inaction grew increasingly dire. Earlier disagreements among Johnson's economic advisors all
but disappeared as the White House rallied around the surcharge as a "right
now measure" that demanded "immediate attention."[103] Without new taxes,
the CEA warned in early 1968, the economy would likely spiral into a "fever-
ish boom that could generate an unacceptable acceleration of price increases,
a possible financial crisis and perhaps, ultimately, a recession."[104]

Despite the "stark reality" of inflation, Congress, led by Chairman Mills,
refused to move on the proposed tax hike. Mills had early on expressed skepticism about the administration's economic forecasts, complaining to Heller
in the summer of 1966 that the administration would not level with him
on the budget and warning that the White House would have to "cut back
expenditures—impound funds if they have to—as a prerequisite to tax action."[105] Ten months later, Mills had not changed his mind; any proposal that
asked Americans to pay more taxes had to be accompanied by a significant
reduction in the rate of government spending.[106] Mills' hostility toward federal spending was well known. During debate on the 1964 Revenue Act he
had made clear his absolute preference for tax reduction over government
spending as the road to economic growth. The Johnson administration, Mills
believed, had chosen the wrong path, and had reneged on its promise to restrain federal expenditures in return for the 1964 tax cut. Without definitive
action by "responsible" members of Congress, the administration would continue to spend: "If we gave him [the president] ten billion dollars more money
to spend, he would spend it if we didn't tie his hands to where he couldn't
spend it."[107]

The chairman also knew he could count on the support of an increasingly conservative Congress, thanks to the "anti-Lyndon Johnson" election
of 1966. After the Congressional midterms, even moderate Democrats had
become reluctant to ally themselves too closely with the embattled president.[108] Buoyed by a friendly Congress and fortified by rising public disenchantment with liberal social projects, Mills dug in his heels. In October, the
Ways and Means Committee officially deferred "further consideration of the
tax increase . . . until such time as the President and the Congress reach an
understanding on a means of implementing more effective expenditure reduction and controls."[109] "What many of us fear," Mills admitted in the fall of
1967, "is that tax increases now make more revenue available for spending

programs in the future. . . . We fear that tax increases not accompanied by real expenditure control can divert us from the free-enterprise road."[110] Both sound economics and public opinion demanded caution. "These actions are not irresponsible, bullheaded, or spiteful, nor are they maneuvers for partisan advantage," Mills insisted. Rather, they were "an expression of the anxiety which many Members of the Congress feel—fortified by the uneasiness they found in their constituencies . . . about the recent sharp rise in federal outlays and the proliferation of federal government activity."[111]

Throughout 1967 and into 1968, Mills resisted the administration's explanation of the cause of inflation as an excess of demand over supply, instead blaming rising wages and prices on collective bargaining agreements and government spending, which pushed up "finished prices no matter how much the demand for goods."[112] According to a laudatory *Fortune* magazine profile, Mills used his "minutely detailed knowledge of just how the economy was doing" to take apart the administration's argument that "new taxes were necessary because demand was excessive."[113] Mills's opposition echoed the conclusions reached by the staff of both the Ways and Means and Joint Economic Committees that because demand was "not excessive at this time" and the economy was "not really booming," a tax increase would do little to control inflation and would only add to the "costs and prices of goods."[114] Wary of the administration's economic forecasts, which had indeed changed dramatically from month to month, Mills said that expenditure control was essential to the nation's fiscal health and economic future.[115] Uncontrolled spending, Mills told the Security Trust Company of Rochester, New York, in May 1967, limited Congress's ability to "develop sound tax policy" by imposing "such a straitjacket on tax policy as to prevent needed adjustments in that policy." Only a "long-range program of periodic tax reduction" could produce stable economic growth. "There is a limit," Mills reasoned, "to the size and number of Federal programs which our economy can support in the future without ever-increasing public debt, balance of payments problems and possible loss of confidence in the dollar by holders abroad."[116] Taxpayers, Mills suggested, had to pay twice to travel down the "government expenditure increase road"—first through the direct burden imposed by rising taxes and second through the "indirect tax" of inflation and economic insecurity. Public spending on welfare and the War on Poverty, Mills and his supporters insisted, jeopardized the postwar social compact's guarantee of economic security and upward mobility.

Early in 1968, the war in Vietnam, deterioration in the international markets, and rapidly escalating prices forced congressional action on the tax front.[117] In late January, the president implored Congress to enact a tax increase to "slow down price increases, cut our balance of payments deficit, maintain a smooth flow of credit, and insure us against risks we should not take."[118] A serious crisis in the international gold markets heightened the need for immediate fiscal restraint, as members of Congress realized "that it would be dangerous to the dollar . . . for the Government to run the expected $20 billion deficit."[119] In March, alarmed by the impending collapse of the international economy, the Senate finally acted. Bypassing both the Ways and Means and Finance Committees, and ignoring parliamentary procedure, Delaware Republican Senator John Williams and Florida Democratic Senator George Smathers worked together to add a 10 percent tax surcharge and a $6 billion spending cut to an excise bill already approved by the House.[120]

In April and May, administration representatives negotiated furiously with members of the House Ways and Means and Appropriations Committees for an expenditure reduction smaller than the $6 billion proposed by Williams and Smathers and demanded by Mills. Though both committees eventually agreed to the $4 billion spending cut suggested by the White House, Chairman Mills declined to support this compromise proposal and continued to press for $6 billion in domestic spending cuts. Once again, the chairman had the administration over a barrel. On 10 May, guided by Mills, the conference committee reported a bill that provided for $10 billion in tax increases and the full $6 billion in expenditure reductions.[121] The administration toyed briefly with the idea of opposing the conference report outright, but ultimately decided to endorse only a motion to instruct the committee to return the bill with no more than $4 billion in spending cuts. When this motion failed at the end of May, the administration resigned itself to the higher figure. The tax hike took priority; failure to raise taxes would, according to the CEA's Arthur Okun, "undermine all our [the administration's] aims and jeopardize the complete world political situation."[122] Holding his nose, and decrying congressional blackmail, the president reluctantly signed off on the Revenue and Expenditure Control Act on 30 May. A few weeks later, the House approved the measure by a vote of 268–150. The Senate followed suit a day later, passing the measure by a substantial 64–16 majority.

Poor Program, Rich Program

Congressional conservatives' determination throughout 1967 and 1968 to limit spending on AFDC and the poverty programs in order to protect the interests of taxpayers stands in marked contrast to their willingness to expand the size and scope of the nation's Social Security program. At the same time that he faced outraged demands to cut spending, especially for welfare and other poverty programs, President Johnson successfully proposed a historic expansion of Social Security. In January 1967, reminding Congress of the "5.3 million older Americans with income below the poverty line," the president urged lawmakers to liberalize Social Security retirement benefits to allow all seniors to take part in the "progress they had worked most of their lives to create."[123] The administration proposal would have provided a 20 percent total increase in Social Security benefits; while most beneficiaries would receive a 15 percent increase in their benefit level, the poorest retirees would receive an increase of almost 60 percent. Costing an additional $4.1 billion, and raising the income of 1.4 million retirees over the poverty threshold, the White House package would, Johnson promised, constitute a "major step toward our goal that every elderly citizen have an adequate income and meaningful retirement."[124] To finance the changes and protect the system's actuarial soundness, the administration proposal relied on the surplus in the Social Security Trust Fund, increases in the payroll tax rate, and changes to the amount of wage income subject to the Social Security tax.[125]

Social Security was easily the most popular and effective part of the U.S. welfare state. By 1968, nearly one American in eight received his or her share of the 15.6 million Social Security checks mailed each year.[126] Federal retirement programs, one presidential task force reported in 1966, reached almost 97 percent of Americans over age sixty-five, and had closed about "two-thirds of the poverty gap" among older Americans.[127] According to economist Paul Samuelson, Social Security was "by a long shot, the most successful program of the modern welfare state."[128] Its political popularity even underwrote the creation of Medicare in 1965, when Johnson administration officials sold the new health insurance program as an extension of the existing retirement system.[129] Yet, by the mid-1960s, the program's growth and success began to worry some policymakers. As *Fortune* reported in December 1967, the "almost reverent tone once adopted" in talking about Social Security had begun to disappear.[130] Indeed, the Ways and Means Committee viewed the president's proposal to increase benefits with considerable skepticism. Recognizing the current popularity of the benefit increases—which had drawn the longest and loudest applause of anything in Johnson's State of the Union address—lawmakers had nevertheless grown concerned about how to pay for them. Although members of Congress were more than willing to take credit for new and higher benefits, they were less eager to raise the effective tax rate on much of the working and middle classes. After hearing for years that Social Security benefits were too low, the *New York Times* reported in March 1967, Congressmen were "now deluged with complaints that Social Security taxes are becoming burdensome."[131] According to one Ways and Means Democrat, the combination of increased payroll tax rates and the proposed increase in the amount of income subject to the Social Security tax, or wage base, might produce a rebellion among workers "sick and tired of politicians playing politics with the old people."[132]

The payroll tax had, in fact, increased dramatically over the course of the postwar period. By 1967, payroll taxes equaled about 4.7 percent of personal income—up from just 1.1 percent of personal income in 1948.[133] If payroll taxes continued to shoot upward, *Fortune* predicted, more and more Americans might "well conclude that Social Security taxes—and the system itself—have become less equitable as they've grown over the years."[134] Even some of the system's staunchest supporters began to question its fairness. Labor leaders George Meany and Walter Reuther each testified that the payroll tax put an undue burden on the "backs of the American worker."[135] Reviving an earlier campaign to introduce general revenue financing into the Social Security system, Reuther argued that continued and "exclusive reliance on the payroll tax" would soon place an "increasing burden on our younger workers who have their own problems raising their own families."[136]

In the end, rising payroll tax burdens did not lead to retrenchment in the Social Security system. Although the Ways and Means and Finance Committees scaled back the administration's proposed benefit increases and changed the financing structure, the final bill still provided retirees with the single largest total dollar increase in the program's history. The Social Security Amendments of 1967, which also included the welfare changes described above, provided for a 13 percent increase in Social Security benefits and improved the progressivity of the system by raising the minimum benefit from $44 to $55 per month. According to the Congressional Research Service, about 23 million people would receive higher benefits as a result of these changes, at a cost of $3 billion in the first year alone.[137] To pay for the new benefits, Congress raised the taxable wage base from $6,600 to $7,800, effective January 1968, and scheduled a tax rate increase for 1969. Social Security also escaped the general budget cutting fervor of 1968. The Revenue and Expenditure Control Act of 1968 explicitly shielded the program—as well as Vietnam-related military expenses, veterans benefits, and interest on the public debt—from any budget cuts. The next year, Congress again voted to increase Social Security benefits, by an average of 15 percent across the board. Three years later, in 1972, Congress approved a 20 percent benefit increase, and perhaps more importantly, voted to adjust benefits automatically for inflation.[138]

This expansion of the Social Security system came at the expense of other social priorities. In November 1966, President Johnson's Income Maintenance Task Force (IMTF), an internal White House working group that included representatives from the Department of Labor, the Treasury Department, the Council of Economic Advisors, and the Department of Health, Education, and Welfare, issued an "administratively confidential" report that warned of the coming conflict between Social Security and other domestic spending programs. Finding "protection against certain of the poverty causing risks"—namely old age and disability—to be far "more complete than . . . protection against others," the IMTF recommended shifting resources away from programs for the aged. With the notable exception of Wilbur Cohen, who represented the DHEW and was known inside Washington as "Mr. Social Security," the task force forcefully recommended a "sharp slowdown in the rate at which OASDI [Social Security] benefits were to be expanded."[139] Arguing that the American social welfare state, already meager in comparison to its European counterparts, was too heavily skewed toward the aged and the nonpoor, the task force recommended significant policy changes to reverse the "basic imbalance within existing transfer systems."[140] Like the authors of the Freedom Budget or the Domestic Marshall Plan, the task force sought to erase the fictive distinction between taxpayers and tax consumers by making visible the role that the hidden welfare state played in securing and defending the rights and privileges of the white middle-class majority.[141] This task, the panel admitted, would require considerable "public re-education" to counter deeply ingrained public attitudes about the " 'deserving' and the 'non-deserving' poor." Failure to do so, however, would mean that the Great Society would remain but a "vision."[142]

The IMTF was particularly concerned about the effect of payroll tax increases on other parts of the U.S. welfare state. Although the Social Security tax had long been "regarded less as a tax than as a premium for insurance . . .

now that rates are high . . . it is coming to be regarded as a tax, and an obvious one at that."[143] Further expansion of both benefits and contributions, the task force worried, would crowd out other social welfare priorities. "In its earlier years," the IMTF reported, "Social Security expenditures probably were not competitive with other governmental expenditures . . . outlays were small and the system separately financed by a payroll tax levied at a modest rate. . . . However, as of 1965, Social Security expenditures constituted about one-quarter of non defense cash outlays . . . and this share has been rising."[144] Further expansion could come only at the "the expense of public willingness to pay income and other taxes," and would create political pressure to reduce "outlays in other programs, particularly on social welfare programs whose budgets are flexible." Unless the administration did something to slow the growth of the Social Security program, the task force warned, the "developing conflict between Social Security . . . and other expenditure programs" would only grow worse.[145] Another member of the Johnson administration, CEA member Gardner Ackley, described this potential trade-off even more succinctly in a November 1966 memorandum to the president on basic issues in income maintenance. "Three billion dollars," he wrote, "would either buy a 15% increase in Social Security—most of which would not go to the poor—or a revolutionary improvement in public assistance programs—all to the poor." According to Ackley "these are getting to be *really competitive, now that the payroll taxes are so high that people know they are an important part of their total tax burden*" (emphasis in original).[146]

The divergent fates of Social Security and AFDC at the hands of congressional budget cutters at the tail end of the "era of easy finance" demonstrate the insoluble dilemma of Democratic liberalism at the close of the 1960s. The resources on which liberals had long relied to create and expand domestic welfare programs no longer served to answer Americans' simultaneous demand for services from the federal government and their unwillingness to pay for them. Advocates of a genuine, national commitment to the economic rights of all Americans found themselves hamstrung by postwar liberal commitments to the individual rights of taxpayers. Ironically, the success of New Deal and postwar social policies in creating the white middle class limited the prospects for a completion of the "rights revolution" promised by President Franklin Roosevelt in his 1944 Economic Bill of Rights. The same features that enabled the expansion of the postwar liberal state—namely its reliance on economic growth, its dedication to low corporate and personal tax rates, and its dependence on earmarked payroll taxes or private and corporate initiative to provide and pay for certain social rights—limited liberals' ability to address the seemingly intractable problem of poverty in the midst of plenty. The contradiction between the rising demands of the nonpoor majority for governmental protection and their resistance to new tax burdens not only shattered the New Deal order, but also profoundly shaped the conservative alternative that sought to replace it.

CHAPTER 4

FED UP WITH TAXES

I n February 1973, a group of thirty St. Louis taxpayers dressed in eighteenth-century costumes celebrated the two hundredth anniversary of the Boston Tea Party by heaving food and medicine crates into the Mississippi River. Carrying signs that read "Fair Taxation or New Representation," the protesters marched through the city, handing out leaflets attacking "unfair" and "burdensome taxes on food and medicine." When they reached the downtown offices of the Missouri Department of Revenue, the protesters stopped briefly to affix their demands for tax justice to the door of the building. Message delivered, the group continued the march to the levee, where its members boarded an awaiting riverboat and sailed away.[1] Two years later, in California, another small group of taxpayers marched through the streets of working-class Chino to protest local property tax laws. Accompanied by a makeshift ambulance pulling an eight-by-sixteen-foot flatbed trailer carrying a dummy on a stretcher, the tax protesters took aim at the state's "sick" tax system.[2] In New Bedford, Massachusetts, some 4,000 taxpayers descended on the mayor's office to protest new property tax assessments. The ensuing riot destroyed the mayor's car and temporarily closed City Hall.[3]

Grassroots tax protests like these, which erupted with increasing frequency over the 1970s, helped put tax politics on the national agenda and keep it there. But it was left to national political entrepreneurs and politicians—liberal and conservative alike—to transform the protesters' inchoate anger and frustration into a coherent and potentially transformative political force. Tax policy became increasingly central to both the Democratic and Republican Parties after 1968, as activists, strategists, and office seekers sought ways to appeal to and win the votes of the nation's 60 million federal taxpayers.[4] Efforts by both left and right to harness the political energies of the emerging tax protest movement reflected the profoundly unsettled nature of American politics in the late 1960s and early 1970s. Conservatives and progressives both interpreted the results of the 1968 presidential election as a rejection of Great Society liberalism; the press blamed a widespread backlash among the white majority for Democratic losses.[5] But if almost everyone agreed that the Great Society had failed, and that the political coalition of African Americans, white Southerners, blue-collar workers, and ideological liberals assembled by Franklin Roosevelt in the 1930s had crumbled, neither left nor right had yet developed a politically viable and ideologically compelling alternative to the New Deal order. After Hubert Humphrey's 1968 defeat, leading Democrats struggled to reinvent the party and offer a coherent post-Great Society liberal agenda. The Republicans, too, experimented with a variety of political programs and rhetorical strategies to consolidate these gains and to strengthen ties to the white working- and middle-class voters of what Richard Nixon called the "Silent Majority."

The wooing of those silent and forgotten Americans widely believed to have become unhinged from the Roosevelt coalition drove both liberal and conservative politics after 1968. Shocked not only by Nixon's victory but also by Alabama Governor George Wallace's strong showing at the polls *outside* the South, leading liberals bent over backward to apologize for the Great Society, to reaffirm their commitment to those, mostly white, citizens allegedly left out of poverty and other federal programs of the 1960s and to pledge their allegiance to the "near poor, the lower middle class, the ethnics [and] the blue collar workers."[6] GOP strategists did much the same. In his widely influential analysis of the 1968 presidential election, Nixon strategist Kevin Phillips painted a portrait of a nation "in motion between a Democratic past and a Republican future."[7] Convinced that workers' allegiance was up for grabs, the Nixon administration adopted an explicitly "blue-collar" strategy to win the votes of this great Silent Majority. As one political analyst rightly predicted in 1969, it was in the "dreams—and the nightmares—of the middle class" that both the Democratic and Republican parties sought the victory formula for 1972 and 1976.[8]

The Forgotten Americans of the Silent Majority—like the tax protest groups they often joined—were neither liberal nor conservative.[9] As noted socialist Michael Harrington pointed out in 1976, the country was moving "vigorously left, right and center all at once."[10] This central tension between radical insurgency and conservative backlash produced a range of confused and often contradictory policies, as policymakers, strategists, and activists tried out a variety of appeals designed to capture the hearts and minds of these "troubled Americans." As much an ideological and political construction as an actual demographic group, Silent Majority voters nonetheless controlled American politics. As public opinion analyst and former Johnson administration staffer Richard Scammon concluded in 1969, Middle America would decide "who sits in the White House."[11]

The courtship of the Silent Majority was a bipartisan affair. Throughout the late 1960s and early 1970s, Republicans and Democrats experimented with ways to appeal to white working- and middle-class voters. Convinced that they had erred in the 1960s by focusing too much on the needs of African Americans and the poor, progressive strategists shifted their attention to what Scammon and his colleague Ben Wattenberg had defined as the "unpoor, unyoung, and unblack" majority.[12] Promising to purge the Democratic Party of the "snobbishness" that had alienated its white working- and middle-class constituents, many leading Democrats tried to reorient the party toward an economic populism that could transcend the cultural and racial fissures that threatened its political future. Grappling for a policy agenda that appeased Middle American voters but maintained the party's commitment to racial and economic equality, many Democrats hoped to fuse together the "base economic interests" of the black and white working and middle classes by fomenting a populist revolt against those "people, classes and institutions . . . which possess an illegitimate amount of wealth and power."[13] Tax politics anchored this new class-conscious majority strategy. Reading the era's emerging tax revolt as a popular uprising against the unfair advantages of wealthy individuals and large corporations, progressive groups like George Wiley's Tax Justice Project and former Oklahoma Senator Fred Harris's New Populist Action sought to transfer the public's well-established hostility to welfare from poor women and their children onto the country's "real welfare recipients"—rich individuals and well-connected corporations that had chiseled "billions of dollars out of the federal treasury."[14] By appealing to "victims of the tax code," over "70 percent of whom were white," Wiley, Harris, and a host of progressive tax reformers hoped they had found the secret to Democratic reconstruction.

Conservatives likewise saw an opportunity in the Forgotten Americans' alienation, frustration, and even anger. Convinced that the GOP's future as a majority party lay beyond the South in the white working-class neighborhoods of the urban North, Richard Nixon developed a decidedly class-conscious political strategy during his first term in office. Crystallized in an April 1970 memorandum drafted by assistant labor secretary Jerome Rosow, the strategy focused in part on forging cultural ties with the rank-and-file of the union movement and rapprochement with union leadership. "Romancing the union leadership," adviser Charles W. Colson reminded Nixon's Chief of Staff Bob Haldeman, "is only one part of the task. . . . Our task is to cultivate local leaders who are anti-student, who are strongly patriotic, and keenly aware on the race question."[15]

Efforts to bind working- and middle-class voters to what Nixon called the "New American Majority," however, went beyond appeals to workers' patriotism or a subtle exploitation of the racial anxiety produced by the Civil Rights revolution. Between 1969 and 1972, the Nixon White House proposed a variety of substantive policies designed specifically to provide material benefits to the white working and middle classes. The Family Assistance Plan (FAP), a 1969 proposal to provide all families with children with a guaranteed annual income, was this strategy's centerpiece. It was only after both the Senate Finance Committee and the public at large rejected the program that the Nixon White House abandoned its efforts to woo the Silent Majority with new or expanded government benefits, and concentrated instead on appealing to these voters as taxpayers overburdened by the costs of liberal welfare programs. The Nixon administration's eventual repudiation of the FAP, and the larger expansionary agenda of which it was a critical part, hastened the transformation of the GOP into what one scholar has aptly termed the "tax cut party."[16]

National politicians and political entrepreneurs hoping to capture the political energy of the nascent tax protests and to attract the white working and middle classes to a new political coalition had to work within the confines of the taxing and welfare states established in the New Deal, World War II, and postwar periods. These institutions at once doomed progressive attempts to fashion a new electoral majority around tax reform and limited the extent to which the right could use tax cuts to mount a meaningful attack on the liberal state. Although the GOP and its conservative allies managed to direct a great deal of anger and frustration against welfare and the variety of liberalism associated with it, they did so only by committing themselves to protecting the host of federally subsidized privileges and prerogatives that most Americans, including the Silent Majority, had come to expect as a matter of right.

Courting the Forgotten American: The Family Assistance Plan

In August 1969, President Nixon unveiled a "new and drastically different approach to the way this country cares for those in need."[17] His proposal, known as the Family Assistance Plan, would have required the federal government to provide all American families with children, including intact two-parent families, with a guaranteed annual income (GAI). Nixon's announcement surprised most political observers. Although it had some conservative adherents, notably University of Chicago economist Milton Friedman, the GAI had a distinctly liberal pedigree. In the late 1960s, progressives frustrated by the limitations of the Johnson administration's antipoverty programs had looked to the GAI, in combination with a full employment agenda, as a critical weapon in the War on Poverty and a way to expand the social and economic rights of those locked out of the opportunity structures of the postwar state. Nixon had a far less lofty goal. The FAP aimed not to eliminate poverty but rather to consolidate electoral gains among white working- and middle-class voters and build a "New American Majority" by extending to these voters the benefits of the visible welfare state.

Influenced by Phillips's discovery of the "emerging Republican majority," journalist Pete Hamill's exposé of the rage of the white lower middle class, and a host of anthropological studies of the frustrated, disillusioned, and angry white majority, the president proposed a policy agenda to incorporate white working- and middle-class voters in a new and lasting political coalition.[18] In the first years of his presidency, Nixon proposed securing the support of the "lower-middle class clerks in Queens, steelworkers in Youngstown, and retired police lieutenants in San Diego" by providing them with tangible material benefits.[19] Rather than rolling back the welfare state, the president aimed to redirect and expand it. Between 1969 and 1971, the Nixon White House proposed an impressive array of domestic welfare policies that promised to extend federal largesse to white working- and middle-class voters reportedly left out of Johnson's Great Society. The administration even considered a new revenue source—the Value Added Tax—to fund these domestic priorities. The FAP, which offered the vast majority of its new benefits to white workers in the North and the South, is best understood as a key element of this initial expansionary phase.

Planning for the FAP began immediately after Nixon took office. After reading an article on fraud and inefficiency in the New York Public Welfare Department, the president ordered his staff to "get charging on it [welfare reform] right away."[20] At first, the task force assigned to the welfare issue took a relatively orthodox approach, proposing only to improve and expand AFDC by imposing national minimum standards and requiring that all states participate in the then-optional welfare program for families of the unemployed.[21] Soon, however, debate within the administration went far beyond these limited reforms. On 17 February 1969, Worth Bateman, a carryover from the Johnson administration, wrote a memo suggesting that the working as well as the nonworking poor be included in any new federal welfare program as a way to minimize existing "inequities in the treatment of male and female-headed families."[22] Soon, a subcabinet-level task force and working group of technical experts submitted a draft proposal that abolished AFDC as a federally aided program, created a negative income tax to benefit poor families and established a national welfare standard for needy adults. Health, Education, and Welfare (HEW) Secretary Robert Finch soon approved the basic outlines of what would become the FAP.

Welfare reform divided the president's advisors. Throughout the spring and early summer of 1969, two groups—an anti-FAP contingent led by presidential economic advisor Arthur Burns and a pro-FAP faction led by Labor Secretary George Shultz, HEW Secretary Finch, and urban affairs counselor Daniel Patrick Moynihan—made their case to the president. The terms of this debate had little to do with the economic implications of the proposal. Rather, both the Burns group—which included Commerce Secretary Maurice Stans and Vice President Spiro Agnew—and the Shultz-Finch-Moynihan group focused on the proposal's implications for the president's support among white working- and middle-class voters. Burns and Stans, for example, pointed out that there had been "no clamor by the working poor for income supplements."[23] "New spending programs, higher taxes, and romantic promises of urban reconstruction," Burns warned Nixon in May, were not "welcomed as words of wisdom by many millions of the white working class." Any plan to "guarantee an income to people who refuse to work or otherwise improve their condition" would only "enhance the growing bitterness of the white lower middle-class and may lead to disaster."[24] Agnew likewise counseled that not only would the FAP fail to "attract low-income groups to the Republican philosophy," but it would also bring the "addictive philosophy of welfare to those who are presently self-reliant."[25]

FAP supporters within the administration too framed their arguments in terms of the proposal's political implications. Shultz, for example, acknowledged Burns's description of the white working and middle classes as a group on the "edge of open, sustained and possibly violent revolt."[26] But, where Burns saw white workers' anger as a warning to the president to drop the FAP lest he add to the existing "uneasiness about handouts that already exists among urban white workers earning $6,000 or more," Shultz saw it as an opportunity to be more responsive to these alienated voters and to distribute the benefits of federal largesse more evenly. The members of the Silent Majority, Shultz reminded the president, were "immigrants or sons of immigrants" who tended to "live in the neighborhoods that blacks are most likely to move into and whose schools black children might attend." These workers, he concluded, felt "insecure about their own place in the mainstream of American society."[27] By reversing the perceived racial logic of the War on Poverty and distributing new benefits to the white working and lower-middle classes, the FAP would ameliorate rather than exacerbate their hostility and insecurity and demonstrate the president's material commitment to the cause of the Forgotten American.

These arguments convinced the president. In August, Nixon unveiled the FAP in a prime-time radio and television address. Lamenting the nation's "urban crisis . . . social crisis . . . and crisis of confidence in the ability of government to do its job," the president attacked the present welfare system as "unfair to the welfare recipient and unfair to the taxpayer."[28] Immediately following the speech, the White House launched a public relations campaign pointing out the benefits the "working poor and taxpayers" could expect from the FAP.[29] Administration press materials highlighted how the program would deliver more than 50 percent of new benefits to the South—a key demographic in Nixon's New American Majority—and include more white (62 percent) than nonwhite families (38 percent).[30] Promising that the FAP would "get rid of the costly failures of the Great Society" and rectify the "unfair" and "inequitable treatment" of the working poor, the White House held out hopes that the welfare reform package, in conjunction with its other domestic priorities, would bind the Forgotten American firmly to Nixon and the GOP.

Things did not go as planned, however. Although initial polls suggested popular support for the proposal, and the Ways and Means Committee, with the blessing of its chairman and ranking member, approved it early in 1970, the FAP stalled in the Senate Finance Committee. The delay proved fatal, allowing anti-FAP forces on both left and right to muster strength, and giving the president time to reconsider. Republican losses in the 1970 midterm elections further undermined Nixon's faith in his plan to use new spending programs to attract lower-middle- and working-class voters into a political coalition.[31] Early in 1971, even as Chairman Wilbur Mills shepherded a new version of the FAP that included stricter work requirements for the employable poor through the House the president began to fear he was "on a bad wicket" with the FAP. In April, Nixon ordered his deputies to drop assistance to two-parent families, by far the most radical element of the proposal, because the public had no interest in "providing aid to working families."[32] By late spring, convinced the proposal was "a political loser" that "would add numbers to the rolls to malinger," Nixon abandoned the FAP altogether.

Conservative opposition to the program, particularly among business groups, combined with public ambivalence and mounting pressure from anti-welfare conservatives like California Governor Ronald Reagan, help explain Nixon's eventual repudiation of what might have been his administration's signature domestic reform. Even before the president announced the FAP in August 1969, the U.S. Chamber of Commerce, a countrywide organization with a membership of more than 3,500 professional and trade groups, had launched an intense campaign to warn business and community leaders about the disastrous economic and social consequences of any guaranteed annual income plan.[33] Chamber members, many representing businesses that relied on low-wage labor, feared that the FAP would reduce the labor supply and exert upward pressure on wages. Representatives from one group of eighteen state Chambers of Commerce testified before Congress that the FAP would create "drastic dislocations of the economy [that] could be serious for the entire country" by enabling poor men and women to opt out of low-wage labor. This concern was particularly pronounced in the South, where the level of FAP benefits far exceeded existing AFDC payments and would destabilize local labor markets. According to one "informal head count" of domestic workers in a small Southern town, for example, the FAP would allow the vast majority of "full-time maids" to withdraw from the labor market.[34] The Southern economy's reliance on low-wage labor may also help to explain Senate Finance Committee Chairman Russell Long's vehement opposition to the FAP. Dismissive of welfare recipients who refused to do so much as "pick up a beer can around their home or even catch a rat" to support their families, the Louisiana Democrat personally bottled up the FAP in committee, and insisted that any "real reform" of the welfare system must include a genuine, and enforceable, work requirement.[35]

Governor Reagan's well-publicized efforts to bring the California welfare system under control also influenced Nixon's decision to abandon the FAP, and at the same time provided an alternative conservative model for welfare reform. Like the president, Reagan hoped to use welfare reform to consolidate his support among the Silent Majority of American workers. In a 1971 interview with the unapologetically antiwelfare U.S. News and World Report, the California governor noted that the "rank and file of organized labor" were "fed up to the teeth" with AFDC.[36] Explaining his proposals to address his state's welfare crisis, Reagan rejected both the guaranteed income approach and the rehabilitative ethos that had informed the War on Poverty; instead he promised to scale back the welfare system, so that only the "truly needy" would be eligible for public assistance. Defending recent changes to the California welfare system—changes that relied on long-standing notions about the deserving and the undeserving poor—the governor often focused on the costs of the existing system and the proposed FAP alternative to individual taxpayers who would have to foot the bill.[37] The California model for welfare reform appealed to the lower middle classes, not as a group unfairly excluded from the benefits of the liberal state, as Nixon had hoped to do with the FAP, but rather as taxpayers who bore the unfair burden of supporting what Reagan called the "loafing classes."[38] Nixon soon appropriated Reagan's appeal to taxpayers and his rhetorical assault on welfare, even going so far as to borrow an apparently apocryphal story—a regular feature of Reagan's antiwelfare rhetoric—about a woman who got up "at a welfare meeting and screamed: 'Don't talk to us about any of those menial jobs!' "[39]

Equally important, the working poor's continued ambivalence about the proposal undercut the original political rationale for the program. Organized labor had endorsed the FAP, but its support was lukewarm at best. Although labor "would join in some coalition efforts" to rally support for the president's plan, Moynihan later complained, "on balance it stood apart, looking to what it perceived to be its own interests."[40] Union leaders objected in particular to work requirements and workfare programs, fearing such policies would drive down prevailing wages. Insofar as such programs provide a federal subsidy to low-wage employers to encourage them to hire former welfare recipients, workers' tax dollars would in effect help to subsidize a program that might jeopardize their own current standard of living. Conservative anti-FAP groups recognized and reinforced these fears, and like Reagan, encouraged workers to consider how a guaranteed annual income would affect them individually as taxpayers.[41]

The FAP also had the unanticipated benefit of dividing the president's liberal opposition. Some liberals welcomed Nixon's proposal, seeing the FAP as a good, albeit inadequate, opening wedge in the struggle to guarantee at least a minimum level of economic security to all Americans. Although the proposed guarantee of $1,600 per year for a family of four would hardly provide an income sufficient to ensure recipients' economic well-being, and fell well below even the miserly federal poverty line of $4,000, many liberal groups held out hope that the program could be improved and expanded in the future. The editors of the liberal *New Republic*, for example, supported the proposal for enshrining the "principle of a . . . guaranteed minimum income" in federal law.[42] Acknowledging the real deficiencies in the FAP, groups like the National Association of Social Workers, the American Public Welfare Association, the League of Cities, Common Cause, the American Jewish Committee, the League of Women Voters, as well as the AFL-CIO, nevertheless rallied behind it and lobbied for amendments to raise benefit levels and soften its most punitive features.

Such compromises seemed impossible and even immoral for other members of the liberal antipoverty coalition. Welfare rights groups, in particular, saw the FAP as a significant threat to the rights and well-being of welfare recipients; they attacked the program as a racially motivated "act of political repression," a "brutal attack upon children," and an "affront to the dignity of humanity" that would send the country "back to the dark ages."[43] Speaking on behalf of current AFDC recipients, the vast majority of whom would receive lower benefits as a result of the FAP, the National Welfare Rights Organization (NWRO) denounced the proposal as a form of "slave labor" and launched a campaign to "Zap the FAP." The organization's strident tone and "militant posture" alienated many liberal organizations otherwise sympathetic to the NWRO's goals and membership.[44]

Absent White House support, with the liberal antipoverty coalition divided and resurgent conservatives arrayed firmly against it, the FAP had no chance. With Nixon's blessing, the Senate Finance Committee delayed consideration of the bill until September 1972, when it finally reported a defanged version to the full Senate. By this time, as Chairman Mills noted, genuine welfare reform was "dead as a doornail."[45] On 3 October, Senate Minority Leader Hugh Scott told the president what he already knew—they were not "getting a bill." Resigned, and concerned only with how his administration would "look in the rubble," Nixon admitted to Scott and to his advisors: "Attitude re welfare very different . . . doubt I would start it again now."[46]

Two days later, almost a year and a half after the full House approved the FAP by a solid 288–132 margin, the Senate agreed only to authorize a limited test of the program and two competing reform alternatives. Although the Senate effectively rejected the FAP, the final bill did *not* roll back the welfare state. In fact, it expanded it exponentially, increasing Social Security benefits by 20 percent and providing that future benefits would be automatically adjusted for inflation. Congress also created a new federal social insurance program—known as Supplemental Security Income (SSI)—to replace the state/federal

Aid to the Blind and Old Age Assistance programs. These changes accelerated the growth of the Social Security program, and provided the blind and
elderly poor with the same degree of protection and economic security af-
forded to other social insurance beneficiaries.[47] But Congress declined to
make any real changes to the AFDC program. From the beginning, the president had framed the FAP as a way to tame the "cumbersome, unresponsive"
welfare bureaucracy created by a "third of a century of social experiments."
By 1972, the structural changes to the welfare system lay abandoned, and only
the residue of welfare reform and a concerted battle against the unwholesome
"dependency" created and subsidized by the "welfare monster" survived.[48]
Equally important, the failure of the FAP and the negative attitudes toward
welfare spending that it revealed and produced set the stage for the return of
tax politics to the center of American political debate.

Mobilizing Taxpayers at the Grass Roots

After the defeat of the FAP, both right and left turned to tax rather than
spending policy to appeal to the Forgotten Americans of Middle America.
The protracted debate over Nixon's welfare proposal had exposed a rift within
the progressive, antipoverty community and only deepened public antipathy
toward welfare. Seeking to reconstruct a new majority around issues of economic justice, the left sought issues with broad political appeal. Tax reform
targeted at corporate loopholes, coupled with tax reduction for lower- and
middle-income workers, grounded this new majority strategy. For its part,
the Nixon administration abandoned the expansionary policies of 1968–72,
turning instead to a domestic agenda that combined significant cuts in social
spending—particularly in Great Society programs associated with the urban,
minority poor—with the promise of tax reductions for the Silent Majority.
Taxpayers themselves, organized at the grass roots in local tax reform associations, and increasingly militant after 1972, helped keep tax policy at the
center of the nation's political agenda.

Economic insecurity created by rising prices and stagnating growth helps
to explain the political salience of tax politics in the 1970s, particularly for
lower- and middle-income Americans. By the end of the 1960s, as the economic growth that had provided the majority of Americans with economic
security and individual mobility throughout the postwar period slowed
down, only to disappear altogether, blue- and white-collar wages stagnated.[49]

Spiraling inflation—on the rise since 1969 and exacerbated by the 1973 oil crisis—in combination with the progressive rate structure imposed large tax increases on taxpayers in the lower- and middle-income tax brackets. According to a 1975 Joint Economic Committee study, personal income and payroll taxes rose twice as fast as prices for food, housing, and transportation. What was more, inflation had affected the tax burdens of low- and middle-income Americans more severely than wealthier taxpayers. In the lowest income brackets, Social Security taxes increased by 13.8 percent and combined personal income taxes increased by 31 percent; in the middle brackets, Social Security taxes rose by 21.6 percent, thanks to artificially inflated incomes and legislation raising the amount of earnings subject to the social security tax, while personal income taxes rose 26.5 percent.[50] At the same time, the federal government collected less and less from the nation's corporations. In 1955, corporate income taxes made up 20 percent of federal revenues; by 1970, they accounted for only 12 percent of the total.[51]

At first, liberals seemed best positioned to capture the nascent middle-class tax revolt and translate it into an ideologically coherent and politically powerful majority coalition. In January 1969, days before Nixon took the oath of office, the Johnson Treasury Department unleashed a firestorm of taxpayer protest when it made public a list of some two hundred "wealthy individuals who had used loopholes in the tax code to reduce, or even eliminate, their federal taxes."[52] At the same time as it drew attention to these so-called "tax millionaires," the Treasury submitted a proposal for comprehensive tax reform comprising eighteen revisions to the individual income tax and four to the corporate tax code. Pointing out the "intricate, subtle and difficult" tax laws that allowed some wealthy taxpayers to escape federal taxation, and aiming to provide some tax relief to those at the bottom of the income scale, the proposal offset $3.4 billion in tax cuts for these brackets with revenue-raising structural reforms aimed at increasing the take from upper-bracket taxpayers and corporations.[53]

The Treasury report helped mobilize taxpayers who were already "sensitive to the amount of taxes" they paid due to the 10 percent income tax surcharge passed the year before.[54] "Rightly aroused . . . about unfairness in taxation," and outraged at a "system that imposes a tax surcharge on the ordinary man while a handful of men with riches beyond imagination pay no taxes at all," irate taxpayers worked with members of Capitol Hill's tax community to push reform onto the national political agenda.[55] The Nixon Treasury Department reported receiving a record 1,930 letters about tax reform in

February 1969 alone; a year earlier, the department had received only 34 such letters.[56] With an intensity that "rivaled the student protests against the Vietnam War," taxpayers inundated Congress and the administration with letters demanding that the tax privileges of the rich be eliminated and ordinary taxpayers' burdens reduced.[57] According to the *New York Times*, the taxpayer revolt was a new fact of political life that politicians ignored at their peril.[58] Lawmakers agreed. Only "meaningful tax reform," Mills told his House colleagues, could prevent a "complete breakdown in taxpayer morale."[59]

By the end of the year, Congress had approved fundamental tax reform over a veto threat from the Nixon White House. The issue provided Democratic liberals with an unexpected policy and political victory and seemed to indicate a way to win back Middle America.[60] Reform advocates on Capitol Hill promised their constituents lower tax bills as a result of the tax revision. According to Indiana liberal Senator Vance Hartke, for example, the bill was nothing less than a "major victory for the forgotten American" who had for too long been "taking it on the chin." Senator Albert Gore praised tax reform and targeted reductions as a way to help out "lower middle income . . . people . . . trying to meet the payment on a home and rear a family of children."[61] Concern over Silent Majority taxpayers likewise drove the Nixon administration's December decision to abandon opposition to the tax revisions. As one presidential aide put it, a "veto would risk alienating such potent groups as the aged as well as a fair portion of the 'great Silent Majority.'"[62] Treasury Secretary David M. Kennedy, budget director Robert Mayo, and CEA chairman Paul McCracken concurred, pointing out that a veto would be "interpreted as denying taxpayers, especially low-income taxpayers . . . advantages offered by Congress while protecting upper-income taxpayers against the loss of their loopholes."[63]

The 1969 campaign for tax reform concentrated the attention of newly formed taxpayer organizations on the issue of fairness or equity in the federal tax code, and tapped into a growing popular resentment toward income taxation. Tax protests continued in cities and towns across the country both before and after the successful 1969 reform campaign. According to some reports, by 1971 more than 2 million taxpayers had joined some 2,300 protest organizations.[64] Like the Forgotten Americans they represented, however, these tax protesters defied easy political categorization and evinced a complex amalgam of reaction and insurgency. Some seemed to embody the popular image of the Silent Majority—white working- and middle-class homeowners who, in the words of tax protester Robert Bartell, had learned from the "radicals" that "all you have to do is get some attention is to shout loud enough."[65] Some groups blamed liberal social policies, including welfare, for rising tax bills. In Fannin County, Georgia, members of a local tax protest organization urged the county board of supervisors to publish the names of food stamp recipients, and questioned the costs of other public services including libraries, jails, and government workers' salaries.[66] Other groups, however, defied the backlash stereotype. In 1970, for example, a group of housewives in affluent Newton, Massachusetts, announced a "mass non-payment of telephone taxes" to register their disapproval of the ongoing war in Vietnam.[67] In Arkansas, California, and Massachusetts, veterans of the welfare rights movement turned their attention and organizational experience to mobilizing low-income taxpayers and directing public attention to corporate tax avoiders.[68]

Liberal politicians and activists hoped to tap this latter vein of tax protest. Tax reform reappeared as a national issue in 1972, when Democratic presidential aspirants again drew public attention to the unfair tax privileges of wealthy individuals and large corporations. "I don't think it's fair," Senator George McGovern of South Dakota said during a 6 March appearance on *Meet the Press*, "to load an undue burden of taxes upon middle-income Americans, upon the wage earner . . . and to let a handful of people in this country . . . literally have every special privilege and every tax loophole that the modern mind and legal fraternity can figure out."[69] Committing the party to combating the "economically depressing effects of a regressive income tax scheme," the 1972 Democratic platform pledged "further revision of the tax law to ensure economic equality of opportunity to ordinary Americans."[70] Uncritically and self-consciously appropriating the defense of the Silent Majority, Democrats vowed to be "responsive to the millions of hardworking lower- and middle-income Americans who are traditionally courted by the politicians at election time, get bilked at taxpaying time and are too often forgotten the balance of the time."[71]

Tax reform seemed even more attractive in the wake of McGovern's disastrous showing at the polls. According to a member of the liberal Coalition for Human Needs and Budget Priorities, progressives had become members of a minority coalition in the "sad position" of "defending social programs against the president's majority against 'welfare' and 'taxes.'"[72] The way out of this dilemma was "obvious, but not easy." Liberals needed to build a "majority coalition" by engaging in a critique of Nixon's domestic policy agenda that went beyond the "great social program cuts" to speak to "the adverse impact of the budget on other constituencies."[73] Throughout the early 1970s, a wide array of liberal activists, including representatives from women's and civil rights organizations, labor unions, civic and religious groups, and antipoverty organizations, struggled to construct such a coalition and to breathe new life into the liberal social compact.

Taxes played a critical role in this campaign. In February 1973, former Senator Fred Harris announced plans to lead a taxpayer revolt aimed at "reforming America's tax laws and 'getting the rich off welfare.'"[74] With an initial budget of $100,000 and plans to raise more from supporters of both Senator McGovern and Governor Wallace, Harris's group, known as New Populist Action (NPA), sought to coordinate a popular campaign to reform the tax system. Concentrating on mobilizing aggrieved taxpayers at the grass roots, the NPA Tax Action Campaign laid out plans to "build local pressure groups to gather support for tax reform," to hold a series of public hearings on inequities in the tax code, and to apply pressure on members of the House Ways and Means and Senate Finance Committees. The group also planned a "National Tax Action Day" to be held on 16 April 1973, the filing deadline for federal taxes.[75]

The NPA attracted support from a variety of traditional liberal organizations.[76] But the organization depended largely on grassroots groups to organize and mobilize taxpayers. Local organizations, rather than the national office, staged and coordinated Tax Action Day events. In Arkansas, local activists organized a "tour of five corporate 'tax avoiders' for a busload of average taxpayers and reporters," making stops at the local offices of the Georgia-Pacific Railroad and Alcoa. In San Francisco, local groups delivered a "blown-up check for $24 million" representing a "welfare payment from average taxpayers" to the city's Alcoa building. Atlanta's Tax Action Coalition organized 250 people in front of the Georgia Power Company to present the utility with a "Tax Avoider" award. In Milwaukee, some five hundred people, many carrying signs protesting the unfairness of the present tax system, marched into the rotunda of the City Hall to attend a rally sponsored by a local Taxes and Taxpayers (TNT) group.[77]

Harris was not alone among liberal strategists and activists in looking to tax politics. In 1973, during a speech at a Conference on Taxes and the Redistribution of Wealth sponsored by the National Council of the Churches of Christ, noted welfare rights activist George Wiley urged his fellow progressives to use the federal tax system itself as a "grassroots organizing tool." Pointing to the ways in which the federal tax code subsidized corporations, millionaires, and oil companies, Wiley blamed corporate tax loopholes for the tax burdens borne by ordinary men and women with no "lobbyists to influence the lawmaking in Congress."[78] Speaking to and on behalf of the "average Middle American taxpayer," Wiley issued a call for a nationwide taxpayers' uprising directed at the "flagrantly unjust tax structure in this country." Mindful of welfare's disastrous reputation among both the public and the policymaking elite, he reminded his audience, "it is not the welfare poor who are picking your pocket, but the welfare rich."[79]

A few months earlier, Wiley had resigned from the NWRO to found a new Movement for Economic Justice (MEJ).[80] Moving beyond the single-issue approach followed by the NWRO, the veteran civil rights organizer hoped to lead a "nationwide grass-roots movement among the many diverse groups of people who have a direct economic stake in more adequate income, better jobs with decent pay, adequate health care and a fairer system of taxation," and to bring the Silent Majority together with the poor and minorities around basic economic security issues.[81] Although Wiley listed housing, wages, health care, consumer issues, welfare, Social Security, and unemployment as key elements of the MEJ political and policy agenda, he chose tax reform as the new organization's first priority. Inequities in the federal tax code, Wiley suggested, affected "people of all interests and backgrounds"; a movement that aimed to challenge and remove those inequities would bind together the "elderly and black Vietnam veterans . . . hospital workers, household employees, women, tenants, farm workers, welfare recipients, mineworkers, day care parents, unemployed workers, Chicanos, Blacks, Puerto Ricans, [and] white ethnics."[82]

In February 1973, the MEJ launched the Tax Justice Project (TJP) to "involve poor, low, and moderate income people in the issue of tax justice." Initially, TJP organizers directed their efforts at individual taxpayers, setting up at least 125 free tax clinics to help people with their tax problems and to demonstrate how these problems were "symptomatic of an entirely unjust system."[83] Usually staffed by volunteers trained by certified public accountants, TJP tax clinics provided a way to contact possible supporters and to recruit them to more explicitly political struggles. A Guide for Volunteers, produced by the TJP, reminded volunteer tax preparers that in addition to helping low- and moderate-income people file the appropriate tax forms, they should also "provide a basic education about the tax system and how it works against low- and middle-income people." The TJP also worked closely with state and local organizations to plan "local tax happenings directed against corporations who avoid their taxes" and to provide these groups with information on the "injustices in the current tax system . . . how to get a free tax clinic started . . .and how [to] get involved in the legislative battle over tax reform."[84] The MEJ and other national organizations, such as Ralph Nader's Tax Reform Research Group, devoted much of their time to setting up "trained local teams who can mobilize quickly and efficiently [to put] maximum pressure . . . on key Senators or Congressmen." The national organizations could provide local groups with "information on elected officials" and help train local activists in the skills needed to effect legislative change. The initial groups might then become the "nucleus" for a larger taxpayers' organization somewhere down the line.[85]

Unions seemed a natural ally in the struggle for tax justice and a key constituency in progressives' plans to construct a new electoral majority, so TJP organizers reached out to organized labor. A tax organizing kit, prepared for union members, included sample press releases, petitions to Congress, fliers, and fact sheets that showed how the unfair tax privileges of the rich and of corporations jeopardized the economic security and mobility of the average worker. TJP materials often stressed how tax loopholes affected individual workers. One flier cast the tax treatment of capital gains income as "welfare for Wall Street" that added "$90 to the tax bill of each and every wage earner."[86] Another blamed corporate and "political pickpockets" for adding $900 to the tax bills of "every American family" to recoup the tax dollars lost through "tax loopholes for big corporations and the rich."[87] Yet another accused Congress of raiding workers' paychecks to "bankroll big oil" (Figure 7).

The TJP also blamed inequities in the tax code for larger problems in the American economy. Tax laws that allowed corporations to pay no taxes on the profits of their foreign subsidiaries, for example, encouraged companies to build new plants and invest profits outside the United States.[88] A sample form letter urged legislators to endorse "tax reform which would take away unfair tax credits, subsidies, depletion allowances and other tax loopholes from the large corporations," while "lowering taxes for middle and lower income families" in order to "put more money in the hands of the people and help our economy."[89] A fact sheet on the need for tax reform likewise tied closing corporate "loopholes amounting to billions of dollars" and a "tax cut for those who are feeling the heaviest burden of inflation" to the revitalization of the American economy, and the fight against recession and inflation.[90] Tax breaks for the rich and for large multinational corporations, argued one tax reform group in 1975, had failed to create jobs or to drive economic expansion. Instead, they had simply passed the cost of government at the local,

Depleting your paycheck to bankroll big oil

Our income tax system is supposed to be fair, with rates based on the amount of one's income.

Yet J. Paul Getty, the oil tycoon who makes about $300,000 a day, pays a lower rate of tax than the average gas station attendant.

And Mobil, Texaco and other big oil companies were able to do record production last year and pay almost no tax at all.

How do they get away with it?

There are several tax loopholes open to the oil industry. But one of the biggest is the "percentage depletion allowance."

It allows an oil company to simply write off 22 percent of its gross income as a business deduction — no matter how little its wells were actually diminished in value.

It has nothing to do with the depletion of oil. What really gets depleted is your paycheck.

With 22 percent of every oil company's income going tax-free, the U.S. Treasury loses about $1 billion a year. And you have to make up the difference.

Of course the oilmen argue that they need this gift as an incentive for finding new oil.

But a 1968 study by CONSAD Research Corporation showed that only one-tenth of the percentage depletion savings for that year were used for exploration. The rest was gravy.

Now we have a fuel shortage and the oil companies are hitting us from both ends — in the paycheck as usual and at the pump with higher prices.

It's time to shut down this welfare plan for big oil. Time for taxpayers to organize and say: "Fair Taxation or New Representation!"

Movement for Economic Justice • 1609 Connecticut Avenue N.W. • Washington, D.C. 20009

Figure 7. In 1973, the Tax Justice Project of the Movement for Economic Justice produced a tax reform organizing kit specifically for the U.S. labor movement. The kit included instructions on "how to make an interesting report at your union meeting," sample letters to Congress, local newspapers, and members of the local union, as well as several posters like this one highlighting big business dependence on corporate welfare. Image WHi-83419. Courtesy of Wisconsin Historical Society, Madison.

state, and federal levels onto the shoulders of "millions of working, productive Americans"[91] (Figure 8)

The progressive tax reform agenda, as well as the larger majority strategy of which it was a critical piece, required liberal agenda setters to abandon "'liberal' catchwords and phrases" such as "welfare."[92] To be sure, these

THIS MAN
makes $10,000 a year.
He pays a bigger tax rate than Texaco, Gulf or Sun Oil*
AND THAT'S NOT FAIR TO YOU OR HIM EITHER!

* He is like millions of other American taxpayers. He is married and the father of two children. He earns $10,000 a year. On that $10,000, John Doe and his family pay taxes at an effective rate of 8 percent.

Texaco Oil Co., with a net income of $928,689,000 in 1971, paid taxes at an effective rate of 3.2 percent.

Gulf Oil Co., with a net income of $628,558,000 in 1971, paid taxes at an effective rate of 4.9 percent.

And, Sun Oil Co., with a net income of $189,265,000 in 1971, paid taxes at an effective rate of 3.9 percent.

In each case, the oil companies with millions of dollars of income, paid a lower effective tax rate than John Doe — and probably you!

The Communications Workers of America, a nationwide union representing more than 550,000 men and women, uges you to join with us in demanding tax equity . . . a fair tax system now.

You can help by writing your U. S. Senators and Representatives today.

Without your efforts, tax reform will be token reform in Congress again this year.

SUPPORT TAX EQUITY... DEMAND TAX EQUITY NOW!

Joseph A. Beirne
President

Glenn E. Watts
Secretary-Treasurer

Distributed by
Local 1101

COMMUNICATIONS WORKERS OF AMERICA
1925 K Street, N.W., Washington, D. C. 20006

Ed Dempsey-Pres.

Figure 8. Communications Workers of America, flier, 1973. Image WHi-83420. Courtesy of Wisconsin Historical Society, Madison.

groups continued to support social spending programs and to insist that tax revision "cut the waste, not the services or the employees."[93] Progressive tax reform groups, in their support for many government programs, distinguished themselves from more conservative antitax groups. As a representative of the left-leaning California Action League (CAL) explained in the last half of the decade, "cutting services or jobs" or the "basic municipal and county services of government . . . critical to the lives of the old and the poor, and . . . important" to the middle class as well was not the solution.[94] Other groups occasionally challenged the arbitrary distinction between taxpayers and tax eaters on the welfare rolls. In 1972, for example, a St. Louis Tax Reform Group assailed the prevailing image of the "lazy welfare chiseler" using "our tax money to feed and clothe her family" by pointing to the $80 in sales and other taxes such a woman would likely pay each year.[95]

Most progressive leaders, however, recognized that direct references to welfare or to spending for the poor—particularly the minority poor—had become a political liability. The "campaign rhetoric of Nixon and [New York Governor Nelson] Rockefeller and the Reagans," coming after decades of bipartisan attacks on welfare as expensive and inefficient, blamed AFDC families not only for rising tax bills on individuals, but also for many other national ills.[96] According to Worth Bateman, one of the original authors of the FAP, welfare would "probably win hands down in any . . . unpopularity poll taken among blue-collar workers."[97] Progressive tax reformers even used the public's negative perception of welfare to deride "handouts" to the very rich. Wiley, for example, made the tongue-in-cheek proposal that the Ways and Means and Finance Committees write "tough means tests and a work requirement for all corporate executives whose firms receive handouts."[98] Bob Loitz, chairman of the National Committee for Tax Justice (NCTJ) and founder of the Ohio Tax Equity Action (TEA) Party, likewise suggested to the Finance Committee that if "big business cannot continue to operate and survive without public assistance, then put them on the dole . . . with direct aid right out in the open, completely above board." This "welfare for the rich," rather than AFDC and other poverty programs, progressive tax reformers argued, best explained the "burden of middle- and low-income U.S. taxpayers."[99]

Progressive political entrepreneurs interested in using tax politics to appeal to white working- and middle-class voters often relied on economic analyses of how special provisions in the tax system had directed "huge sums of money" to particular industries, activities, or classes of persons.[100] In the mid-1960s, a group of tax insiders—most of them professional economists employed by Congress, the executive branch, or policy think tanks—had rallied around the cause of broadening the tax base by reducing wasteful or economically inefficient tax preferences. With a powerful ally in Chairman Wilbur Mills, this group of professional tax reformers undertook a thorough review of the Internal Revenue Code, which revealed the extent to which the tax code had been used as an alternative to direct spending. These tax reformers did not want to eliminate all tax expenditures; rather, they wanted to trim outdated provisions from the tax code, to promote economic efficiency, and to ensure that taxpayers with roughly the same incomes faced approximately the same taxes. These reformers could claim a great deal of credit for the 1969 tax bill, which embodied some, if not all, of their reform proposals.[101] Because, as Mills put it, the tax code required constant revision to meet "changing underlying economic and institutional conditions," these tax experts continued to produce quantitative studies of the Internal Revenue Code and build a case for further reforms.[102]

Progressives hoped to use these studies to build a case against the federal income tax code as unfairly rigged in favor of wealthy individuals and large corporations.[103] In the 1972 election cycle, Democratic candidates seized on one study produced by this tax reform faction—a Brookings Institution report by Joseph Pechman and Benjamin Okner that uncovered nearly $77 billion in annual tax spending hidden in the Internal Revenue Code. For Democratic politicians, the study revealed a huge source of untapped revenues and a potential political gold mine. If these loopholes were closed and the revenues recouped, the Democratic Policy Council promised in 1972, the country would have more than enough to "pay for almost any foreseeable increase in expenditures that may become necessary."[104] On the campaign trail, Senator McGovern promised that tax reform to close "loopholes" that enabled wealthy individuals and corporations to avoid paying their "fair share," in conjunction with reductions in military spending, would free up $54 billion—more than enough to allow the country to "move forward with new programs."[105]

But the Brookings study of the federal tax code described a far more complicated reality. The tax subsidies it uncovered included not only glaring and regressive corporate loopholes, such as the Oil Depletion Allowance, but also more pedestrian tax preferences, including the deduction for mortgage interest, which cost the federal government $4.9 billion in lost revenue in 1976, as well as certain tax preferences for married couples. Although some on the political left appropriated the Pechman and Okner study to anchor political attacks on the "tax millionaire," the actual report concluded that at current tax rates—that is the rates used to derive the $77 billion figure—10 percent of increased tax collections would come from those with total incomes under $10,000 and another 43 percent from those with total incomes between $10,000 and $25,000.[106] Indeed, while the base-broadening reforms recommended by the study would "improve immeasurably the equity of the income tax," they might mean tax increases for the Silent Majority and would be "unpopular with large masses of voters."[107]

Nor could tax reform alone pay for huge new social programs—as many progressive tax reformers had hoped and promised. As a rule, members of the academic and professional tax reform community resisted efforts to yoke tax reform to new spending programs. Most of these tax reformers viewed base broadening as a way to pay for lower overall tax rates—not new spending— and insisted that any reform package be revenue neutral. Economist Stanley Surrey made this point in a March 1973 economic roundtable sponsored by the Kennedy School of Government. Speaking directly to Wiley, the former Treasury Department official argued that efforts to "advance welfare reform" and to "pay for it at the same time through tax reform" simply would not work. "Tax reform can't pay for welfare reform," he said.[108] Surrey and his fellow economist, Richard Musgrave, also expressed considerable doubt about progressive tax reformers' most basic assumption: that tax reform could join the economic interests of the middle and working classes to those of the poor. It was "dangerous and not realistic," Musgrave told Wiley, to tie the "$15,000 wage earner with welfare recipients," because it is "difficult to simultaneously talk about tax reform that will work changes for both groups."[109]

Events bore out the economists' warnings. Although Wiley had hoped that the "new movement in the suburbs among the middle class on abolishing property taxes" could be "shaped and directed" to the left, he soon discovered that many local tax groups had little interest in broader issues of economic justice. Nor did many of these groups include a membership that extended to "blacks, Chicanos or Indians."[110] Local organizers likewise recognized the potential danger in tax reform politics. Although his organization had worked hard to "build a 'majority constituency' around this [property tax reform] issue," CAL organizer Mike Barnes admitted, other, more conservative forces representing "older, white homeowner type[s] and their taxpayers/ homeowners associations" might well capture the issue.[111]

The continued deterioration of the national economy—a combination of rising unemployment, stagnating growth, and spiraling inflation that violated the basic terms of the postwar liberal social compact—further undercut the potential of tax reform to underwrite a new progressive majority. Inflation pushed many middle- and lower-income taxpayers into higher marginal tax brackets. This bracket creep, as it was called, meant substantial increases in federal tax bills at what must have seemed exorbitant rates. Rising Social Security tax bills further increased the tax burden of the Silent Majority. Just as President Johnson's Income Maintenance Task Force and Council of Economic Advisors had predicted in 1967, payroll taxes increased dramatically over the 1970s. By the end of the decade, they accounted for 22 percent of all federal tax collections, up from 13 percent at the beginning of the decade. Based on earnings rather than wealth, as well as highly regressive, the Social Security tax took the largest bite out of the income of the working and middle classes. According to the Joint Committee on Taxation (JCT), by 1978, about 5.8 percent of the average worker's earnings went to Social Security. Thirty years earlier, it was only 1 percent.[112] The conjunction of economic decline and rising tax burdens created what political scientist Michael Brown has aptly termed a "pincers effect" on lower- and middle-income workers, who felt themselves stuck with a "sharply rising tax burden that appeared to yield no tangible benefits."[113]

Liberal tax reform discourse and policies offered little to these middle- and working-class homeowners and taxpayers "squeezed" by inflation and high taxes.[114] Eager as they were to broaden their appeal among the ranks of the taxpayers of the Silent Majority, progressive tax reformers were largely silent on the ways the federal tax code subsidized those working- and middle-class Americans supposedly forgotten by liberal policymakers.[115] Indeed, progressive tax reformers repeatedly declined to challenge the narrowed definitions of both the welfare state and taxpaying citizenship produced in the 1940s, 1950s, and 1960s. They accepted at face value the claims that the Silent Majority had been forgotten by federal policy and made to pay for expensive social experiments that brought them little benefit. The Forgotten American's conviction that "there was no welfare state for him," of course, ignored the vast benefits that the white working and middle classes had received from federal programs put in place during the New Deal, World War II, and postwar years.[116] Even the Great Society—the target of much of the Silent Majority's frustration and anger—had directed substantial resources to the middle and working classes in the form of Medicare and federal aid to education.

Progressive reformers might have pointed out, as the authors of the Domestic Marshall Plan and the Freedom Budget had done, that the white working and middle classes had benefited significantly from the welfare state. They also could have challenged the narrow definition of welfare that included only AFDC. But they did not. In fact, some reformers went out of their way to protect the special status of the middle-class welfare state. Harris's Tax Action Campaign, for example, explicitly rejected any efforts to point out the welfare elements of the Social Security program, or to challenge the discursive fiction that distinguished payroll taxes from other forms of federal taxation. Worried about alienating "important lobby groups, key members of Congress and former Social Security officials," the group sought to "preserve the 'insurance' rhetoric" and opposed any efforts to characterize Social Security "contributions" as a "tax or a regressive payroll tax."[117] Progressive organizations also rejected claims that the Silent Majority had benefited from existing forms of tax welfare. Although in theory the "little guy can share in some of the largesse conferred by loopholes," one group said, in "practice it doesn't work out that way."[118]

The institutions and ideological commitments of the postwar welfare and taxing states limited progressives' ability to answer the growing anger of taxpayers, at the same time as they enabled conservatives to translate the inchoate but powerful taxpayer revolt into a transformative political force. Responding to the reintroduction of tax politics during the 1972 Democratic primary, GOP strategists developed a powerful political rhetoric that blamed rising tax burdens almost exclusively on "irresponsible" and "wasteful" Democratic programs. Hostility toward Great Society programs, in combination with revived hostility to welfare stoked by the protracted debate over the FAP, gave these arguments coherence and salience. By the 1972 election, conservatives had not only successfully co-opted poverty warriors' arguments that welfare led to "family break up and instability," but also appropriated liberal attacks on the "rigged" tax code and turned them against federal spending in general.[119]

Capturing the Insurgency: Tax Politics and the New GOP

In October 1971, Patrick Buchanan, a member of President Nixon's press team and one of the administration's conservative Young Turks, sent top presidential aide H. R. Haldeman a memorandum outlining a new political strategy to capture the allegiance of the white working and middle classes. Entitled "Dividing the Democrats," the memo outlined several "fissures" in the Democratic Party that "could be exploited to the benefit of the President." Although most analyses of this memorandum have focused on Buchanan's explication of "cultural politics," his economic strategy is equally, if not more, important. Convinced that the expansionary posture of the administration's first term had been a dismal failure, succeeding only in alienating "our conservative foot soldiers," Buchanan recommended that the president use taxes to develop a class-conscious appeal to the alienated working-class members of the crumbling Roosevelt coalition. Where the "economic interests" of the New Deal coalition had once been "complementary" and "harmonious," Buchanan concluded, over the 1960s core Democratic constituencies—namely African Americans and white workers—had begun to compete for the same, increasingly scarce economic resources. By taking "a hard line on welfare," the president could at once consolidate support among the white working and middle classes and force the Democrats to "choose between the working class outraged by the excesses of the program and the welfare class." If the president dropped the FAP and picked up the cause of tax relief, Buchanan promised, he could secure his reputation as "the visible and outspoken champion of the Forgotten Americans, the working people of this country," and force a final and fatal "division within the Democratic Party." The administration's expansion strategy—including the FAP and Revenue Sharing with the states—had failed. The president's conservative base had grown "sullen, bitchy [and] angry." "Our little old ladies in tennis shoes," Buchanan warned, "are not at all enamored of HR 1 [FAP] and price controls and $100 billion in deficits."[120] Unless the president forced the Democrats to choose between their liberal support and the white working and middle classes, he would be left with "welfare reform, revenue sharing, environment, while they [Democrats] are talking about reducing the tax burden of the workingman."[121]

Buchanan had some reason to worry. Although national polls generally agreed that Nixon would easily win reelection in 1972, the public gave the president low marks for his handling of the economy in general, and tax reform in particular.[122] One poll, taken only a month before the election, found that the "tax-reform issue could be one of the strongest working for McGovern in this final month of the election."[123] The president had already found himself on the losing end of the tax issue in 1969, when he publicly opposed the proposals introduced by the Johnson administration and endorsed by the Democratic Congress. Instead of stoking the anger of taxpayers, the president had opted in 1969 to *defend* taxes as giving "life to the people's purpose in having a Government to provide protection, service and stimulus to progress."[124] The president's initial commitment to the expansion of the welfare state to the white working and middle classes, even led the White House to consider a new Value Added Tax (VAT) to offset the costs of "revenue sharing, depreciation reform, tax relief on tuition costs and child care costs for the working wife, integration of personal and corporate taxes and local property tax relief."[125] The failure of the FAP and the rest of the administration's expansionary domestic agenda to challenge the president's reputation as "enemy of the poor and unemployed" transformed the administration's tax agenda.[126] Buchanan joined Treasury Secretary John Connally, a former Democrat, in urging the president to link tax reduction for "lower- and middle-income groups" to a hard line on the "issue of federal spending."[127]

The national Democratic Party unwittingly gave credence to GOP claims that Democratic tax reform would help the "welfare class" at the expense of the "working class" when its nominee for president linked comprehensive tax reform plans to a controversial $1,000/family "demogrant" that was almost universally seen as a guaranteed annual income. According to pollster Lou Harris, middle-income voters feared that, if elected, McGovern would "raise their taxes to pay for higher welfare payments."[128] By tying tax reform to income redistribution, White House economic advisor Herbert Stein observed, McGovern effectively shifted economic politics from "unemployment-inflation issues to the income distribution-tax reduction issues where [the administration] position is stronger," and allowed the White House to align itself with the "apparently popular position against tax increases."[129] The White House and the president's election team launched an extensive campaign linking McGovern to the "Democratic liberal establishment that passed all the huge spending programs of the fifties and sixties"—programs that had "bankrupted the workingman" and "taxed to death the middle class," while doing little to "help the poor."[130] Recasting the Democrats' tax reform proposal as a thinly disguised tax increase intended to pay for a new welfare program for the minority poor, the Nixon campaign constantly reminded voters that the middle class and working class not simply the rich would have to "foot the bill for McGovern's schemes."[131] AFL-CIO president George Meany, who had declined to give the union's endorsement to either candidate in 1972, agreed. "Our guy," he told Labor Secretary Shultz, "thinks he's paying his taxes so that somebody else can get welfare."[132]

The transformation of tax politics in the Nixon administration is a critical, if understudied, aspect of the larger transformation of the GOP and of American politics. Where the administration had once embraced an expanded welfare state as a way to appeal to Forgotten Americans, by 1972 it had adopted the politics of tax reduction. By "really" hitting "hard" on the "issue of federal spending," Nixon and the GOP articulated an appeal to voters simultaneously angered by the expansion of the visible welfare state and jealous of the economic and social privileges they understood as part of the postwar social compact. Focusing on tax reductions for the "little guy" also helped remake the GOP's image and prepare it for majority status. As outlined in a June "Assault" memorandum written by Buchanan and Kenneth Khachigian, Nixon's election-year tax strategy should be to erase the persistent perception that the Republican Party was "sleek, fat and incumbent" and allow the president to "shed the 'in bed with Big Business' image" long associated with the GOP.[133]

The journey of tax politics from left to right during Nixon's first term both mirrored and produced the larger shift in American politics. Progressive tax reform schemes, which at first promised a way around the racial backlash of the late 1960s and early 1970s, foundered on the institutions and ideological commitments of the postwar liberal state itself. The collapse of the FAP pointed the way toward a conservative realignment around the issue of taxation. By promising tax cuts, and blaming welfare for rising tax burdens, the right was able to build a popular, if unstable, electoral majority, and more importantly to shift the terms of debate for the rest of the twentieth century. What is more, in the wake of the FAP, and in the context of economic collapse and widespread distrust of the government's stewardship of the economy, the GOP successfully embraced a political agenda that promised to lower taxes on the increasingly overburdened Silent Majority *without* jeopardizing the privileges delivered and secured by the middle-class welfare state. This was antistatism in name only, one that depended on the widely accepted but inaccurate perception that the federal government provided "welfare" to only a narrowly defined and morally unworthy group. The popular iteration of conservative antitax politics thus drew significantly on the legacies of postwar liberalism, and ultimately reproduced many of the same contradictory impulses and promises that had at once sustained the liberal state and led to the collapse of the political coalition and consensus that had created and defended it.

CHAPTER 5

GAME OVER

Early in the summer of 1980, Robert Johnson and Ron Pramschuffer, two enterprising Maryland businessmen of the "Archie Bunker persuasion," figured out how to translate the rage of the "white lower middle class" into a board game.[1] Their brainchild, *Public Assistance: Why Work for a Living When You Can Play This Great Welfare Game*, hit the stores later that year, just in time for the holiday shopping season.[2] Modeled after *Monopoly*, the game retailed for about $16 and included a game board, four playing pieces, four identical pieces representing each player's live-in or spouse, a set of cardboard pieces representing illegitimate children, and a supply of play money. The rules were simple. Players rolled a set of dice and moved accordingly along one of two tracks: the "Able Bodied Welfare Recipient's Promenade," or the "Working Person's Rut." Whoever ended the game—usually twelve trips around the board—with the most money won.

The game reflected Johnson and Pramschuffer's belief that the federal government exploited "poor hardworking taxpayers like themselves."[3] Not surprisingly, life on the "Working Person's Rut" was expensive and dangerous. Players might be asked to pay out money for gas, for property taxes (ten times a roll of the dice), for school tax ($50), for a new tire ($50 towing charge), for rent (also ten times the dice) or for a monthly parking fee ($30). Their children faced violence at the hands of "ethnic gangs" and the threat of being "bussed back to inner-city schools"; their relatives risked being killed by a "'rehabilitated' murderer," or "raped by a paroled rapist"; their daughter's "ethnic boyfriend" might cost them $150 in hospital bills; government "over-regulation" or affirmative action programs for "ethnic immigrants" and "'disadvantaged,' minority, homosexual, Buddhist female[s]" might put them out of a job. With few exceptions, players unlucky enough to land on the "Working Person's Rut" found themselves "burdened by oppressive taxes, strangled by government regulations, and victimized by reverse discrimination."[4]

On the other hand, players on the "Able-Bodied Welfare Recipient's Promenade" experienced what journalist Nicholas Lemann described as a "pleasantly racy round of looting, gambling, drinking, having illegitimate children, and of course, collecting government benefits."[5] The game provided ample opportunities to cheat the government out of money. Players on the "Promenade" might expect to gain $500 by selling "tranquilizers . . . to distraught housewives," to collect another $700 in "emergency grants" from "five different welfare offices on [their] way to Atlantic City," to scam Social Security out of a $300 burial benefit; or to earn $200 from an ethnic politician interested in getting out the welfare vote. Of course, the easiest way for "Able Bodied Welfare Recipients" to collect additional money was simply to have more children. Players could collect $200 for the first, and $100 for each additional illegitimate child with no restrictions on the number of children on whom they might collect. Life on the "Promenade" was not only more lucrative than life in the "Working Person's Rut," it was also more fun. "Able-Bodied Welfare Recipients" could use their welfare benefits to "play the ponies" or the state lottery; working stiffs had no time or money for such pursuits.

The *Welfare Game*, in short, presented a world where the demands of welfare recipients and the federal government explicitly threatened the rights and well-being of taxpaying citizens. Drawing on hoary racial and gendered stereotypes, the game visually insisted on the zero-sum competition between tax eaters and taxpayers that, by the 1980s, had become central to mainstream discourse about welfare in particular, and liberalism in general. "We didn't invent this game," Johnson later insisted, "Government liberals did. We just put it in a box."[6] Not only did the game provide separate paths for Able-Bodied Welfare Recipients and Working Persons, it also made explicit that workers' burdens were *caused* by the behavior of both welfare recipients and their federal enablers. For example, any time a player on the Welfare Promenade landed on a "Have an Illegitimate Child" square, each player in the Working Person's Rut had to pay that player $50 out of his or her pocket. Most of the setbacks dealt to Working Persons came at the hands of the federal government or the social work establishment. And even if a player in the Working Person's Rut somehow managed to beat the odds and finish the game with the most money, that player would still owe taxes (anywhere from 10 to 50 percent) to the "custodian of the taxpayers' hard earned dollars."

By 1980, the connection between welfare—narrowly defined as means-tested assistance for poor women and their children—and taxes had been well established. So too had the idea that the legitimate rights and interests of taxpayers competed with and were jeopardized by the suspect rights and illegitimate interests of tax eaters on the welfare rolls. Liberals, as well as conservatives, had been instrumental in producing this discursive and policy framework, but, by the mid-1970s, the GOP had claimed the tax issue as its own. Republicans consolidated this position in the late 1970s as both a faltering economy and a precipitous decline in the public's trust in government institutions lent credence and popular support to the party's new antitax identity. By decade's end, the Republican right had successfully articulated a coherent and politically viable alternative to postwar liberalism that centered on the twin issues of taxes and illegitimate, even harmful, welfare spending. Appropriating liberals' traditional defense of individual rights and economic mobility, the GOP successfully cast itself as a bulwark against a liberal establishment determined to ignore public wishes by building public programs that succeeded only in imposing a "major burden on the budget and the nation" and making "people dependent on government."[7] Tax and spending issues framed and gave life to this political agenda.

The right's tax and spending agenda owed its success to the ways the liberal taxing and welfare state had at once obscured the role that government had played in securing and creating the (white) middle class and identified welfare—an allegedly wasteful and residual program—as the public face of government. By 1978, even before the nationwide tax revolt unleashed by California's Proposition 13, the GOP had succeeded in capturing tax politics, casting the federal income tax as the lifeblood of a discredited liberal state and a gross violation of individual taxpayers' property rights. Welfare provided the alchemical spark that allowed the GOP to articulate a public politics attacking the liberal state and, at the same time, pledge to protect the economic and social privileges of the majority of Americans.

Reagan-era domestic policy combined growth-oriented tax cuts for taxpayers in the upper brackets with reductions in federal expenditures aimed at the poor. In 1981, the Reagan administration, with the assistance of newly ascendant congressional conservatives and little opposition from a chastened Democratic opposition, shepherded a massive tax cut and significant budget reductions through Congress. This "revolution" in tax and spending policy lasted for only a year. In 1983 and 1984, President Ronald Reagan, mindful of skyrocketing deficits, accepted the need for significant tax increases; in 1986, his administration led the way in pushing a base-broadening income tax reform bill through Congress. Although the administration successfully reduced spending commitments for means-tested programs, it was unsuccessful in its attempts to dismantle either the Great Society or the New Deal welfare states—particularly those programs benefiting the broad middle class. According to one study of the Reagan record, after an initial year of "overwhelming legislative victories," the White House had "little additional success in advancing its agenda."[8]

The Reagan revolution succeeded initially because its program—and the rhetorical defense of that program—was grounded firmly in the language of American liberalism.[9] Both the liberal framing of Reagan's tax and spending policies, and the long reach of the New Deal, World War II, and postwar taxing and welfare state limited the extent of the right turn in American politics. The GOP's new antitax agenda, first articulated during the height of the early 1970s welfare crisis, depended on a very narrow definition of welfare and a perceived link between rising tax burdens and rising welfare rolls. When the Reagan White House turned its attention to the larger, more costly, and more popular parts of the liberal welfare state—including Social Security and Medicare—the "revolution" stalled. Here, Reagan ran into the same problem that Johnson-era liberals had encountered in their attempts to build the Great Society, namely how to reconcile Americans' taste for federal benefits with their unwillingness to pay for them.[10]

The End of Tax Reform as We Know It

In 1972, the Nixon campaign seized on the anger of ordinary taxpayers to develop a powerful political narrative of working- and middle-class victimization and a potent political formula to further weaken the New Deal coalition and scuttle progressives' new majority strategy.[11] Four years later, President Gerald Ford, in the midst of a neck-and-neck contest with Governor Jimmy Carter of Georgia, brushed off the old Nixon campaign script, labeling his opponent a "big spender" who would raise taxes on the top half of income earners to help the bottom half.[12] But it was Ronald Reagan who best articulated this political appeal, pledging himself to protect the "little taxpayers" against the "big tax spenders" in the Democratic Party.[13] Taking aim, in his first inaugural address, at a government that had "grown beyond the consent of the governed" and a tax system that "penalizes successful achievement," Reagan blamed the federal establishment for the nation's manifold social, cultural, political, and economic problems.[14]

The transformation of the GOP and the political success of its antitax agenda make sense only within the economic context of the 1970s. The rising cost of living, in particular, provoked discontent and insecurity among the Silent Majority.[15] Between 1973 and 1981, as the inflation rate climbed from about 6 percent to more than 13 percent, Americans listed "the high cost of living" as the "most important [issue] facing the country," mentioning it more frequently than any other issue.[16] By the summer of 1979, political journalist Theodore White reported, "no other issue could rival inflation as a pressure on the American mind, its mood and family planning for the future."[17] Almost everyone, it seemed, from business and professional people to manual workers, described inflation as the "nation's most important problem."[18] Outraged consumers occasionally took matters into their own hands, as in 1973, when a 75 percent increase in meat prices led shoppers to set up picket lines and organize a weeklong nationwide meat boycott. But, for the most part, the economic crisis seemed beyond the control of ordinary Americans, threatening not only their well-being in the present but also "their plans for the future."[19]

What was worse, the federal government seemed impotent in the face of economic disaster. Economists were at a loss even to explain how inflation and stagnation—"stagflation"—could be present at the same time, much less design a policy to address them. The economic crisis thus bred a kind of intellectual and cultural crisis that undermined faith in the bedrock institutions of American life.[20] By the end of the decade, public opinion expert Daniel Yankelovich reported, mistrust in national institutions had reached historically unprecedented levels.[21] This was especially true with regard to government. One 1976 survey of 2,000 families in four American cities found that the average citizen held the "government and the politicians" responsible for the nation's "economic ills."[22]

At the same time, the percentage of Americans who believed "people in government waste a lot" of tax money rose from 47 to 78 percent.[23] Although most scholars have focused their attention on the public's rising distaste with *what* the government did with tax money, the other side of the equation—the public's perception of how much money they were sending every year to "people in government"—was equally, if not more, important. The progressivity of the tax code, in the context of the inflationary crisis of the 1970s, pushed taxpayers into higher and higher marginal tax brackets and produced rapidly rising tax burdens that seemed to have little relation to *real* improvements in living standards. This phenomenon—known as "bracket creep"—in combination with the decade's chronic economic and energy crises and persistent and seemingly inexplicable stagflation translated previous calls for tax reform into strident demands for tax reduction.[24] In concert with the general economic collapse and mounting economic insecurity, rising tax burdens helped to generate public hostility to taxes in general—a hostility the resurgent GOP, a new generation of Republican political entrepreneurs, and the new conservative counterestablishment were more than happy to exploit.

The Revenue Act of 1978, the last tax bill of the decade, provided a dress rehearsal for the tax politics of the Reagan era.[25] In January, President Carter had recommended a relatively modest $34 billion tax cut for individuals and businesses offset by some $9 billion in revenue-raising reforms. Casting himself as a populist crusader, Carter promised to crack down on those "few individuals" who were "able to live extravagantly at the expense of general revenues," and to protect the interests of "low- and middle-income workers struggling to make ends meet."[26] Even though the package promised tax benefits to almost everyone with an income below $100,000 a year, or about 96 percent of the population, it ran quickly into opposition from both the left and the right.[27] Indeed, two days *before* the package was officially unveiled, the National Urban League condemned the anticipated tax proposals as inadequate to meet the needs of the nation's black communities.[28] A day later, Democratic Ways and Means Chairman Al Ullman of Oregon announced that his committee would not accept the president's proposal to "tighten up on business expense accounts."[29]

The Carter administration never managed to get control of the tax debate. Democrats' efforts to generate populist anger against the tax advantages of those at the top end of the income scale and harness the tax revolt as they had done in 1969 fizzled and died.[30] The chairmen of the House Ways and Means and Senate Finance Committees repeatedly warned that any revenue-raising or loophole-closing reforms would face an uphill battle in their committees.[31] By April, Ways and Means Committee members, including some liberal Democrats, had begun to entertain the possibility of a "tax cut without tax reform."[32] And by the end of the summer, Congress, including a substantial number of Democrats, had completely rejected the president's package, instead passing a relatively regressive tax measure that provided the largest benefits to those in the upper tax brackets. According to Robert Brandon, the director of the liberal Tax Reform Research Group, the Revenue Act of 1978 reversed "over ten years of tax reform efforts." Public Citizen agreed, calling the bill a "significant step backward in our efforts to make our tax system sound and the tax burden fairer."[33] "Carter and liberal Democrats," *Congres-*

sional Quarterly concluded toward the end of the year, had been caught off guard by a "coalition of Republicans and conservative Democrats" who rejected the "traditional belief that tax bills should 'redistribute income.' "[34]

The debate over two amendments to the 1978 tax bill—the first a GOP proposal to return capital gains tax rates to their pre-1969 levels and the second a Democratic amendment to require periodic congressional reauthorization of certain tax expenditures—illustrates the weaknesses of Carter's pleas for tax reform and provides a preview of Reagan-era tax policy and politics. Together, these amendments to the bill suggest the historical specificity of the right turn of the 1970s and 1980s—its link to the unraveling of the American economy and the Keynesian consensus that sustained it, and to the institutions and ideologies of the liberal state it sought to undo.

With many of the most controversial revenue-raising reforms proposed by the president more or less dead on arrival, the tax debate quickly centered on an amendment introduced by Representative William A. Steiger of Wisconsin, a young legislator "widely regarded as one of the [GOP's] most promising political figures," to reduce the tax rate levied on capital gains.[35] A similar bill in the Senate claimed sixty cosponsors, including twenty-five Democrats. Although the Carter administration remained firmly resolved against any reduction in the capital gains rate—denouncing it again and again as a "fat-cat amendment" and the "Millionaires' Relief Act"—the idea of cutting the tax had apparently unstoppable momentum on Capitol Hill.[36]

The debate over capital gains reductions tested and proved the political viability of supply-side economics. In the late 1960s and early 1970s, as inflation mounted and economic growth slowed, some academic economists and political figures began to challenge the Keynesian theories that had for decades guided American economic policy and both justified and underwritten the expansion of the liberal state (see Chapter 2). As the Keynesian consensus weakened, academic economists offered several substantive critiques to the reigning orthodoxy—from Milton Friedman's 1967 evisceration of the Phillips curve to Martin Feldstein's "new public finance" and Robert Lucas's "rational expectations theory."[37] By the mid-1970s, the economic crisis had bred a kind of intellectual crisis within the field of economics, as Keynesian economics seemed unable to explain, much less address in any practical way, the problem of stagflation.[38] This failure, in combination with the weakening of the Keynesian consensus within the economics profession as a whole, opened up political space for the manufacture and marketing of new economic theories and policies.

The most politically salient of these ideas—supply-side economics—rejected the Keynesian emphasis on stimulating consumer demand in favor of revived attention on the problems of supply. Reaching back to the nineteenth century and the work of French economist Jean Baptiste Say, supply-side enthusiasts accused Keynesians of ignoring the human incentives to work and to invest, and turned their attention to how government policies—namely taxation and regulation—had "hobbled the economy" by forcing large quantities of labor and capital to withdraw from the market.[39] One supply-side economist, Norman Ture, estimated that misguided Keynesian fiscal policies had cost the nation as much as half a billion dollars each year in lost growth.[40]

Supply-side economics drew on intellectual insights from within the economic mainstream, but took shape in the "overtly politicized world of public policy and advocacy journalism" produced by the New Right counterrevolution.[41] Although the supply-side idea was generally in the air in the early 1970s, it took legislative and political form within the network of relationships established and mediated by new conservative institutions.[42] According to most accounts, the idea for a supply-side tax cut originated in 1974, when, over drinks, University of Chicago economist Arthur Laffer demonstrated its basic principles on the back of a cocktail napkin to Jude Wanniski, of the *Wall Street Journal*, and Dick Cheney, then an official in the Ford administration.[43] Throughout 1974 and 1975, Wanniski, Laffer, and Robert Mundell, a Columbia University economist, met regularly to "plot and scheme how to take over economic policy."[44] The group soon included other conservative insurgents, including future Office of Management and Budget (OMB) Director David Stockman and Jack Kemp, a second-term congressman from upstate New York whose "evangelical" enthusiasm for tax cutting rocketed "him from the back benches of the House to become a star attraction at GOP gatherings around the country."[45] Kemp's conversion and Wanniski's "missionary work" also brought *Wall Street Journal* editor Robert Bartley into the supply-side fold and transformed the paper's editorial page into the doctrine's "quasi-official voice."[46]

Supply-side arguments got an early test run in 1978 during the debate over the capital gains rate cut. Supporters did not usually label the capital gains cut as a supply-side policy, but the arguments marshaled in favor of the rate cut echoed the concerns of true believers like Wanniski and Kemp. Like supply-siders, supporters of the capital gains cut focused on investment rather than consumer demand as the engine of economic growth, and blamed liberal policies for the economic travails of the 1970s. The amendment's chief sponsor, Representative Steiger, for example, blamed "redistributive" taxation for reducing the nation's capital stock and limiting the country's ability to invest and create jobs. By cutting capital gains taxes, Steiger argued, Congress could automatically spur capital formation, generate new investment, and create several hundred thousand new jobs.[47]

Witness after witness repeated these arguments during the Senate Finance Committee's hearings on the tax bill. Not surprisingly, business interests, including the National Association of Manufacturers (NAM) and the National Chamber of Commerce endorsed the rate cut. According to the NAM spokesman, reductions in the capital gains rate would go a long way toward improving the "general tax climate for productive investment" and relieve the burden of middle-income taxpayers.[48] Jack Carlson, chief economist for the Chamber of Commerce, went further, claiming that cutting the capital gains rate would most help "the disadvantaged, older people, minorities, women and teenagers."[49] These arguments even managed to convince normally stalwart Democratic liberals like New Jersey Senator Harrison Williams and Vermont Senator Patrick Leahy to sponsor a similar proposal in the Senate.[50] Former Senator Eugene McCarthy, whose unsuccessful 1968 bid for the presidency had inspired thousands of idealistic college liberals to "go clean for Gene," lent his support to the cause in an editorial for the *Washington Evening Star*, in which he argued that reduced capital gains taxes would encourage savings and investment, increase jobs, raise the GNP, and even, "all things being more or less equal," reduce the federal budget deficit.[51] Indeed, as the editors of the *Washington Post* noted, by 1978, the idea that the federal income tax took "too much from the prosperous," once the exclusive "property of the more rigorous among the Republicans," had gained significant bipartisan support.[52]

The debate over the Steiger Amendment—and the slightly smaller capital gains tax cut sponsored by Oklahoma Democrat Jim Jones—also tested the strength of progressive attacks that labeled supply-side economics as a thinly veiled version of unpopular "trickle down" economics that benefited the rich and corporations at the expense of the working and middle classes. As the editors of the *New York Times* noted in April 1978, the Steiger Amendment would most benefit persons earning more than $200,000.[53] Andrew Biemiller, the legislative director for the AFL-CIO, lambasted the tax bill as a "grossly inequitable" measure that would primarily benefit higher income taxpayers, individuals with large amounts of sheltered income, and corporations.[54] The Americans for Democratic Action likewise criticized the measure for failing the tests of "fairness and equity" and for providing too little relief "where it . . . is really needed."[55] Treasury Secretary Michael Blumenthal argued that the rate cut would cost the Federal Treasury more than $2 billion, with little impact on new investment.[56] Carter himself denounced the proposed rate cut as providing "huge tax windfalls for millionaires and two bits for the average American."[57] Although this kind of populist tax politics had produced a tax revolt aimed at "tax millionaires" less than a decade earlier, by 1978 it failed to generate much interest at all. Indeed, according to a Harris Poll conducted in March that year, although a slight majority of those polled believed that the capital gains rate was too high, 46 percent had no opinion at all on the matter.[58]

A second proposal, this one offered on the Senate floor by Ohio Democrat John Glenn, illuminates another aspect of tax politics in the late 1970s and reflects the increasingly narrow definition of "public spending." Glenn's amendment, also known as the Sunset Tax Act, would have required Congress to reauthorize certain "tax expenditures," including special tax exclusions, exemptions, deductions, credits, deferrals, or preferential tax rates, every five years.[59] The proposal was relatively modest, and reflected the consensus among tax experts that tax spending was the functional equivalent of direct spending.[60] Congress had given its approval to this concept in 1974, when it required both the Treasury Department and the Joint Committee on Taxation to publish an annual tax expenditure budget.[61] Senator Edward Kennedy, Democrat of Massachusetts, appropriating the right's antitax and antiwaste rhetoric, called tax expenditures "nothing more than a permanent appropriation through the Internal Revenue Code" that often "subsidized low priority, unjustifiable and wasteful programs."[62] Glenn insisted that there was not a "single argument made on behalf of the basic sunset bill" for direct expenditures that did not "apply in spades to the tax incentive side of the equation."[63]

Despite its modesty, however, opponents ferociously resisted the Glenn Amendment. In the week preceding Senate consideration of the proposed change, both the chairman and the ranking member of the Senate Finance Committee attacked the bill as a hidden tax increase. Others accused Democratic proponents of assuming that "all income belongs to the government."[64] Indeed, in spite of broad expert support for the concept, congressional conservatives in both parties dismissed "tax expenditures" as a liberal invention contrary to the American tradition of individual property rights and a "whole new concept of jargon."[65] According to Senate Minority Leader Ted Stevens of Alaska, the tax expenditure concept represented a fundamental threat to individual rights by eliminating the "areas providing decisions on an individual basis" and prohibiting "John Q. Citizen" from "utilizing" his "decision-making power."[66] Senator Clifford Hansen of Wyoming likewise argued that "implicit in any argument on tax expenditures is the assumption that the Government has a prior right to all of the taxpayers' income."[67] In an essay in *Newsweek*, conservative economist Milton Friedman similarly claimed that liberal tax policy jeopardized fundamental rights. "The preservation of liberty," he wrote, "is the primary justification for private property." Appropriating a slogan first used by the radical student left of the 1960s, Friedman asked, "Is it not time that we rebelled against the doctrine that each of us has stamped on his back, 'Property of the U.S. Government. Do not fold, spindle or mutilate'?"[68] Although debate over the Glenn Amendment took the better part of two days and survived a motion to table, the amendment was ultimately ruled out of order, and did not even receive an up or down vote from the Senate.

Both the capital gains reduction and the failure of the tax expenditure sunset provision pointed to a changed tax policymaking climate on Capitol Hill—one that reflected and reinforced a growing public dissatisfaction with and distrust of government. Study after study demonstrated that, in general, Americans did not "trust those in positions of leadership as much as they used to" and felt "isolated and distant from the political process."[69] Declining political trust likely undercut the Carter administration's populist attack on "fat cats." According to some analysts, by the late 1970s, attacking the "malefactors of great wealth" had "suddenly become stale politics." "When you have an unpopular leader of an unpopular institution attacking the fat cats," the Hoover Institution's Seymour Martin Lipset noted in 1978, "it becomes a case of the pot calling the kettle black."[70]

Diminished political trust decreased the political efficacy of appeals grounded in claims to redistributive justice, such as those made by the Carter administration against the capital gains rate reductions, even when those appeals were made on behalf of the majority of American taxpayers.[71] The routine identification of welfare with the federal government further enhanced the appeal of anti-redistributionist policies and rhetoric. The widely perceived—if wholly specious—link between rising welfare caseloads and rising taxes, and the perception of inefficient and even corrupt government, effectively pushed tax policy to the right. Supply-side economics, which looked to the private sector rather than to the state as the engine of economic

growth, capitalized on rising dissatisfaction with government. But conservative defenders of the market relied, not surprisingly, upon the institutions and
ideologies of the liberal state itself, which had long assigned primary credit
for national prosperity to the private sphere. Together, these trends produced
not only the relatively conservative Revenue Act of 1978 but also the Proposition 13 "property tax revolt" then sweeping across California.

Sponsored by two conservative political entrepreneurs with links to the
real estate industry, and approved by more than two-thirds of California voters in June 1978, Proposition 13 placed sharp limits on California's ability to
raise property taxes and seemed to signal a nationwide revolt against taxes.[72]
The referendum had an immediate effect on national tax and spending policy. Speaker of the House Tip O'Neill of Massachusetts almost immediately
pulled President Carter's comprehensive welfare reform proposal, the Program for Better Jobs and Income, off the House's legislative calendar; legislators in both parties began acting as if "taxpayers were converging on them
like killer bees."[73] GOP lawmakers, sensing an opportunity to score points
against their Democratic opponents, planned a "nationwide blitz" to convince voters that Democratic tax and spending policies had put the American
dream out of the average citizen's reach.[74]

Most people viewed the California tax revolt as a massive rejection of
liberal government; opinion data, however, suggest a far more complicated
story.[75] Dissatisfaction with the tax system had indeed mounted over the
course of the 1970s, but public opinion polls show no dramatic shift in opinion leading up to the vote on Proposition 13.[76] Moreover, while voters expressed a general dissatisfaction with government, they remained committed
to most governmental activities. Americans continued to support increases
in government spending for the environment, health care, crime prevention,
drug treatment, and education.[77]

The significant exception to this broad support for the service state was
welfare. A CBS/*New York Times* poll taken shortly after Proposition 13 found
that 43 percent of Californians favored large cutbacks in welfare and social
services.[78] This should come as no surprise. Not only was welfare the most
obviously redistributive program on the list (which included services such
as police, library hours, garbage collection, and public transportation), but it
had long been on the receiving end of political condemnations—from both
the left and the right—for being both inefficient and corrupt. From the 1950s
attacks on "welfare loafers," to the Great Society's commitment to providing
a "hand up, rather than a handout," to Ronald Reagan's factually inaccurate

but nevertheless powerful condemnations of a Chicago "welfare queen" who had "used 80 names, 30 addresses" and "12 Social Security numbers" to bilk taxpayers out of $150,000 in "tax-free cash income," American political discourse had long identified welfare with an inefficient, and possibly immoral, use of taxpayer dollars.[79] Proposition 13 supporters made this association explicit. "The people who wrote the Constitution," quipped the initiative's septuagenarian cosponsor Howard Jarvis, "said the people of the United States shall be protected in their life, liberty and property. They didn't say life, liberty and welfare or life, liberty and food stamps."[80] By reducing government spending to welfare and food stamps, Jarvis, and political entrepreneurs like him, suggested that taxes could be cut without endangering services or jeopardizing the social entitlements of middle-class citizens. Predictably, public opinion polls found that the majority of Americans believed that Proposition 13, or similar proposals, would not result in any substantial cuts in necessary services.[81] Surveys conducted in the weeks leading up to the June 6 referendum found that 73 percent of Proposition 13 supporters believed that "local governments can get by on a lot less money." An even larger percentage (84 percent) believed that the federal government was "somewhat" or "very" inefficient.[82] A sign displayed proudly on the front lawns of thousands of Californians enjoined voters to "Help Make Government Efficient: Yes on Prop. 13."[83]

The campaign for Proposition 13 demonstrates the important connection between the right turn in American tax policy and rising public hostility toward welfare. The public identity of welfare helped to drive conservative tax politics, not only in California but across the nation. Exploiting the public's rising dissatisfaction with government, the long-standing association between welfare, waste, and inefficiency and the reality of rising tax burdens and economic insecurity, conservative political entrepreneurs developed a policy program around tax and spending cuts that all but ignored the enormous privileges enjoyed by the middle-class white majority. "The American Dream of a good and comfortable life," the Republican National Committee (RNC) warned in 1979, "is in jeopardy," threatened not by "some foreign power but from the misguided policies of [the] president." Blaming high tax rates and inflation on Democratic social spending policies, the GOP committed itself to a reorientation of federal priorities in line with "public concern about government spending."[84] Appropriating the language of the Civil Rights movement but reversing its implications, conservative strategists invoked a kind of victimization narrative powerfully present in another popular Proposition 13 yard sign: "Save our Homes, Yes on 13."[85]

This narrative, and the political agenda it defended and sustained, drew on the ideological and institutional legacies of postwar liberalism. Throughout the postwar period, policymakers had pursued a low-tax agenda designed to encourage economic growth and capital investment and to assuage constituent fears about the growth of the state. Combined with the bipartisan invocation of a rights rhetoric, low taxes became something of a civic creed and a central component of the postwar social compact.[86] The tax rights movement of the late 1970s drew middle-class voters into a political alliance based on their identity as overburdened taxpayers, rather than as relatively privileged beneficiaries of federal largesse. By hiding the institutions of the middle-class welfare state in the interstices of the federal tax code, postwar liberals played an active role in the production of the interests that ultimately produced the liberal-bashing Reagan revolution in taxing and spending.[87]

The collapse of the New Deal order represented a crisis for postwar liberalism, but conservatives recognized in the unraveling of the Roosevelt coalition an opportunity to channel politics to the right and to consolidate their own political power. Eager to escape the party's traditional image as the stooge of "big business," strategists in the Republican Party developed a class-conscious political agenda and language that constructed Democratic efforts to use government power to reduce socioeconomic and racial inequality as an illegitimate and ultimately futile abuse of power. This agenda derived support from a host of public intellectuals who, with the financial support of new conservative foundations, and the ear of ambitious politicians, described, at great length the abuses of the liberal state. Where Barry Goldwater and the conservatives of the 1950s and 1960s had opposed federal welfare policies as *unconstitutional*, the conservatives of the 1970s and 1980s dismissed them as *ineffective* and *immoral*. Charles Murray, for example, claimed to show that the Great Society and War on Poverty bore direct responsibility for the current debased condition of the African American poor by tracing a host of allegedly pathological behaviors—including unwed motherhood and low work effort—to liberal welfare programs.[88] George Gilder accused liberalism of imposing "new forms of bondage and new fashions of moral corruptions to poor families." Relegating racism to the past, and claiming that the "idea that America is still oppressive and discriminatory" was "genuinely difficult to sustain," Gilder, like Murray, blamed the War on Poverty and the resulting "explosion of welfare" for any and all problems faced by the poor minority and the minority poor.[89]

Ronald Reagan—the spokesman for the kind of antiwelfare, antitax conservatism born in the suburban enclaves of the postwar Sunbelt—rode the 1970s tax revolt and the larger dissatisfaction with government into office by capitalizing on the public's growing hostility toward welfare and growing taste for tax reductions.[90] Yet, even after Reagan had been in office for eight years, the system of social protections—both formal and informal—that many Americans had come to expect as a matter of right remained in place, limiting the extent of the Reagan revolution and setting the stage for a prolonged period of political stalemate. The conservative ascendency may have contained the liberal state but it did not break it.[91]

Liberalism and the Reagan Revolution

In August 1981, President Reagan signed into law two landmark bills that marked both the beginning and the end of the Reagan revolution in domestic policy. The first, the Omnibus Budget Reconciliation Act (OBRA), promised to "restrain the size and cost of government" by slashing federal budget expenditures by $130 billion over three years.[92] The second, the Economic Recovery and Tax Act (ERTA), made major changes to the nation's corporate income tax, provided for a 25 percent three-year, across-the-board reduction in marginal individual income tax rates, and, perhaps most importantly, required that individual tax brackets be annually adjusted—or indexed—for inflation.[93] Introduced as a comprehensive economic recovery package in February, and passed with significant Democratic support, the tax and spending bills marked a major victory for the White House. According to Richard Darman, Reagan's deputy chief of staff, together OBRA and ERTA made up the "largest single spending control bill and the largest single tax bill in the history of the Republic."[94] For the president, the tax and spending bills signaled nothing less than a domestic revolution, "a turnaround of almost a half-century of a course this country has been on . . . an end to the excessive growth in government bureaucracy and government spending and government taxing."[95]

Tax and budget cuts emerged as politically meaningful issues in the context of a stagnant economy plagued by spiraling inflation and a widely perceived crisis of political and economic leadership. The overwhelming popularity of California's Proposition 13 alerted policymakers to the political value of tax cuts. Enterprising politicians, convinced that the New Deal coalition had all but shattered, turned to tax cuts to bind together a new political majority. The federal income tax, in particular, had grown increasingly unpopular over the course of the 1970s. According to a May 1980 study by the Advisory Council on Intergovernmental Relations, the number of Americans who believed the federal income tax was the "worst" or "least fair" tax rose from 19 percent in 1972 to 36 percent in 1980, an increase of almost 90 percent.[96] This general dissatisfaction, however, did not necessarily translate into political action. Although most Americans surveyed agreed that their taxes "were too high," few believed that high taxes were among the "most important" problems facing the nation. In other words, tax cuts aroused sufficient public enthusiasm once offered, but the public did not take a leading role in demanding them. Indeed, despite the Reagan administration's repeated claims to the contrary, its tax and spending cuts did not simply answer the transparent demands of the people.[97] Rather, they were designed and sold to the general public by political entrepreneurs within the Republican Party and the larger conservative counterestablishment of the 1970s. Richard Nixon had first recognized the potential of tax cut politics in the wake of the debate over the FAP, but it was not until the late 1970s, in the midst of a severe economic crisis, that tax cuts moved decisively to the front of the Republican agenda.

The widely noted, if overstated, dissolution of the liberal consensus in the late 1960s raised conservative hopes about effecting a major political realignment. Nixon and his supporters talked enthusiastically of the "passing of the New Deal," and of their rendezvous "with a great historical hinge and moment of reversal."[98] Although this first attempt to build a conservative new American majority made several false starts, by 1972, Nixon and his aides had recognized the potential of tax politics to create a new conservative majority and make inroads among middle- and even working-class voters. The power of tax politics only increased over the decade, as rising unemployment and stagflation undercut the Democratic Party's historical advantage on economic issues and provided the material basis for a cross-class alliance among taxpayers.[99] Not surprisingly, federal income taxes had grown particularly unpopular among members of the lower-middle class. While 36 percent of all Americans in the ACIR poll listed the federal income tax as the "worst" tax, 47 percent of Americans in the $10,000–14,999 income bracket felt this way.[100] Ambitious conservative politicians, as eager as Nixon had been to create a new conservative majority, recognized the political potential in the discontent of taxpayers and developed a policy program and political appeal that bound these voters to the GOP and the GOP to the conservative movement.

Tax and budget cuts were the key to this political and policy agenda. The transformation of the GOP into the tax cut party began in the early 1970s, accelerated during the Carter presidency, and was complete by June 1978, when the overwhelming majority of California voters approved Proposition 13. As a candidate, Ronald Reagan early endorsed the conservative tax cut agenda, voicing his support for Proposition 13 and for the 30 percent, three-year supply-side tax cut sponsored by Senator William Roth of Delaware and Representative Jack Kemp of New York (better known as the Kemp-Roth bill).[101] Tax policy played a key role in both the GOP primaries and the general election campaign. The Republican platform unveiled at the party's 1980 convention, for example, contained a full 115 sentences about tax policy; twenty years earlier, the platform had contained only 2 sentences on tax policy. Indeed, according to one study, tax policy became increasingly important to both parties' platforms after 1968—the moment of the supposed liberal crack-up—as both Democrats and Republicans hoped to use tax policy to anticipate, discover, and even generate majority demands.[102]

Once elected, the Reagan administration moved quickly on the tax and spending agenda outlined during the campaign. Within thirty days of taking the oath of office, the president committed himself to what his supporters described as a four-part program for economic recovery based on Reagan's campaign and reflective of the "overwhelming mandate on which he was elected."[103] Although many of the president's advisors, concerned about the effect that massive deficits might have on capital markets and interest rates, suggested that the administration first offer a smaller tax cut that targeted only the top rates in order to encourage saving and investment, Reagan stuck to his guns, insisting that everyone's taxes be cut.[104] His goal, tax historian W. Elliot Brownlee and Reagan Treasury Department veteran Eugene Steuerle conclude, was to "exploit broad popular support for a tax cut . . . and produce a more profound realignment of voters."[105]

The case for the tax cuts thus depended not only on economics—though the supply-side theory did provide some intellectual justification for the proposed rate reductions—but also on a populist appeal to voters as taxpayers. This appeal, in turn, depended on public hostility toward government in general, and on the perceived link between rising tax burdens and "ballooning" welfare costs. Cutting spending and taxes, the Reagan administration promised, was a win-win proposition; taxpayers could "trade off . . . less government in return for more take-home pay and economic prosperity."[106] Indeed, throughout the campaign for both the ERTA and the OBRA, the Reagan administration stayed on message, routinely blaming "too many years of politics as usual—of the Congress spending and taxing at an ever-growing rate" for the repeated and worsening rounds of inflation, unemployment, and economic stagnation that had sapped the nation's economic strength and jeopardized its position in the world.[107] Only by ending counterproductive policies and lifting the "punitive taxes on initiative and saving" could the nation expect to renew its economic vitality and bring about an "American economic renaissance."[108] Current economic travails, which the newly elected president described as the "worst economic mess since the Great Depression," did not indicate a "breakdown of the human, technological, and natural resources upon which the economy is built"; rather, they were the unfortunate consequence of government policies and of the unchecked growth of the state in previous decades.[109] Freeing the market of unnecessary constraints, in the form of both taxes and regulations, and divesting the government of unnecessary spending programs, the White House claimed, would once again allow the country to prosper.

The economic recovery package faced an uncertain future. Although the public generally supported the president's proposals, his overall approval rating in mid-March was relatively modest, and at 60 percent, was actually *lower* than the ratings of Jimmy Carter, Richard Nixon, John Kennedy, and Dwight Eisenhower at similar points in their presidencies.[110] Moreover, while some people had interpreted Reagan's victory at the polls in 1980 as an indication that the electorate was becoming increasingly conservative, public opinion data showed no significant changes in the proportions of self-described liberals or conservatives. Nor could the president claim a mandate for his proposed tax and spending policies. In April, Andrew Kohut, president of the Gallup Organization, concluded that the president's "mandate" was "fragile" at best.[111] The tax cut in particular generated considerable skepticism. *Newsweek* reported that although the president's $48 billion package of budget cuts was "steaming through Congress," the three-year 10 percent tax cut proposal seemed to "have run aground."[112] A CBS/*New York Times* poll in early 1981 found that far more Americans favored balancing the budget (70 percent) than wanted large tax cuts (23 percent). Democrats likewise sensed the administration's vulnerability on the tax issue.[113] According to Montana Democratic Representative Max Baucus, the Democrats had considerably "more room on the tax side. . . . Even the Republicans are nervous about Kemp-Roth."[114] South Carolina Representative Ken Holland, a leader of the Conservative Democratic Forum and one of the administration's key Democratic allies, admitted in May, "there is not a huge sentiment out there anywhere for any tax bill."[115]

Indeed, Reagan's proposal to slash taxes succeeded largely thanks to broad popular support for his budget package. According to a 1982 report by the Center for Tax Justice—a left-leaning research and advocacy organization—the administration's "decisive victory" on the budget in late May both "dispirited" the Democratic resistance and "buoyed" the White House's stance on the tax bill.[116] Speaker O'Neill later admitted that his party did little to fight the president's tax and spending agenda, out of fear that there "would be hell to pay in the midterm elections."[117] The president's victory on the budget bill not only divided and disheartened the Democratic resistance, it also clarified the political justification for the tax cut by cementing the association between welfare and liberal government, undercutting Democrats' objections that the tax cuts would be unfair and would jeopardize important and necessary social programs. Calling for massive, long-term reductions in both discretionary and entitlement spending, Reagan introduced the budget package in early March with the promise that his administration would move quickly to restrain the size and cost of government and allow the "people" to decide "how to dispose of the majority of" the country's bounty.[118] The White House further promised that the budget package, in concert with the proposed tax reductions, would help to produce a healthy and growing economy and ensure that all families, states, and regions would gain more in higher after-tax income, increased purchasing power, and more jobs and growth than they would give up in government benefits.[119]

In his first press conference, Reagan had promised that his review of the budget would include all spending programs, warning that no one would be "exempt from being looked at for areas in which we can make cuts in spending."[120] OMB Director David Stockman, a former two-term representative from Michigan, likewise promised to end the era of "permanent government" by "curtailing weak claims" rather than "weak clients."[121] But, from the beginning, the White House put a significant part of the federal budget off limits, safeguarding "Social Security benefits for the elderly, basic unemployment benefits, cash benefits for the elderly, disabled and for dependent families [SSI], social obligations for veterans, summer jobs for youngsters."[122] As the president's first chief domestic policy advisor, Martin Anderson, later admitted, the White House chose to protect these programs for purely political reasons, using the term "safety net" strategically to "describe a set of social welfare programs that would not be closely examined on the first round of budget changes because of the fierce political pressures that made it impossible to even discuss these programs."[123] Altogether, these entitlement programs accounted for about 60 percent of domestic expenditures, and at least 50 percent of the "off-limits" programs were subject to annual cost-of-living adjustments that automatically drove up their costs.[124] Given these restrictions, and the administration's commitment to increasing defense expenditures, it is hardly surprising that about 70 percent of the proposed cuts came from discretionary and entitlement programs for the poor. According to a 1984 Urban Institute study, the Reagan administration did little to "reduce rapidly rising expenditures for Social Security, Medicare, government employee pensions and other predominantly middle-class programs that" had been "the chief source of growth in the federal budget since the 1950s."[125]

The administration's budget proposal included reductions in annual spending for social programs of about 17 percent, or nearly $75 billion, by fiscal 1985. About 60 percent of these savings were to be found in the smallest component of all federal social spending—the welter of fixed-dollar grant programs that allowed state and local governments to provide education, health, employment, and other social services. Another 28 percent of the cuts came from federal programs for the poor. These included changes to child nutrition and housing assistance programs, as well as cuts in AFDC, Medicaid, and Food Stamps.[126] The administration proposed to reduce spending on these programs largely by making it more difficult for people to qualify for assistance and by offsetting welfare benefits more fully for earnings and other sources of income. The elimination of the so-called "30 and a third" earnings exemption in AFDC, for example, caused somewhere between 400,000 and 500,000 of the working poor to lose both AFDC and Medicaid benefits.[127] More than a million poor Americans lost food stamp assistance due to COBRA's more stringent eligibility requirements.[128]

By promising to reduce the size of government while leaving untouched the largest social welfare programs, the Reagan administration recognized and reinforced these programs' special status and reprised the postwar script that more often than not equated government spending with a narrow definition of "welfare." The 1981 budget campaign capitalized on the public's negative feelings toward welfare and, in fact, used AFDC as a kind of shorthand for morally suspect and ineffective government spending.[129] Attacks on the state borrowed heavily from postwar discourse about welfare, particularly the enervating effects of dependency on family formation and individual freedom. "The growth of government programs," Reagan told Congress in February, had not only promoted "dependency," but had also reduced "real economic opportunity for many minority groups" by creating a "new kind of servitude . . . to the power of the state itself." As if that weren't bad enough, the problems of welfare, unless contained, would slowly sap the nation of its economic vitality and individual Americans of their personal liberty by "turning producing Americans into people looking to Washington for funds" and allowing "government to sit over them as a distant entity, doling out funds . . . [and] doling out controls."[130]

Widespread beliefs about the "fraud, inefficiency and abuse" within the welfare system buttressed the administration's claims that the proposed budget cuts would have little effect on the "truly needy" or on necessary (or at least popular) social safety net programs. Administration rhetoric strengthened this belief. In late March, for example, staffers in Martin Anderson's office pulled together a list of "typical . . . stories" about fraud and abuse in AFDC to counter claims that the budget unfairly targeted the poor. This "fact sheet"—designed as a set of talking points for White House surrogates—bore an uncanny resemblance to many of the scenarios spelled out in the *Welfare Game*. Focusing on individual narratives—a Philadelphia native who continued to collect AFDC, Medicaid, and food stamps even after she had died; Ohio steelworkers out on strike who "coerced" the county into providing "food stamps at the Union Hall"; or a St. Louis woman who "claimed to be indigent" but "in fact owned a four-family flat . . . [and] drove a Cadillac (Coupe de Ville)" while receiving both welfare and unemployment insurance—the White House strategy aimed not only to minimize resistance to budget cuts, but also to build support for the president's tax program.[131]

As it had after the failure of the FAP, this attack on welfare went largely unchallenged. The supposed revolt of the Silent Majority pushed many on the left to abandon welfare—a program identified with poor, black, single mothers. Both in and outside Congress, progressive forces for the most part distanced themselves from welfare recipients, choosing instead to stress the implications of the president's proposed budget cuts for the middle-class majority.[132] The left's repudiation of welfare left poor women and their families unprotected. Thanks to the combined effects of these program cuts and the severe recession of 1982 and 1983, the official poverty rate rose from 11.7 percent in 1979 to 15 percent in 1982—its highest level since the beginning of the Great Society and the War on Poverty.[133] But this discrediting of welfare not only undercut support for specific programs, it also left uncontested the conservative claim that all government programs were, like welfare, inefficient, expensive, and morally hazardous. As one result, even when the public turned against Reaganism and its budget cuts, it did not suddenly embrace either welfare or the liberalism that supposedly created and sustained it.

The battle over the budget culminated in late May 1981, when the Senate and a significant majority of the House approved it. The final budget resolution reduced overall federal expenditures by about $1.1 billion in fiscal 1982, and called for larger cuts in later years. In cutting AFDC, it placed limitations on work support and earnings that made it more difficult for poor Americans—mostly poor women with children—to combine low-wage work with public assistance. These policy changes, intentionally or not, further reduced political support for welfare by reinforcing the program's image as one used only by women who did not work at a time when more and more nonpoor women were entering the workforce.[134]

Reagan's budget victory not only served to cow the Democratic opposition, it also set in motion a set of political calculations that made approval of the tax proposals almost inevitable. The final push for the tax cut no doubt benefited from the mobilization of the newly organized conservative counterestablishment, which not only provided an economic defense of the tax program—in the form of the supply-side doctrine—but also generated support from the grass roots though a direct-mail campaign that, according to one White House insider, "dwarf[ed] what conservatives did for the fight against the Panama Canal Treaties."[135] The White House staff, and in particular the OMB's Stockman, also successfully exploited the complex rules of the budget process to move the president's proposals through Congress.[136] But, in the end, it was the administration's success in linking welfare and rising taxes that pushed Reagan's tax agenda forward.[137] Here again, the Reagan White House drew sustenance from postwar liberal structures and discursive commitments. The taxing and welfare state constructed by liberal state builders in the postwar period, and liberals' embrace of a political language and policy apparatus that subordinated the role of the state to that of the free market in assigning, protecting, and sustaining individual freedoms and prosperity, held the institutional and ideological seeds of the Reagan revolution.

Convinced of a genuine grassroots taxpayer revolt among lower- and middle-income workers—the heart of the Roosevelt coalition—Democratic leaders in Congress admitted the need for broad and significant tax cuts for individuals and business, and all but abandoned defending the federal government as an instrument of economic justice. Although the Democratic leadership attacked supply-side economics as a dangerous "roll of the dice" based on the "untested faith" that some "mystic combination of tax cuts and spending cuts" would defeat "inflation, low productivity, etc., as the morning sun dissipates the evil vapors of the night," the party ultimately offered a tax package similar to—if smaller than—the president's proposal.[138] The Democratic compromise, reported by the Ways and Means Committee in late June, included a two-year tax cut that reduced marginal rates across the board. Hoping to woo back the Silent Majority voters who had abandoned the party in 1980, the Democratic alternative showered specific benefits—including a partial abatement of the so-called marriage penalty and a larger standard deduction—on middle-class Americans overburdened by "the adverse effects of inflation and increased payroll taxes."[139]

The Democrats' embrace of tax cuts, and their attempts to focus those benefits more squarely on the middle classes, were a matter of political calculation. As the *New York Times* noted, although the party had historically portrayed itself as the "party of the 'little man,'" in Reagan's America, Democrats were more interested in the "middle class, the families earning from $20,000 to $50,000, voters that deserted the Democrats in droves last year [1980]."[140] But, these strategic calculations ultimately undermined the larger liberal project and diminished the Democratic Party's "intellectual credibility."[141] By accepting the need for tax cuts, Democrats gave credence to conservative attacks on the state itself. Although some Democrats argued that the fact that the "average American is better off today than ever before" indicated that "government must have been doing something right," the party as a whole accepted the existence of a national consensus behind "slowing the growth rate of federal spending, reducing the size of government—including its maze of regulations—and providing tax relief to those whose taxes have grown because inflation has forced them into higher tax brackets."[142] Democrats' attempts to capture the tax issue only muddied the waters.[143] In the absence of any kind of ideologically coherent alternative to the Reagan program and in light of the president's personal popularity—magnified by his aplomb in the wake of the unsuccessful attempt on his life—voters ultimately came to accept the "necessity—and efficacy—of [the] . . . measures" proposed by the administration.[144]

Only days before the House and Senate were scheduled to vote on the tax cut, Reagan again addressed the nation.[145] Since February, when he had first announced the tax and spending program and apprised viewers of the "grim and disturbing" state of the economy, the tax fight had, the president claimed, developed into something of a populist uprising with ordinary Americans sending a message—in telegrams, letters, phone calls, and even "personal visits"—that they "wanted a new beginning." In doing so, the president claimed, these voters had stood up against "all the lobbying, the organized demonstrations and the cries of protest by those whose way of life depends on maintaining government's wasteful ways" and reaffirmed the "mandate . . . delivered in the election" the previous November. Should Congress ignore that mandate and reject the tax cut, it would bring the nation "full circle to the source of our economic problems, where the government decides that it knows better than you what should be done with your earnings, and in fact, how you should conduct your life." [146]

The appeal worked. The next day, Speaker O'Neill, who had staked a great deal of his personal and political prestige on defeating the tax and spending packages, admitted he had been beaten. To "devastating effect," Congress had been "blitzed" by support for the president's tax package in a way "this nation [had] never seen."[147] The final bill, which received significant Democratic support, provided for cumulative reductions in the individual income tax rates of 1.25 percent in 1981, 10 percent in 1982, 19 percent in 1983, and 28 percent in 1984 and subsequent years. The bill also reduced the top marginal tax rate from 70 percent to 50 percent and included special provisions to benefit certain groups, including higher-income married couples, higher-income retirees, and the savings and loan industry.[148] Most important for the future of tax and spending politics in the United States, not to mention the fate of the Democratic and Republican parties, ERTA also provided for indexation of tax brackets to inflation, beginning in 1985 (see Table 1).

Throughout early 1981, the Reagan White House made its case for tax and spending cuts by defending the rights and privileges of taxpayers against the illegitimate rights claims of welfare recipients. In doing so, however, Reagan ultimately limited the extent to which his administration could actually reduce the size of the state and the extent to which his would be a truly transformative presidency. Indeed, by framing his own antistatism as a "war" on welfare—a target of very limited value in the context of all federal spending—Reagan undermined the larger conservative project of shrinking the state to a size where, in right-wing tax reformer Grover Norquist's memorable phrase, it could be "drowned in the bathtub."[149] "Starving the beast" singularly failed to reign in the growth of the federal government. Thanks to both the effects of tax cuts that failed to generate the economic growth promised by supply-

Table 1. Estimated Revenue Effects of Individual Income Tax Provisions (millions of dollars)

Provision	1981	1982	1983	1984	1985	1986
Rate Cuts	------	-25793	-65703	-104512	-122652	-143832
20% rate on capital gains for Part of '81	-39	-355	------	------	------	------
Deduction for 2-earner married couples	------	-419	-4418	-9090	-10973	12624
Indexing	------	------	------	------	-12941	-35848
Child and dependent care credit	------	-19	-191	-237	-296	-356
Charitable contributions deduction for non-itemizers	------	-26	-189	-219	-681 -	-2696
Rollover period for sale of residence	Negligible	>$10 million	>$10 million	>$10 million	>$10 million	>$10 million
Increased exclusion on sale of residence	Negligible	-18	-53	-63	-76	-91
Changes in taxation of foreign earned Income	------	-299	-544	-563	-618	-696
Total	-39	-26929	-71098	-114684	-148237	-196143

Source: U.S. Congress, Joint Committee on Taxation, Summary of HR 4242: The Economic Recovery Tax Act of 1981, 5 August 1981, 97th Cong., 1st sess. (Washington D.C.: GPO, 1981), 58, table 2.

side prophets, accelerated defense spending, and automatic growth in entitlement spending for the middle-class welfare state, the federal deficit ballooned during Reagan's tenure in office. Between 1981 and 1988, the national debt grew from $930 billion to $2.6 trillion.[150] What is more, despite its claim of a popular mandate to restrain the size of government, the Reagan administration failed, with a few exceptions, to dismantle the New Deal, postwar, or Great Society welfare states. By 1985, although the administration had succeeded in slowing the growth of domestic spending, federal spending as a proportion of GNP had actually risen by a half a percentage point.[151] Even welfare spending seemed little affected by the 1981 budget changes. By the time Reagan left office, federal welfare spending was higher than when he had taken office. In subsequent legislation—most importantly in the Family Support Act of 1988, which was hailed at the time as the most important welfare reform measure since the New Deal—Congress rejected OBRA's approach, combining work requirements with increased federal spending for various "work supports."[152] The so-called revolution in tax policy was also short-lived. Within months of signing the ERTA into law, Reagan proposed, with little fanfare, what amounted to a substantial tax increase, billed as a revision "in the tax code to curtail certain tax abuses and enhance tax revenues." In 1982 and 1984, he supported and signed two tax laws—the Tax Equity and Fiscal Responsibility Act (TEFRA) of 1982 and the Deficit Reduction Act (DEFRA) of 1984—that together raised more tax revenues than any peacetime tax bill in U.S. history.[153]

But, if the Reagan revolution was less transformative than its supporters hoped and its detractors feared, the revolutionary moment did permanently change the character of fiscal policy and politics in the United States. This change in turn affected the tenor and content of larger political debate by shifting the country's political agenda "from problem solving to budget cutting," and replacing the postwar period's emphasis on the benefits of citizenship with a new focus on its costs.[154] The provision in ERTA requiring that income tax brackets be indexed for inflation was particularly significant because it ensured that federal revenue would no longer automatically rise alongside inflation. By 1990, indexing alone had reduced federal revenues by $180 billion.[155] By eliminating the revenues automatically generated by rising wages and incomes, the ERTA made it far more difficult for lawmakers to raise additional funds and ensured that taxes would become a perennial political issue.[156] With entitlement and military spending more or less locked in place, resources available for new programs—or for the expansion of existing ones—all but disappeared.[157] The defense of taxpayers' rights, which had appeared periodically during the postwar period—particularly in times of economic stress—became, in the wake of the ERTA and the indexation of tax brackets, the fundamental principle and overriding concern of American domestic and even foreign politics.

At the same time, by hitching the defense of taxpayers to a limited war on a very narrow segment of illegitimate welfare spending, the right limited the extent of the ideological realignment that accompanied the GOP's electoral successes. Most recent studies suggest that the country has not grown more conservative since Reagan took office, even though policy, and the elected leaders that make policy, have shifted definitively to the right.[158] Indeed, the consequences of a liberal consensus that promised the cost-free *expansion* of the activist state and a conservative counterrevolution that promised its cost-free *contraction* has been a political and ideological stalemate, the terms of which have at once foreclosed the possibility of new liberal policies because of an emphasis on the costs to the taxpayer and a fear of "government intervention," and inhibited a genuine conservative revolution of the antistate variety because of the popularity of the largest and most expensive components of the liberal state.

STALEMATE

The tax and welfare politics described in this study continue to shape American social and economic policy and to define American politics. Although "welfare as we knew it" no longer exists, thanks to the Personal Responsibility and Work Opportunity Act of 1996, the specter of welfare hangs over domestic policymaking. In the 2008 presidential race, Senator John McCain, who had fallen behind Senator Barack Obama in the polls, turned to tax and welfare politics as the closing argument in his effort to win over undecided voters.[1] "When politicians talk about taking your money and spreading it around, you'd better hold onto your wallet," McCain told an enthusiastic Miami crowd. "[Obama's] plan is to give away your tax dollars to those who don't pay taxes. That's not a tax cut; that's welfare."[2] McCain's opponent responded in kind. "The only 'welfare' in this campaign," Obama countered the next day, "is John McCain's plan to give another $200 billion in tax cuts to the wealthiest corporations in America."[3] More recently, the accusations of waste, fraud, and abuse historically aimed at "welfare queens" have been leveled against the "bank bailouts" and the 2009 economic stimulus package. Meanwhile, resistance to any tax hikes has become almost pathological, especially in light of sharply rising deficits and a looming shortfall in revenues needed to pay for Social Security, Medicare, and other entitlements. The GOP has led the antitax crusade, raising the threat of higher taxes to stymie an array of Democratic reform proposals—from cap-and-trade plans to reduce greenhouse gas emissions to the health care reforms enacted under the Patient Care and Affordability Act of 2009. Democrats—liberals, moderates, and conservatives alike—have hardly rallied to defend taxes, or to challenge a political discourse that focuses almost exclusively on the *costs* of American citizenship.

This book has sought to understand the contours of contemporary American politics in their historical context by tracing the complicated and interlocking relationship between the American taxing and welfare states in the twentieth century. The modern taxing state, grounded in the Revenue Act of 1942, and elaborated and secured in subsequent legislation, not only underwrote the welfare state—providing state builders with the revenue necessary to build institutions extending economic security to the majority of Americans—but also constituted an important element of that regime of social protection. As this study has suggested, throughout the postwar period, liberals yoked promises of economic and social security to an equally important commitment to impose only relatively low tax burdens on individual citizens. Paying close attention to the *politics* of taxation, and understanding low taxes as a critical element of the New Deal, World War II, and postwar liberal social compact, this study has called into question both left- and right-wing visions of the "liberal golden age" and the conservative retrenchment that succeeded it. Indeed, close examination of the contested politics of taxes and welfare reveals the insufficiency of either the "right turn" or the "liberal consensus" to describe, much less explain, the complicated nature of American politics in the post-World War II period.

Thanks to the Revenue Act of 1942, taxpaying emerged in the postwar period as the primary obligation of national citizenship and the most visible connection between citizens and the federal state. This tax regime has proved remarkably durable. Even in the wake of Proposition 13 and the nationwide "revolt against taxes" it is supposed to have unleashed, conservatives found themselves largely unable to overturn the existing tax structure.[4] The welfare state, broadly construed, likewise survived the right turn of the 1980s. The U.S. government today spends more money than ever on programs designed to provide both economic security and well-being.[5] Moreover, much of this expansion, including the 2003 addition of a $190 billion prescription drug benefit to the existing Medicare program, can be attributed not to "tax and spend" liberals but to conservative Republicans.[6] With social provision accounting for more than a third of the federal budget, and extending assistance to the vast majority (92.8 percent) of Americans, it would seem that reports of the death of the U.S. welfare state have been greatly exaggerated.[7]

Yet, despite the durability of the taxing state and the political popularity of *most* federal welfare programs, antigovernment sentiment remains high. Declining trust in the government has recently found its most public expression in the so-called Tea Party movement, but it has been a persistent fact of political life for the last forty years.[8] According to one study, the "trust in government" index has fallen from its 1966 peak of 61 to 26 in 2008.[9] The rising percentage of Americans who believe that "people don't have a say in what government does" reflects a growing alienation from the political system, manifest in low levels of interest in political and civic affairs and plummeting voter participation rates.[10] The American right has both benefited from and encouraged this erosion of public trust with its oft-repeated insistence that government is the problem rather than the solution.[11]

Yet conservative rhetoric alone cannot be held accountable for the shift in public attitudes toward the state. Nor can the right turn and the subsequent retrenchment of liberal social policies be attributed exclusively to a racialized backlash against the Civil Rights movement or Great Society liberalism. Rather, as this study has shown, understanding the paradox of contemporary American politics—Americans' mounting disenchantment with a state that has provided citizens with large and growing resources that enable them to enjoy at least a modicum of social and economic security—requires us to re-examine the institutions of the postwar liberal state and the ideological terms of the postwar liberal social compact.

In recent years, political scientists, historians, and others have challenged the description of the United States as a "reluctant" or "laggard" welfare state. By focusing on the structure of the welfare state—rather than its size—scholars like Jennifer Klein, Christopher Howard, Jacob Hacker, and Monica Prasad have called attention to the unique policy mix that constitutes the American social safety net. While systems of direct provision may be stingy and punitive, like Aid to Families with Dependent Children (AFDC) or its 1996 replacement Temporary Assistance to Needy Families (TANF), or, like Medicare and Social Security, limited to well-defined and politically popular groups, other forms of economic and social security—usually provided directly or indirectly through the tax code—are relatively generous.[12] If we include public regulations like the minimum wage or the Employee Retirement Income Security Act (ERISA), the U.S. welfare state appears even more robust.[13] Both the regulatory state and the tax expenditure system have depended on close cooperation between the public and private sectors. Encouraged by federal policy, and under pressure from organized labor, during the postwar period many corporations put into place a kind of adjunct social safety net that included pensions and employer-provided health insurance. Although these benefits were delivered and administered by private entities, the federal government encouraged and subsidized them through the federal income tax code. "The American social welfare experience," Hacker has rightly concluded, "is exceptional . . . not because social spending is low in comparative perspective, but because so much of it comes from the private sector."[14]

These stealth forms of public provision enabled postwar state builders to overcome Americans' hostility to federal taxation and direct government intervention. As Brian Balogh has recently pointed out in his study of nineteenth-century associationalism, the "fear of intrusion into private and local affairs has always touched a particularly sensitive nerve in the United States."[15] But the form social provision took in the postwar period did not simply reflect an antigovernment ethos unique to the American character. Rather, it can be seen as the product of historically specific choices made by liberal state builders. As I argued in Chapter 1, postwar liberals abandoned their quest for a comprehensive welfare state in light of the attacks launched at local welfare programs in the name of beleaguered taxpayers. Convinced that these state and local welfare crises, in combination with an increasingly conservative Congress, presented an insuperable obstacle to more generous forms of social provision, liberal welfare experts turned their attention to rehabilitation, while their progressive allies in the American labor movement concentrated on securing employment-based welfare benefits from private employers.[16]

For a time, this strategy was remarkably successful. Taking advantage of the prolonged economic growth of the postwar period and relying on payroll taxes, automatic revenue increases, and hidden tax expenditures, liberal state builders built a relatively generous—if very complicated—system of economic and social security. By 1965, more than 122 million workers had some form of private health coverage, 47 million enjoyed life insurance benefits, 28 million had access to temporary disability coverage, and 25 million participated in employer-provided pension plans.[17] That same year, almost 98 percent of senior citizens received some assistance from the Social Security system, which had reduced poverty rates among the aged by more than 60 percent.[18] By 1998, Social Security had become even more poverty-effective, moving out of poverty almost 75 percent of the elderly who "would have been poor in the absence of government programs."[19]

In the long run, however, liberals' reliance on automatic revenues, earmarked taxes, and hidden tax expenditures to build the social safety net held important implications, not only for the future of the welfare state, but for the trajectory of twentieth-century politics. The most generous, effective, and popular parts of the U.S. welfare regime—both direct and indirect—expanded both economic security and economic opportunity to a wide swath of Americans. However, because these forms of social provision were either provided through private intermediaries or attached to participation in the private labor market, they reproduced rather than challenged existing social and economic (not to mention racial and gender) hierarchies. By yoking economic security directly and indirectly to labor force participation, the U.S. welfare state reinforced the long-standing distinction between the "deserving" and the "undeserving" poor. Social Security and Medicare could be defended as entitlements duly earned after a lifetime of labor; tax expenditures could be either ignored or, more and more frequently, seen as a way of returning to taxpayers what was rightfully theirs anyway. But programs that provided direct cash assistance to the poor could easily be attacked as an unwarranted giveaway to the lazy and the shiftless and an illegitimate transfer from taxpayers to tax eaters.

Perhaps more importantly, the shape and structure of the U.S. welfare state undermined popular support for the political actors—activist Democrats and liberal Republicans alike—who had helped to build it. Indirect forms of social provision, like tax expenditures —which make up an increasing part of the American social safety net—are less likely than direct forms of social entitlement to create positive attitudes toward government because they do not feel like social benefits at all.[20] If this is true of tax expenditures granted directly to individuals, such as the home mortgage interest tax deduction and deductions given for state and local taxes, it is even more true for those tax breaks given to employers to provide certain economic security programs, including health insurance and pension plans, to their employees. Insofar as these benefits are hidden in the tax code and directly provided by private employers (rather than the state), it could hardly be surprising that most people have no idea that the "government is . . . [already] deeply involved" in providing health and retirement security programs to many Americans.[21] The hidden character of tax expenditures has made it difficult for liberal legislators to claim credit for the security and protection they engendered and provided. The largely hidden nature of the federal subsidy under middle-class economic security and upward mobility enabled the production of a historically inaccurate but politically persuasive narrative that equated liberal interventionism with welfare and blamed both for endangering the American dream and jeopardizing middle-class economic security. In other words, by hiding the state in plain view, liberals enabled and even encouraged the middle-class majority to see itself as the victim, rather than the beneficiary, of the taxing and welfare state.

Rising economic insecurity in recent decades has compounded these problems for liberal policymakers. As Mark Smith has argued, contrary to most conventional wisdom, the GOP, not the Democratic Party, has most benefited when the electorate is focused on economic issues.[22] Since 1972—the same year President Richard Nixon embraced the politics of tax cuts—the GOP has been seen as the "party of prosperity" by the majority of voters, despite the relatively poor performance of the U.S. economy during periods of Republican rule. By adhering closely to a "limited set of principles"—namely that tax cuts are good for both the individual and the economy at large—the GOP has secured for itself a "reputational edge" on economic questions.[23] These issues have grown increasingly important to electoral politics as economic insecurity has risen and the average American has become more and more vulnerable to economic shocks. Although income volatility sometimes means large increases in annual income, social mobility in general has not increased substantially since 1970.[24] Ironically, the economic insecurity that has apparently buttressed the GOP is the result of a crumbling social safety net. Although efforts have been made to prop or patch up the safety net built in the postwar period, these efforts have done little to protect ordinary Americans securely against what President Franklin Roosevelt once called the "hazards and vicissitudes of life."[25]

This study has aimed to put these contemporary trends—rising economic insecurity, the emergence of a politically powerful conservative movement, the continued expansion of the welfare state, and widespread hostility toward and distrust of the activist state itself—into historical perspective. Taking the long view calls into question many commonly held notions about our recent political past and helps to explain, at least in part, some of the major dilemmas of contemporary politics. First, this study has pointed out some important—and often ignored—continuities between the so-called liberal consensus and the apparently conservative retrenchment period that succeeded it. The "tax and spend" liberal of the popular imagination is largely a fiction. Throughout the postwar period, liberals consistently defended low tax rates on ordinary Americans as an essential element of the social compact negotiated during the New Deal, World War II, and postwar eras. Even during the New Deal of the 1930s and the Great Society of the 1960s—the two boom periods of liberal state building—liberal presidents with substantial Democratic margins in both houses of Congress never tried to tie new social benefits to tax increases on the majority of taxpayers. Yet, as this study has also shown, tax politics has proved itself a weak foundation for progressive politics. Although some groups successfully used their identity as taxpayers to claim expanded citizenship rights, progressives have found themselves largely unable to capture and channel the politics of taxation.

The failure of progressive tax politics in the 1970s, and the emergence of the GOP as the "tax cut party," should remind us that the structure of systems of social provision—that is, how benefits are delivered and how costs are collected and distributed—is vitally important. The economic downturn of the 1970s placed new pressures on the jury-rigged, Rube Goldbergesque system of social and economic provision put in place in the post-World War II period, and allowed a resurgent right to capitalize on the nascent revolt of the taxpayer and to recover its political footing after the Goldwater rout of 1964. As the postwar economic expansion slowed and eventually gave way to inflation and stagnation, the American right rallied behind a tax-cutting agenda that helped to focus attention on the *costs* rather than the *benefits* of the activist state. The structure of the welfare and taxing states both limited the Democratic Party's ability to respond to changes in the international and domestic political economy and allowed the GOP—dominated increasingly by its conservative wing—to reinvent itself as the populist defender of taxpayers' interests. Because so much of the liberal welfare state had been hidden in plain sight, Democratic liberals found themselves unable to answer convincingly the vexing question that public opinion expert Ben Wattenberg posed to Lyndon Johnson on behalf of the "working man, the union man" in 1967: "What have you done for me lately?"[26]

But if the GOP successfully claimed the tax revolt as its own, and through the indexation of tax brackets in the Economic Recovery and Tax Act of 1981 managed to "fiscalize" domestic politics, the American right has been far less successful in dismantling the welfare state.[27] Even if the right has managed to convince the majority of American voters that the government *is* the problem, it has not yet convinced most Americans that they should let go of the public benefits they currently enjoy or that spending on most welfare state activities should be cut back significantly. According to the Pew Research Center on the People and the Press, in 1997 Americans still registered strong support for government programs to ensure "affordable health care," provide a "decent standard of living for the elderly," and reduce poverty.[28] Even among "strong Republicans," support for most welfare state activities remains high.[29]

Welfare of course is the exception to this otherwise robust support of state economic security programs and social priorities. Public support for welfare—never strong to begin with—all but disappeared in the early 1970s, even as assistance to the poor remained an important and popular public priority. In 1981, the Advisory Commission on Intergovernmental Relations conducted two separate surveys to determine American attitudes toward taxes and government. In both, the Commission asked respondents to identify public programs most appropriate for "curtailment." In the first poll, the commission included "public welfare" in its list of choices; in the second, it listed "aid for the needy" instead. This change in terminology produced dramatically different results: 39 percent of those surveyed targeted "public welfare" for retrenchment; only 7 percent believed that "aid to the needy" should be reduced.[30] Such results suggest that welfare—defined since the early 1950s to refer almost exclusively to need-based cash assistance to the very poor—has held political implications disproportionate to its size or its cost to the average taxpayer. As the middle-class welfare state that delivered economic security to millions of Americans became increasingly difficult to see, welfare emerged as the public face of the liberal state. Criticized by the left as insufficient and inefficient and by the right as irresponsible and immoral, and attacked by all as riddled with waste, fraud, and abuse, welfare served at once to diminish public support for the liberal state it supposedly represented, and to provide lawmakers with a way to reconcile the public's demand for low tax rates *and* generous social benefits.

Given this history, it is hardly surprising that President Bill Clinton, a New Democrat who pledged to find a "third way" between traditional Democratic liberalism and Republican conservatism, chose "ending welfare as we know it" as a way to make good on his campaign promise to bring the "era of Big Government" to a close. The Personal Responsibility and Work Opportunity Act of 1996—which replaced AFDC with the new state block grant program known as TANF and effectively ended welfare's status as an entitlement—complemented the major antipoverty initiative of the Clinton administration: the expansion of the Earned Income Tax Credit (EITC).[31] Introduced in the mid-1970s by Senator Russell Long, the Louisiana Democrat who once referred to welfare recipients as "brood mares," the EITC provides a refundable tax credit to the working poor. The program grew slowly in the early 1980s, but increased rapidly later in the decade and throughout the 1990s as lawmakers expanded eligibility, increased the value of the credit, and indexed it for inflation. Indeed, by 1996, the federal government spent more on the EITC than it did on AFDC.[32] By 2000, the program cost the federal government $32 billion and provided financial assistance to 19.3 million taxpayers.[33] Six years later, the cost and reach of the program had increased to $44.4 billion spread out over 23 million tax filers.[34] Sold as a kind of tax cut for working families and offered up as an alternative to "failed" welfare programs, the EITC has enjoyed considerable political support. In 1999, when the Republican leadership of the House of Representatives proposed to save $8 billion by deferring EITC payments for one year, political leaders on both sides of the aisle moved quickly to defend the program. President Clinton refused to sign any measure that would mean an "effective tax increase on the most hard-pressed, working Americans." In 1999, Governor George W. Bush of Texas, then the leading candidate for the 2000 GOP presidential nomination, agreed, chiding fellow Republicans for "balancing the budget on the backs of the poor."[35]

The EITC has undoubtedly provided much needed financial assistance to the working poor, but it is limited in terms of its larger political implications. Like all hidden forms of social provision, the EITC does little to foster political consciousness and its receipt does not generally translate into support for the activist state. The same holds true for other forms of spending through the tax code. As Suzanne Mettler has argued, most taxpayers who benefit from hidden tax spending are often "unaware of how much they actually gain from these policies" and may not "perceive the tax breaks to be social benefits at all."[36] Although the United States devotes an increasing share of social welfare revenues to these hidden tax programs, the rate of return, in terms of political capital, is rather low. While tax expenditures may have salutary effects on the economic well-being of individuals and families, they do little to enhance the reputation of the activist state or to create politically powerful constituencies interested in their survival or expansion.

The invisibility of the role the federal government has historically played—and continues to play—in underwriting at least a degree of economic security and opportunity for the majority of American citizens, stands in stark contrast to the visibility of the institutions of the American taxing state. As Sven Steinmo has pointed out, the means by which the government collects tax revenue determines both the "level of public spending" and the politics surrounding questions of taxing and spending.[37] American reliance on both a progressive federal income tax and earmarked payroll taxes makes the *burdens* of government painfully apparent, at the same time as the *benefits* of that same government have become increasingly hard to discern. As both the protracted struggle over the 1968 income tax surcharge and President George H. W. Bush's decision to raise taxes to fight the deficit in the early 1990s demonstrate, visible tax increases carry enormous political risks.

The political risks of tax increases have become even greater in recent years. The indexation of federal tax brackets means that lawmakers can no longer count on automatic, inflation-generated revenues to pay for new programs or to improve existing ones. The budget rules adopted in 1990, which required that any new spending be offset either by reductions in other areas of the budget or by new revenue enhancements, have also raised the political cost of new programs.[38] One result of this new fiscal calculus has been rising deficits, as policymakers are reluctant either to raise taxes or to cut popular programs. This new "austerity" has also sparked heated competition among and between programs for scarce resources. This trend, already apparent in 1965 when the Income Maintenance Task Force warned President Johnson that further expansion of Social Security could come only at the cost of diminishing support for other spending priorities, has since devolved into what one observer has called a "fierce Darwinian struggle for fiscal survival."[39] The emergence of a conservative movement dedicated to the politics of tax cuts has raised the political stakes even further. The transformation of the GOP into the "tax-cut party" began in the early 1970s, as strategists in the Nixon administration recognized in the nascent revolt against state and local taxes an opportunity to capture the political loyalty—or at least the votes—of the so-called Silent Majority of white, working- and middle-class Americans. Throughout the 1980s and early 1990s, fiscally conservative deficit hawks within the GOP caucus restrained this tax cut agenda, but by the mid-1990s these forces had been all but sidelined within the party, as enthusiastic and well-funded antitax groups, including Americans for Tax Reform and the Club for Growth, spent considerable effort and money to increase the number of dedicated tax cutters in Congress.[40] The result has been near unanimity among members of the Republican Party that tax cuts are good policy and good politics, regardless of their effect on the deficit. As Vice President Richard Cheney is reported to have said during a 2002 White House tax policy strategy session, "Deficits don't matter."[41]

Much like the liberals who dominated national politics between the end of the World War II and the early 1970s, Republican conservatives have seen their agenda founder on the basic dilemma of contemporary American politics: Americans demand more and more services from the federal government as a fundamental right of citizenship, but they don't want to pay for them. Liberals reconciled these twin demands by drafting a social compact whose terms included both low tax rates and access to new systems of economic security and opportunity. Liberals' fealty to a low tax agenda, and their faith in the benevolence of the free market, ultimately produced a set of political institutions and ideologies that privileged individual self-interest over any sense of collective obligation, and decoupled the obligations of citizenship—namely, the burden of taxation—from its benefits. Liberal institutions and ideologies, as this study has shown, fostered a political discourse that distinguished taxpayers from tax eaters, and, more often than not, privileged the rights and interests of the former over the needs and rights claims of the latter. When the economy faltered in the 1970s, conservatives were well positioned to use liberals' traditional commitments to low tax burdens and individual rights to capture the allegiance of white middle-class voters who saw themselves as the victims of the liberal state. Legitimated by a newly assertive conservative counterestablishment, the GOP's antitax politics celebrated the rights of taxpayers and linked targeted attacks on a limited definition of the state to a much-needed economic revival. Like liberal state builders before them, conservatives found welfare a useful tool in advancing their social policy agenda. Whereas liberals had used the failure of welfare to justify new investments in social policy and the creation of new welfare state institutions, conservatives have used the "failure" of welfare to condemn the state itself. And like liberal state builders before them, conservatives have found themselves constrained by a postwar social compact that promised both new forms of social protection and low individual tax burdens.[42]

NOTES

Introduction: Tax Matters

1. Figures for 1960 from Susan B. Hansen, *The Politics of Taxation: Revenue Without Representation* (New York: Praeger Special Studies, 1983), table 3.2. Figures for 2008, author's calculation from 2008 Democratic and Republican Party platforms. See 2008 Republican Party Platform and 2008 Democratic Party Platform, "Renewing America's Promise," in John T. Woolley and Gerhard Peters, eds., *The American Presidency Project* (Santa Barbara: University of California, 1999–) (hereafter Woolley and Peters), http://www.presidency.ucsb.edu/ws/?pid=78545, 78283.

2. Franklin Roosevelt, "Statement on Signing the Social Security Act of 1935," 14 August 1935, in Woolley and Peters, 14916. In recent years, scholars have expanded our understanding of the U.S. welfare state. Traditional analyses that tend to treat the European welfare state model as normative have focused almost exclusively on social insurance, including Old Age Insurance, or "Social Security," and Unemployment Insurance, or direct welfare grants. Recognizing that the United States has traditionally relied less on social insurance or grants than on loan guarantees, regulation, and, perhaps most important, tax policies that provide indirect benefits to individuals and employers, scholars have begun to include these policy tools in their assessments of the U.S. welfare state. The Organization for Economic Cooperation and Development (OECD) has recently lent its imprimatur to this definition by collecting data on "untraditional" and indirect forms of social welfare spending. See Christopher Howard, *The Welfare State Nobody Knows: Debunking Myths About U.S. Social Policy* (Princeton, N.J.: Princeton University Press, 2007); Jacob Hacker, *The Divided Welfare State: The Battle over Public and Private Social Benefits in the United States* (New York: Cambridge University Press, 2002); Jennifer Klein, *For All These Rights: Business, Labor, and the Shaping of America's Public-Private Welfare State* (Princeton, N.J.: Princeton University Press, 2003).

3. C. Eugene Steuerle, *Contemporary U.S. Tax Policy* (Washington, D.C.: Urban Institute Press, 2004), 228.

4. Over the last several decades, in an effort to explain the "right turn" in American politics, historians and others have often focused on the ways conservative politicians, ideologues, and political entrepreneurs have manipulated public anxiety over the broad social and cultural changes unleashed by the Civil Rights and sexual revolutions of the

1960s to foment a kind of pseudo-populist backlash against liberal ideas and lawmakers. More recently, other historians have challenged these top-down narratives by revealing the serious and sometimes violent grassroots challenges to the liberal consensus in the 1940s and 1950s. This study builds on the backlash literature and its grassroots challengers, but brings the focus back to the liberal policymakers who designed, institutionalized, and defended the welfare and tax systems that make up the modern American state. For a good example of "backlash" literature, see Dan T. Carter, *From George Wallace to Newt Gingrich: Race in the Conservative Counterrevolution* (Baton Rouge: Louisiana State University Press, 1996); and Thomas B. Edsall and Mary Edsall, *Chain Reaction: The Impact of Race and Rights on American Politics* (New York: Norton, 1991). Studies on grassroots challenges to the liberal order build on Thomas Sugrue's pathbreaking study, *The Origins of the Urban Crisis: Race and Inequality in Postwar Detroit* (Princeton, N.J.: Princeton University Press, 1996). See also Matthew D. Lassiter, *The Silent Majority: Suburban Politics in the Sunbelt South* (Princeton, N.J.: Princeton University Press, 2006); Robert O. Self, *American Babylon: Race and the Struggle for Postwar Oakland* (Princeton, N.J.: Princeton University Press, 2003).

5. Republican National Committee, *Fact Book 1978*, in Paul Kesaris, ed., *Papers of the Republican Party* (Frederick, Md.: University Publications of America, 1978), Reel 15, Frame 252. See also Martin Andersen, *Welfare: The Political Economy of Welfare Reform in the United States* (Stanford, Calif.: Hoover Institute Press, 1978), 56.

6. Ronald Reagan, First Inaugural Address, 20 January 1981, in Woolley and Peters, 43425.

7. Barbara Gottschalk and Peter Gottschalk, "The Reagan Revolution in Historical Perspective," in *Remaking the Welfare State: Retrenchment and Social Policy in America and Europe*, ed. Michael K. Brown (Philadelphia: Temple University Press, 1988), 59–72.

8. Analysts estimate that Medicare Part D will cost about $190 billion by 2023. For more, see Steurle, 228. For an analysis of the role Republican lawmakers have played in building and expanding the welfare state, see Howard, chap. 4.

9. Suzanne Mettler, "The Transformed Welfare State and the Redistribution of Political Voice," in *The Transformation of American Politics: Activist Government and the Rise of Conservatism*, ed. Paul Pierson and Theda Skocpol (Princeton, N.J.: Princeton University Press, 2007), 191.

10. For an analysis of the political consequences of political trust, see Marc J. Hetherington, *Why Trust Matters: Declining Political Trust and the Demise of American Liberalism* (Princeton, N.J.: Princeton University Press, 2005).

11. Humphrey Taylor, Harris Poll 21, 16 February 2011, Harris Interactive, http://www.harrisinteractive.com/NewsRoom/HarrisPolls/, accessed 21 February 2011. Of those polled, 80 percent opposed cutting Social Security benefits, 71 percent opposed cutting spending for education, and 67 percent opposed cutting federal health care programs. The majority also opposed cutting spending for federal revenue sharing with states (55 to 28 percent), federal jobs programs (56 to 33 percent), federal aid to cities (55 to 34 percent), federal highway spending (59 to 31 percent), pollution control (54

to 37 percent), and the food stamp program (51 to 40 percent). The only program cuts to command a clear majority were reductions in foreign aid spending (69 to 20 percent). Only a bare majority (51 percent) of respondents favored cuts in federal welfare spending—historically the most unpopular domestic spending priority. These results suggest that while the idea of cutting federal spending is popular, support disappears when Americans are asked to make specific cuts. The poll's author, Harris Poll chairman Humphrey Taylor, concludes, "many people seem to want to cut down the forest but to keep the trees."

12. Julian Zelizer, "The Uneasy Relationship: Democracy, Taxation and State Building Since the New Deal," in *The Democratic Experiment: New Directions in American Political History*, ed. Meg Jacobs, William J. Novak, and Julian Zelizer (Princeton, N.J.: Princeton University Press, 2003), 276–300.

13. Bertram Harding, *A Narrative History of the War on Poverty*, 18, in Lyndon B. Johnson Library (hereafter LBJL), White House Central Files (hereafter WHCF), Administrative History, Office of Economic Opportunity, Box 1 (Crisis of 1967), File: Vol. 1, Part 2, Narrative History 3 of 3.

14. For a brief history of the Social Security Act, see Blanche Coll, *Safety Net: Welfare and Social Security, 1929–1979* (New Brunswick, N.J.: Rutgers University Press, 1995); James Patterson, *America's Struggle Against Poverty in the Twentieth Century* (Cambridge, Mass.: Harvard University Press, 2000).

15. In FY 1994, Federal social welfare spending totaled $867 billion, 59 percent of total federal outlays. With a combined price tag of almost $458 billion, Medicare and Social Security accounted for the majority (53 percent) of federal welfare spending; support payments to the states (AFDC) cost about $16.5 billion. See Dawn Nuschler, *CRS Support for Congress: Social Welfare Spending in Fiscal Year 1994: A Fact Sheet* (Washington, D.C.: Congressional Research Service, 8 November 1994).

16. Paul Malloy, "The Relief Chiselers Are Stealing Us Blind!" *Saturday Evening Post*, 8 September 1951; Rufus Jarman, "Detroit Cracks Down on Relief Chiselers," *Saturday Evening Post*, 223, 14 (10 December 1949): 122.

17. See Michael B. Katz and Lorrin Thomas, "The Invention of 'Welfare' in America," *Journal of Policy History* 10, 4 (1998): 401.

18. Roosevelt, "Annual Message to Congress," 4 January 1935, Woolley and Peters, 14890; President William J. Clinton, "Address Before a Joint Session of Congress on the State of the Union," 23 January 1996, in Woolley and Peters, 53091; Clinton, "Address Accepting the Democratic Nomination at the Democratic National Convention in New York," 16 July 1992, Woolley and Peters, 25958.

19. The term "gate-less poverty" is taken from President Johnson's 1965 commencement address to the graduates of historically black Howard University, in Washington, D.C. In the speech, Johnson pledged a new direction for Civil Rights legislation, one that reached beyond formal equality to provide "equally as a fact and equality as a result." "Commencement Address at Howard University: 'To Fulfill These Rights,'" 4 June 1965, in Woolley and Peters, 27201.

20. Josephine Brown, *Public Relief, 1929–1930* (New York: Holt, 1940), quoted in Patterson, 55.

21. Patterson, 55–59. See also William Leuchtenburg, *Franklin D. Roosevelt and the New Deal* (New York: Harper and Row, 1963). Americans turned first to welfare capitalist schemes initiated in the prosperous 1920s, ethnic and fraternal organizations and mutual benefit societies that offered temporary financial assistance, private charities, and family organizations. Only after these traditional institutions proved inadequate did people begin to look to the government for assistance. Even then, state and local governments rather than the national government provided most of the assistance. See Lizabeth Cohen, *Making a New Deal: Industrial Workers in Chicago* (New York: Cambridge University Press, 1990).

22. Roosevelt, "Annual Message to Congress," 4 January 1935.

23. Ibid.

24. Committee on Economic Security, "Technical Board Report," August 1934, quoted in Coll, 39.

25. The major categorical assistance programs—OAA and ADC—built on existing programs aimed at alleviating the desperate poverty of the unemployable poor. The law required the federal government to match state and local contributions to relief programs for "deserving" but unemployable groups like the aged poor, single mothers with dependent children, and the blind. Because they provided federal assistance only to discrete groups and required financial contributions from state and local governments, these relief programs promised to be relatively cheap and to limit federal involvement in, and interference with, local practices. The system ensured that public assistance grants varied widely between poorer and richer states and that local caseworkers had a great deal of discretion in administering the programs. With federal law vague on eligibility and silent on benefit levels, states were free to limit eligibility through such prejudicial criteria as suitable home and substitute father regulations that often rendered unwed mothers ineligible for assistance, and to provide grants far below even minimum subsistence levels. For more on the existing "pension" programs for women, children, and the aged, see Theda Skocpol, *Protecting Soldiers and Mothers: The Political Origins of Social Policy in the United States* (Cambridge, Mass.: Belknap Press of Harvard University Press, 1992); Joanne Goodwin, "Employable Mothers and 'Suitable Work': A Re-Evaluation of Wage Earning and Welfare in the Twentieth Century," in *Mothers and Motherhood: Readings in American History*, ed. Rima D. Apple and Janet Gordon (Columbus: Ohio State University Press, 1997). For a brief summary of the kinds of laws imposed by states to reduce single mothers' access to ADC benefits, see Bureau of Public Welfare, *Illegitimacy and Its Impact on the Aid to Dependent Children Program* (Washington, D.C.: GPO, 1962). For the legal challenges to these criteria, see Gwendolyn Mink, *Welfare's End* (Ithaca, N.Y.: Cornell University Press, 1998); Elizabeth Bussiere, *(Dis)Entitling the Poor: The Warren Court, Welfare Rights, and the American Political Tradition* (University Park: Pennsylvania State University Press, 1997).

26. In choosing to rely exclusively on dedicated payroll taxes, the president rejected the advice of many New Dealers in Congress and a great many social insurance experts who rightly pointed out that these taxes would weigh most heavily on lower-income workers. But Roosevelt held firm, insisting that money for the new programs be "raised by contribution rather than by an increase in general taxation." Administration insiders, including Harry Hopkins and Rexford Tugwell, urged the president to pay for the new unemployment and retirement programs at least in part out of general revenues. Social insurance experts and economists attacked the payroll tax as regressive and inefficient. The proposed Social Security system, charged one social insurance advocate, amounted to little more than a "system of compulsory payments by the poor for the impoverished." Harvard economist Alvin Hansen questioned the economics behind a program that took money out of consumers' pockets, in the form of compulsory payroll taxes, in both good and bad economic times. See Mark J. Leff, "Taxing the 'Forgotten Man': The Politics of Social Security Finance in the New Deal," *Journal of American History* 70, 2 (September 1983): 363. See also Abraham Epstein, *Insecurity: A Challenge to America: A Study of Social Insurance in the United States and Abroad* (New York: Random House, 1936); Edwin E. Witte, *The Development of the Social Security Act: A Memorandum on the History of the Committee on Economic Security and Drafting and Legislative History of the Social Security Act* (Madison: University of Wisconsin Press, 1962). On professional economists' opposition to social insurance financing, see Edward D. Berkowitz, "Social Security and the Financing of the American State," in *Funding the Modern American State, 1941–1995: The Rise and Fall of the Era of Easy Finance,* ed. W. Elliot Brownlee (Washington, D.C.: Woodrow Wilson Center Press, 1997), 148–93.

27. Julian Zelizer, "The Forgotten Legacy of the New Deal: Fiscal Conservatism and the Roosevelt Administration, 1933–1938," *Presidential Studies Quarterly* 30, 2 (June 2000): 335.

28. J. Douglas Brown, Columbia University Oral History Project, Pt. 3, "Social Security," 113, quoted in Michael K. Brown, *Race, Money, and the American Welfare State* (Ithaca, N.Y.: Cornell University Press, 1998), 57.

29. Ellen S. Woodward, "America's Further Needs in Social Security," Address to the National Conference on Family Relations, Cleveland, 22 May 1943, National Archives and Records Administration (NARA) II, College Park, Md., RG 235, Family Security Agency (FSA), Office of Information Reference Files, 1934–1946, Box 26, File: SSB Addresses. Not all social security experts accepted the political wisdom of using the language of private insurance to sell the new unemployment and retirement security programs. Ewan Clague, for example, counseled that insurance imagery would only "create a new set of misunderstandings and fallacies" that would limit the programs' ability to provide meaningful economic security to all Americans and constrain the eventual growth of the social safety net. Ewan Clague to Arthur Altmeyer, 1 July 1937, Folder 011, "June–December 1937," Central Files of the Social Security Board (1935–1947), NARA, RG 47, quoted in Jerry Cates, *Insuring Inequality: Administrative Leadership in Social Security* (Ann Arbor: University of Michigan Press), 34.

30. Named for California physician Francis Everett Townsend, the Townsend movement claimed as many as 30 million members at its peak in 1936. Townsend proposed to provide all retired persons over age sixty a lump payment of $200/month provided it all was spent within that month. The proposal, estimated to cost up to $24 billion/year—or about half the annual national income in the mid-1930s—would have depended on a kind of "transaction tax" to finance benefits. For more, see Coll, 50–51.

31. "Tax Strike Stops Chicago Police Pay," *NYT*, 17 May 1931, 15; "Chicago Tax Strike Laid to Overload," *NYT*, 7 November 1932, 2.

32. Quoted in David Beito, *Taxpayers in Revolt: Tax Resistance During the Great Depression* (Chapel Hill: University of North Carolina Press, 1989), 8; For state-level responses to the tax revolts, see Michael K. Brown, 36–37.

33. For the alternatives to the administration's economic security package, see Linda Gordon, *Pitied But Not Entitled: Single Mothers and the History of Welfare* (New York: Free Press, 1994), chap. 8.

34. As Robert Lieberman has pointed out, the administrative structure of the new Social Security Board also helped to minimize taxpayer resistance to the new program. Charged with setting up an entirely new federal program that required employers in covered industries to submit wage statements for each of the 30 million employees enrolled in its programs, the SSB delegated responsibility for the collection of this information— and of payroll tax contributions—to the Bureau of Internal Revenue. The SSB itself took care of the distribution of benefits. This ingenious arrangement not only allowed the Board put the new security policies in place relatively quickly, but further distanced social insurance entitlements from the taxes that paid for them, helping insulate social insurance entitlements when public opinion turned against the tax collector. See Lieberman, *Shifting the Color Line: Race and the American Welfare State* (Cambridge, Mass.: Harvard University Press, 1998), 76–77.

35. Over the course of the 1930s, as the Great Depression wrecked individual incomes and decimated corporate profits, the top-heavy income system played an increasingly marginal role in the U.S. tax system. Between 1926 and 1930, for example, individual income and corporate taxes together accounted for 64 percent of federal tax revenues. Excise taxes, including those on tobacco, alcohol, and manufacturers, made up just 16 percent. By the end of the decade, corporate and individual income taxes made up 40 percent of annual federal tax collections, excise taxes 32 percent, and social insurance payroll taxes, borne largely by lower- and middle-income workers, another 13 percent. See Mark J. Leff, *The Limits of Symbolic Reform: The New Deal and Taxation, 1933–1939* (Cambridge: Cambridge University Press, 1984), 12, table 1, Components of the U.S. Federal Tax Structure, 1925–1980 (percentages of annual collections).

36. "25 Percent in Nation Held Unaware of Taxes," *NYT*, 21 June 1939, 5.

37. For more on the gendered assumptions that underwrote the Social Security Act, see Alice Kessler-Harris, *In Pursuit of Equity: Women, Men, and the Quest for Economic Citizenship in Twentieth-Century America* (New York: Oxford University Press, 2001); Gwendolyn Mink, *The Wages of Motherhood: Inequality in the Welfare State* (Ithaca,

N.Y.: Cornell University Press, 1994). For a brief overview of the racial dynamics of New Deal welfare policymaking, see Jill Quadagno, *The Color of Welfare: How Racism Undermined the War on Poverty* (New York: Oxford University Press, 1994). For an analysis that challenges common scholarly assumptions about the role of race and the political economy of the American South in the making of the Social Security Act, see Martha Derthick and Gareth Davies, "Race and Social Welfare Policy: The Social Security Act of 1935," *Political Science Quarterly* 112, 2 (Summer 1997): 217–35.

38. Testimony of Social Security Board Chairman Arthur Altmeyer, House Committee on Ways and Means, *Social Security Act Amendments of 1949: Hearings*, 81st Cong., 1st sess, 28 February, 1–4, 7–11, 14–18 and 21–23 March 1949, quoted in Gilbert Steiner, *Social Insecurity: The Politics of Welfare* (Chicago: Rand McNally, 1966), 22.

39. Elizabeth Wickenden Oral History Project, Interview 1, 5 April 1966, Folder 5, Box 16, Elizabeth Wickenden Papers, Wisconsin Historical Society, quoted in Jennifer Mittelstadt, *From Welfare to Workfare: The Unintended Consequences of Liberal Reform, 1945–1965* (Chapel Hill: University of North Carolina Press, 2005), 29.

40. Alvin Hansen, "Economic Progress and Declining Population Growth," *American Economic Review* 29 (March 1939): 4, quoted in Robert M. Collins, *More: The Politics of Economic Growth in Postwar America* (New York: Oxford University Press, 2000), 6. As Collins has pointed out, however, while Hansen's analysis of "secular stagnation" exerted a great deal of influence on New Deal economic policymaking, New Dealers' "embrace of scarcity economics and stagnationism was often ambivalent, a source of tension and contention" (7).

41. Testimony of Illinois State Chamber of Congress, Senate Committee on Finance, Social Security Revision: Hearings, 81st Cong., 2nd. sess., 8 February 1950, quoted in Steiner, 22. The Social Security Committee of the CIO likewise testified before the House Ways and Means Committee that the organization viewed "public assistance as residual." See House Committee on Ways and Means, Amendments to the Social Security Act, Part 8, 79th Cong., 2nd sess., 7 May 1950, 961.

42. Harry S Truman, "Letter to the President of the Senate on a Pending Bill to Increase Public Assistance Benefits," 18 July 1951, in Woolley and Peters, 13842.

43. Arthur J. Altmeyer, *The Formative Years of Social Security* (Madison: University of Wisconsin Press, 1966), 205, quoted in Cates, 71.

44. Lieberman, 67.

45. See Steiner.

46. Epstein, *Insecurity* (New York: Smith and Haas, 1933), 23, quoted in Kessler-Harris, 78.

47. Arthur J. Altmeyer, "Making Social Security a Reality," Address to 63rd Annual Convention for the American Federation of Labor, Boston, 5 October 1943, NARA II, Family Security Agency, Office of Information, Reference Files, 1939–46, Box 26, File: SSB Addresses.

48. Harold Ickes, "To Have Jobs," *Negro Digest* (1943): 73, quoted in Michael K. Brown, 64. See also John Kirby, *Black Americans in the Roosevelt Era: Liberalism and Race* (Knoxville: University of Tennessee Press, 1980).

49. For more on the racially unequal consequences of New Deal labor policy, see Ira Katznelson, *When Affirmative Action Was White: An Untold History of Racial Inequality in Twentieth-Century America* (New York: Norton, 2005), chap. 3.

50. Senate Committee on Finance, Revenue Act of 1932, Hearings on HR 10236, 72nd Cong., 1st sess., 6 April 1932, quoted in Leff, *The Limits*, 16.

51. Benjamin Stolbert and Warren J. Vinton, *The Economic Consequences of the New Deal* (New York: Harcourt Brace, 1935), 73, and "Mr. President, Begin to Tax!" *Nation* 141 (6 March 1935): 64, quoted in Leff, *The Limits*, 97, 103.

52. Benjamin Marsh, House Committee on Ways and Means, Proposed Taxation: Hearings, 74th Cong., 1st sess., 8–13 July, 1935, quoted in Leff, *The Limits*, 105.

53. The survey, conducted by George Gallup's American Institute of Public Opinion, asked voters whether single men earning between $15 and $20 per week should be required to pay any federal income tax. By a margin of 88 percent to 12 percent, the public answered "no." The public opposed requiring married men earning between $40 and $50 to pay income tax by a slightly less (64 percent) though still significant margin. See "Cut in Exemption on Tax Opposed," *NYT*, 12 March 1939, 59; cited in Leff, *The Limits*, 113.

54. *New York Herald Tribune*, quoted in "Press at Odds on Tax Message," *NYT*, 2 June 1937, 16; also quoted in Leff, *The Limits*, 112. In 1935, under pressure from the Townsend Old Age Pension Movement and Louisiana Senator Huey Long's (D-La.) Share Our Wealth campaign, the president proposed to raise taxes on the incomes and assets of the very wealthy—the so-called "malefactors of wealth." Introducing the 1935 Revenue Act—commonly referred to as the Wealth Tax—to Congress and the nation, Roosevelt criticized the "great and undesirable concentration of control in a relatively few individuals over the employment and welfare of many, many others." The new tax law imposed a graduated tax on corporations, a new tax on the dividends that holding companies received from the corporations they controlled, and new surtaxes on the incomes of the very wealthy, made the income tax more progressive, and subjected the wealthiest Americans to higher taxes. By 1936, the top 1 percent of taxpayers paid an effective income tax rate of 16.4 percent, higher than at any time since World War I. See Franklin Roosevelt, "Message to Congress on Tax Revision," 19 June 1935, in Woolley and Peters, 15088. See also W. Elliot Brownlee, *Federal Taxation in America: A Short History*, new ed. (Cambridge: Cambridge University Press, 2004), 85–90; Leff, *The Limits*, chap. 2.

55. See Ronald King, *Money, Time, and Politics: Investment Tax Subsidies and American Democracy* (New Haven, Conn.: Yale University Press, 1993), chap. 3; see also Alan Brinkley, *The End of Reform: New Deal Liberalism in Recession and War* (New York: Knopf, 1995), chap. 1 and epilogue.

56. See Lizabeth Cohen, *A Consumers' Republic: The Politics of Mass Consumption in Postwar America* (New York: Knopf, 2003).

57. The law accomplished this by significantly lowering the personal exemption allowed to each taxpayer and his or her dependent, thus lowering the threshold for federal

income tax liability. For a detailed description of the 1942 law, see Roy G. Blakely and Gladys C. Blakely, "The Federal Revenue Act of 1942," *American Political Science Review* 36, 6 (December 1942): 1069–82; see also Brownlee, *Federal Taxation*, 114–19.

58. See Mark J. Leff, "The Politics of Sacrifice on the American Home Front in World War II," *Journal of American History* 77, 4 (March 1991): 1296–1318.

59. In one animated short, entitled "The New Spirit," Donald Duck fills out his income tax return for the first time, and finds the job both easier and less financially painful than he had feared. In another, "Spirit of '43," Donald is torn between spending his paycheck immediately and saving his money to meet his new income tax obligations. As he falters, his uncle—the thrifty Scotsman, Scrooge McDuck—reminds his nephew not to "forget our fighting men." When Donald chooses the responsible path, the spendthrift who had been tempting him to spend his "dough" in the local bar is revealed to be a Nazi (complete with toothbrush mustache) as the swinging doors of the saloon behind him close to reveal a swastika. "This is our fight, the fight for freedom," the narrator reminds viewers at the end of the short. Walt Disney Pictures, "The New Spirit," 23 January 1942; "The Spirit of '43," 7 January 1943. For an analysis of the Treasury Department's attempt to create a "culture of taxpaying," see Carolyn C. Jones, "Mass-Based Income Taxation: Creating a Taxpaying Culture, 1940–1952," in Brownlee, ed., *Funding*, 107–47. See also James T. Sparrow, "Buying Our Boys Back: The Mass Foundations of Fiscal Citizenship in World War II," *Journal of Policy History* 20, 2 (2008): 263–86.

60. "The Spirit of '43"; Dorothy Ducas, "Wartime Taxes," 7 December 1942, in Occasional Publications, 1942–1943, Miscellaneous Publications on War Subjects, 1942–1943, Records of the Office of War Information, RG 208, quoted in Jones, 114. Even those hostile to the federal income tax defended other forms of taxation in similar patriotic terms that stressed the equality of sacrifice. For example, one Ohio businessman, writing to Senator Robert A. Taft (R-Ohio) on behalf of a national sales tax, insisted that the "duty and burden to win the war is everyone's." See W. H. Moores to Senator Taft, 24 October 1942, in Robert A. Taft papers, LoC, Box 824, File: Taxes 1942.

61. Sparrow, 271.

62. Office of War Information, "Battle Stations for All," February 1943, in Pamphlets, 1942–1943, Records of the Office of War Information, RG 208, quoted in Jones, 114; Franklin Roosevelt, "Excerpts from a Press Conference," 28 December 1943, in Woolley and Peters, 16358.

63. Altmeyer, "Making Social Security a Reality."

64. Ewan Clague, "Social Security During Demobilization: Address Delivered Before 1944 Biennial Conference and Institutes of the Wisconsin Welfare Council," 28 October 1944, NARA II, RG 235, FSA, Office of Information, Reference Files, 1939–1941, SSB, Box 27, File: SSB Articles, Publications, etc.

65. The Wagner-Murray-Dingell bills of 1943 and 1945 would have liberalized eligibility requirements for retirement programs, eliminated occupational exclusions written into the 1935 law, fully federalized Unemployment Insurance, created a new national health insurance program, and replaced ADC and the other categorical public assis-

tance programs with a "comprehensive . . . general public assistance system providing aid on the basis of need. For more on the legislative history of the Wagner-Murray-Dingell Bills, see Edwin Amenta and Theda Skocpol, "Redefining the New Deal: World War II and the Development of Social Provision in the United States," in *The Politics of Social Policy in the United States*, ed. Margaret Weir, Ann Shola Orloff, and Theda Skocpol (Princeton, N.J.: Princeton University Press, 1988), 81–122. See also National Resources Planning Board, *Security, Work, and Relief Policies: Report of the Committee on Long-Range Work and Relief Policies* (Washington, D.C.: GPO, 1942); John Jeffries, "FDR and American Liberalism: The 'New' New Deal," *Political Science Quarterly* 5, 3 (Autumn 1990): 397–418.

66. On the history of national health insurance in the United States, see Colin Gordon, *Dead on Arrival: The Politics of Health Care in Twentieth-Century America* (Princeton, N.J.: Princeton University Press, 2004).

67. "Wider Security Is Debated Here," *NYT*, 12 February 1943, 33; Letter to the Editor, "Financing Social Security," *NYT*, 19 February 1943, 18.

68. Informal minutes of the Social Security Board, 22 July 1936, SSA, Woodlawn, Md., quoted in Cates, 29–30.

69. Franklin Roosevelt, quoted in Luther Gulick, Memorandum for the File, "Memorandum on Conference with FDR Concerning Social Security Taxation, Summer 1941," Social Security History Online, http://www.socialsecurity.gov/history/Gulick.html.

70. For the institutional logic that permitted and even impelled Social Security's postwar growth, see Lieberman.

71. Recent research suggests that indirect forms of social spending are less likely than direct provision to produce positive attitudes toward government. For an analysis of the GI Bill of Rights that demonstrates how public policy can engender citizenship, see Suzanne Mettler, "Bringing the State Back into Civic Engagement: Policy Feedback Effects of the G.I. Bill for Rights for World War II Veterans," *American Political Science Review* 96, 2 (June 2002): 351–65.

72. Jude Waninski, "Should a GOP Scrooge Shoot St. Nick? The Two Santa Theory," *National Observer*, 6 March 1976, 7, 14.

73. See Pierson and Skocpol, eds., *Transformation of American Politics*.

Chapter 1. Defending the Welfare and Taxing State

1. Howard M. Norton, "Public Welfare: A Business Without a Business Manager," *Baltimore Sun*, 15 February 1947, I 1. For a narrative account of the Baltimore "probe," see Benjamin J. Lyndon, "Relief Probes: A Study of Public Welfare Investigations in Baltimore, New York, Detroit, 1947–1949" (Ph.D. dissertation, University of Chicago, 1953), part 1.

2. Howard M. Norton, "Public Welfare: 11 Million Dollars and How It Is Spent," *Baltimore Sun*, 9 February 1947, I 1.

3. Jacob Panken as told to Hal Burton, "I Say Relief Is Ruining Families," *Saturday Evening Post* 223, 14 (30 September 1950): 113, 25.

4. Donald Howard, "Public Assistance Returns to Page One," *Social Work Journal* 29 (April 1948): 47.

5. See Blanche Coll, *Safety Net: Welfare and Social Security, 1929–1979* (New Brunswick, N.J.: Rutgers University Press, 1995). On politics of welfare reform and child support enforcement, see Gwendolyn Mink, *Welfare's End* (Ithaca, N.Y.: Cornell University Press, 1998).

6. Commission on Governmental Efficiency and Economy, *The Department of Welfare: City of Baltimore* (Baltimore, December 1947), 13.

7. Sen. Robert A. Taft (R-Ohio), quoted in Gary Donaldson, *Truman Defeats Dewey* (Lexington: University of Kentucky Press, 1999), 34–35. See also Susan Hartmann, *Truman and the 80th Congress* (Columbia: University of Missouri Press, 1971).

8. For more, see Christopher Howard, *The Hidden Welfare State: Tax Expenditures and Social Policy in the United States* (Princeton, N.J.: Princeton University Press, 1997); Ira Katznelson, *When Affirmative Action Was White: An Untold History of Racial Inequality in Twentieth-Century America* (New York: Norton, 2005); Jacob Hacker, *The Divided Welfare State: The Battle over Public and Private Social Benefits in the United States* (New York: Cambridge University Press, 2002); John Jeffries, "FDR and American Liberalism: The 'New' New Deal," *Political Science Quarterly* 5, 3 (Autumn 1990): 397–418; Edwin Amenta and Theda Skocpol, "Redefining the New Deal: World War II and the Development of Social Provision in the United States," in *The Politics of Social Policy in the United States*, ed. Margaret Weir, Ann Shola Orloff, and Theda Skocpol (Princeton N.J.: Princeton University Press, 1988), 81–123.

9. David Lawrence, "What Is Right in the Left?" *U.S. News and World Report*, 20 January 1950, 35.

10. Robert M. Collins, *More: The Politics of Growth in Postwar America* (New York: Oxford University Press, 2000), 42.

11. Michael K. Brown, *Race, Money, and the American Welfare State* (Ithaca, N.Y.: Cornell University Press, 1998), 169

12. "Illustrations of OASI 'Bargains' for Some Favored Retirants," in Taft Papers, LoC, Box 799, File: Social Security, 1950.

13. Allen Otten, "Tax Overhaul: Universal Sales Levy? Income Tax Ceiling? No More Excises?" *Wall Street Journal*, 21 April 1953, 1.

14. On the meaning of security, and its centrality to both the New Deal and postwar social compacts, see Jennifer Klein, *For All These Rights: Business, Labor, and the Shaping of America's Public-Private Welfare State* (Princeton, N.J.: Princeton University Press, 2003).

15. Herbert Lehmann, quoted in Jonathan Bell, *The Liberal State on Trial: Cold War and American Politics in the Cold War* (New York: Columbia University Press, 2004), 20.

16. George Bigge, "The Goal of Social Security," Address Given at Christ Church Forum, New York, 21 September 1944, in National Archives and Records Administration II (hereafter NARA II), RG 235, Office of Information, Reference Files, 1939–1946, SSB, Box 26, File: SSB Addresses.

17. See Herbert Stein, *The Fiscal Revolution in America* (Chicago: University of Chicago Press, 1969); Robert M. Collins, *The Business Response to Keynes, 1929–1964* (New York: Columbia University Press, 1982); Lizabeth Cohen, *A Consumers' Republic: The Politics of Mass Consumption in America* (New York: Knopf, 2003).

18. Commission on Governmental Efficiency and Economy, 1, 83–84.

19. D. Howard, 48; Lyndon, 14.

20. New York State Department of Social Welfare, *Public Social Services in 1948*, 82nd Annual Report, 1 January 1948–31 December 1948 (New York, 1948), Legislative Document 7638, 38.

21. Commission on Governmental Efficiency and Economy, 13.

22. For a history of relief practices in Depression era Baltimore, see Jo Ann E. Argersinger, *Toward a New Deal in Baltimore: People and Government in the Great Depression* (Chapel Hill: University of North Carolina Press, 1988), chap. 2.

23. Lyndon, 20.

24. Ibid., 24.

25. Quoted in ibid., 25.

26. "To Understand the Workings of Our Public Welfare System," *Baltimore Sun*, 10 February 1947, I 24.

27. Norton, "Public Welfare: 11 Million Dollars," 1.

28. Ibid, 3.

29. For Baltimore numbers, see Lyndon, 20, and Commission on Governmental Efficiency and Economy, 8; for New York numbers see "State Relief Increased Month by Month in Year," *NYT*, 22 May 1947, 2; and Department of Administration, Mayor's Executive Committee, *Report on the New York City Department of Welfare*, 24 October 1947 (New York, 1947).

30. "Family on Relief, Evicted, Lodged in Hotel by City at $500 a Month," *NYT*, 10 May 1947, I 1.

31. "A Crisis for the Mayor," *NYT*, 24 May 1947, I 14.

32. *Indianapolis Star*, 21 October 1951, quoted in Hilda Arndt, "An Appraisal of What the Critics are Saying About Public Assistance," *Social Service Review* 26 (1952): 470; D. Howard, 51.

33. Gallup Poll, Survey #367-K, Question 2, 30 March 1946, in George Gallup, ed., *The Gallup Poll, 1935–1971*, (New York.: Random House, 1972), 1: 566.

34. See Paul Boyer, *By the Bomb's Early Light: American Thought and Culture at the Dawn of the Atomic Age* (New York: Pantheon, 1985).

35. "The Boom," *Fortune*, June 1946, 99.

36. Gallup Poll, Survey #375-K, Question 14a, in Gallup, 1: 594. According to the Gallup Poll, 60 percent expected this "serious business depression" to materialize within a decade.

37. Chester Bowles, quoted in Meg Jacobs, *Pocketbook Politics: Economic Citizenship in Twentieth-Century America* (Princeton, N.J.: Princeton University Press, 2005), 222. For a contemporary analysis of the political effects of inflation and economic insecurity,

see Robert J. Samuelson, *The Great Inflation and Its Aftermath: The Past and Future of American Affluence* (New York: Random House, 2008); Jacob Hacker, *The Great Risk Shift: The Assault on American Jobs, Families, Health Care, and Retirement, and How You Can Fight Back* (New York: Oxford University Press, 2006).

38. Franklin D. Roosevelt, Jr., Letter, no date, WHS, ADA, Series 1, File: Office of Price Administration, Correspondence, 1946 June–January 1947; William O'Dwyer, Letter, 30 April 1946, WSHS, ADA, Series 1, File: Office of Price Administration, Correspondence, 1946 June–January 1947.

39. For more on the political effects of inflation and consumer politics, see Jacobs and Cohen.

40. See D. Howard, 51; Rufus Jarman, "Detroit Cracks Down on Relief Chiselers," *Saturday Evening Post* (10 December 1949): 122; Paul Malloy, "The Relief Chiselers Are Stealing Us Blind!" *Saturday Evening Post*, 8 September 1951. The case of the "lady in mink" too captures this obsession with relief recipients' tastes for "expensive baubles." The so-called "lady in mink" came to the public's attention in the fall of 1947, when the *NYT* ran a three-column, front-page headline, in the best spot in the paper that read: "Woman in Mink with $60,000 Lived on Relief in a Hotel Inquiry by State Discloses." The subhead continued the tale of iniquity: "42 Cases Analyzed; Investigator Says City Agencies Held Client Is Always Right; One 'Front For Bookies'; Deal Apparently Involved Her Living on Aid While Husband Paid $14,000 in Bad Checks," *NYT*, 30 October 1947, 1.

41. Gallup Poll, Survey 414-K, Question 2b, March 1948, in Gallup, 1: 721.

42. Samuel Lubell, *The Future of American Politics* (New York: Harper, 1952), 216.

43. Commission on Governmental Efficiency and Economy, 80; D. Howard, 51.

44. Brown, tables 8a b, 178.

45. Arthur Altmeyer, "The Need for Social Security," quoted in Andrea Campbell and Kimberly Morgan, "Financing the Welfare State: Elite Politics and the Decline of the Social Insurance Model in America," *Studies in American Political Development* 19, 2 (Fall 2005): 197; Ellen Woodward, "America's Further Needs in Social Security: Address to the National Conference on Family Relations," Cleveland, 22 May 1943, in NARA II, HEW, Family Security Agency, Office of Information Reference Files, 1939–1946, Box 26, File: SSB Addresses.

46. For an analysis and description of the Social Security Amendments of 1950, see Martha Dethrick, *Policymaking for Social Security* (Washington, D.C.: Brookings Institution, 1979), chap. 11; Julian Zelizer, *Taxing America: Wilbur D. Mills, Congress and the State, 1945–1975* (Cambridge: Cambridge University Press, 1998), chap. 4; For an analysis of the contest between Social Security experts and public assistance officials, see Jerry Cates, *Insuring Inequality: Administrative Leadership in Social Security, 1935–1954* (Ann Arbor: University of Michigan Press, 1983). See also Edward Berkowitz, *Mr. Social Security: The Life of Wilbur J. Cohen* (Lawrence: University of Kansas Press, 1995).

47. OAA's importance continued to wane for another two decades until Congress finally replaced it with a new social insurance program, known as Supplemental Security Income, in 1972.

48. Wilbur Mills, U.S. House, *Congressional Record*, 81st Cong., 1st sess., 5 October 1949, 13905, quoted in Zelizer, *Taxing America*, 75.

49. For an example of this argument, see George Bigge, "Social Security and Private Enterprise in a Post-War World," Address to the Advertising Board of Cleveland, 1943, NARA II, HEW, Family Security Agency, Office of Information, Reference Files, 1939–1946, SSB, Box 26, File: Bigge Speeches and Articles, Social Security. See also Advisory Commission on Intergovernmental Relations, *The Federal Role in the Federal System: The Dynamics of Growth: Public Assistance, The Growth of a Federal Function* (Washington, D.C.: GPO, 1980), 42.

50. According to a 1960 report by the Advisory Council on Public Assistance (ACPA), nationally, states met only about 85.7 percent of need. The problem was worse in the South, where the average ADC grant was more than 30 percent below minimum levels. See Advisory Council on Public Welfare, Staff Paper, "Greater Adequacy of Income for Needy People: Recommendations Made to the Advisory Council on Public Welfare," 9 September 1965, table B-24, NARA II, RG 363, Box 1, Advisory Council Files, File: "Advisory Council Actions Taken or Deferred."

51. The National Resources Planning Board anticipated this result in its 1943 report, and indeed, in the late 1930s and early 1940s many states *had* taken legislative action to shift women and children to ADC to reduce the burden on unsubsidized general relief programs. See U.S. National Resources Planning Board, Committee on Long-Range Work and Relief Policies, *Security, Work, and Relief Policies, 1942: Report of the Committee on Long-Range Work and Relief Policies to the National Resources Planning Board* (Washington D.C.: GPO, 1943), 470–73; 90–94.

52. Arthur Altmeyer to Oscar Ewing, "*Chicago Tribune* Article Under Date of December 16," 5 January 1948, NARA II, RG 235, DHEW, FSA, Office of the Administrator, General Classification Files, September 1944–December 1950, Box 308, File: 1948.

53. Lubell, 217, also quoted in James T. Sparrow, "Buying Our Boys Back: The Mass Foundations of Fiscal Citizenship in World War II," *Journal of Policy History* 20, 2 (April 2008): 263–82.

54. Edward Folliard, "Alone in a Leftist World, We're Veering Farther Right," *Washington Post*, 27 October 1946, B1.

55. Joseph Martin, *My First Fifty Years in Politics* (New York: McGraw-Hill, 1960), 179, quoted in Donaldson, 34.

56. Sen. John M. Vorys (R-Ohio), Papers, Election Materials (1946), quoted in Hartmann, 8.

57. Sen. Robert A. Taft, Radio Address, quoted in Donaldson, 34–35.

58. Rep. Earl Wilson (R-Ind.), quoted in Hartman, 36.

59. Sen. George Malone (R-Nev.), 18 July 1947, quoted in Bell, 49; Senate Committee on Finance, *Report: Individual Income Tax Reduction Act of 1947*, 80th Cong., 1st sess., 9 July 1947, (Washington D.C.: GPO, 1948), 1, 11; Rep. Harold Knutson (R-Minn.), quoted in Brown, 120.

60. Malone, 18 July 1947; and Senate Committee on Finance, 1, 11.

61. Rep. Joseph Martin (R-Mass.), speech to annual meeting of Pennsylvania Manufacturers' Association, 25 February 1947, quoted in Bell, 48.

62. Sen. Malone, Address on Senate Floor, 80th Cong., 1st sess., 18 July 1947, *Congressional Record* 93, 9277, quoted in Bell, 49.

63. To capitalize on the popular appeal of tax cuts, and to head off the familiar accusation that GOP policies favored the wealthy few at the expense of the working and middle classes, the tax plan introduced in early 1947 provided the largest rate reductions to those in the lower income brackets, and promised an "immediate reduction in individual income taxes" to "give relief to all those persons bearing heavy tax burdens." Under the bill, taxpayers with net incomes of $1,000 or less after exemptions would receive a 30 percent reduction in their income tax liabilities; taxpayers with net incomes of $1,000–$1,400 would receive a tax cut of between 20 and 30 percent; taxpayers in the $1,400–$4,000 tax bracket would receive a 20 percent tax cut; taxpayers with more than $4,000 in annual taxable income would receive a 20 percent cut on the first $4,000 and a 10 percent break on the remainder. The final bill reduced individual tax rates by 10 to 30 percent, with the larger rate reductions granted in the lower tax brackets, and raised the personal exemption from $500 to $600, at a cost of about $6.55 billion in lost revenue. See House Committee on Ways and Means, *Report: Revenue Act of 1948*, 80th Cong., 2nd sess., 27 January 1948 (Washington, D.C.: GPO, 1948), tables 1, 3. See also Senate Committee on Finance, 11.

64. W. E. Clow to Taft, 18 November 1947, Taft Papers, Box 892, File: Taxes 1947.

65. Tax Foundation, *U.S. Federal Individual Income Tax Rates History, 1913–2010*, http://www.taxfoundation.org/publications/show/151.html.

66. Jon Bakja and Eugene Stuerle, "Individual Income Taxation Since 1948," *National Tax Journal* 44, 4 (December 1991): table A.1.

67. Coll, 177.

68. Claude Robinson, Letter, 1946?, Taft Papers, Box 786, File: Republican Party: Wilkieism. According to the Opinion Research Center's study, the Democratic Party enjoyed a significant advantage over the GOP. Although voters viewed the Democrats as "unbusinesslike" and profligate spenders, they also saw the party of Roosevelt and Truman as the internationally minded "friend of the common man." On the other hand, while the GOP got high marks for being "budget minded" and an "efficient administrator," the party was also seen as the "Friend of the Wealthy" and "out of date on foreign policy." According to the report, 36 percent of those polled associated the Democrats with the terms "common man; working man; poor." "Free trade" and "New Deal/liberalism" (10 percent) were second and third most mentioned attributes. As for the GOP, 21 percent respondents listed "big business/capitalism" and 19 percent "rich; upper class" (19 percent) as the party's most salient characteristic.

69. Broadcast, Sen. Robert A. Taft, Columbia Radio Network, 25 May 1947, Taft Papers, Box 832, File: Tax Reduction Bill 1947.

70. Claude Robinson, "Confidential/Background Report: Truman, the Republicans, and 1948," Opinion Research Corporation, Princeton, N.J., July 1945, in Taft Papers, Republican Policy and Propaganda.

71. This campaign originated in the late 1930s when Emanuel Celler, a Democratic representative from Brooklyn, introduced a proposal to repeal the Sixteenth Amendment and replace it with a new constitutional provision stipulating that in "no case shall the maximum rate of taxation" on income, estates, and gifts "exceed 25 percent." Celler Amendment (HR 722), as cited in Godfrey Nelson, "Tax Revision Held Key to Prosperity," *NYT*, 24 July 1938, 38.

72. In the past, all changes to the Constitution had originated in Congress and were ratified by the states. Limitation advocates planned to flip this equation by persuading enough state legislatures to petition Congress to call a constitutional convention to consider tax limitation—an untested procedure. For an analysis of the constitutionality of this proposal, see Joint Committee on the Economic Report and House Select Committee on Small Business, *Constitutional Limitation on Federal Income, Estate, and Gift Taxes*, 82nd Cong., 2nd sess. (Washington, D.C.: GPO, 1952).

73. The states that considered and approved the measure before or during World War II, and the years of passage, are Mississippi, Rhode Island, 1940; Iowa, Maine, Massachusetts, Michigan, 1941; Alabama, Arkansas, Delaware, Illinois, Indiana, New Hampshire, Pennsylvania, Wisconsin, 1943; Kentucky, New Jersey, 1944. For a short history of the tax limitation movement and its fiscal implications, see ibid..

74. Ibid., 8–10.

75. See for example such a characterization by the Guaranty Trust Corporation in "Tax Shift Seen as Postwar Need," *NYT*, 27 June 1947.

76. Rep. Ralph Gwinn (R-N.Y.), cited in "Realty Men Favor a U.S. Tax Ceiling," *NYT*, 4 December 1949, 77.

77. Chalmers Roberts, "Biggest Tax Tangle May Occur in '53," *Washington Post*, 11 June 1953, M6.

78. "House Group Opens PAC Inquiry Here," *NYT*, 13 November 1944, 25. The Committee found itself in deep water with Congress, when, in 1944, its executive secretary Dr. Edward A. Rumely refused to comply with a subpoena issued by the House Campaign Expenditures Committee requiring the organization to release a list of donors that had contributed more than $100 to the Committee. Rumely was indicted on the charge of "willful default" in the production of the subpoenaed records, but a federal jury ultimately acquitted him of all charges. See "Rumely Indicted for Holding Data," *NYT*, 3 October 1944, 13; "Rumely Warrant Issued," *NYT*, 4 October 1944, 38; and "Dr. Rumely Acquitted," *NYT*, 19 April 1946. Rumely had already been in jail once, sentenced as a German agent during the First World War. See Drew Pearson, "Foundation Accused as Lobby," *Washington Post*, 24 March 1949, B15.

79. "Financial Backers of Lobbies Sought by House Inquiry," *NYT*, 27 May 1950, 7.

80. Drew Pearson, "The Washington Merry-Go-Round: Ike Held Duped by Rep. Gwinn," *Washington Post*, 18 June 1949, B13.

81. "Disguised Propaganda," *Washington Post*, 29 May 1950, 8.

82. House Select Committee on Lobbying Activities, *Report Citing Edward A. Rumely*, 81st Cong., 2nd sess., 30 August 1950 (Washington D.C.: GPO, 1950), 11.

83. Ibid., 2.

84. "Rumely Bars Data to Lobby Inquiry," *NYT*, 28 July 1950, 11; "Rumely Is Cleared of House Contempt," *NYT*, 10 March 1953, 21; Select Committee on Lobbying Activities, 13.

85. "Top Tax: One Fourth of Income?" *U.S. News and World Report*, 8 June 1951, 54.

86. "Tax Ceiling Pressed: Proponents See Chance to Force Congress to Take Action," *NYT*, 21 December 1952, 37.

87. Gallup Poll, Survey489K, Question 35, 12 July 1952, in Gallup, 2: 1075. The question read: "It has been suggested that a law be passed so that the Federal Government could not take more than 25 percent, or one fourth, of any person's income in taxes, except in wartime. Would you favor this 25 percent top limit?"

88. See, e.g., Mrs. Arthur G. Rotch for Americans for Democratic Action, Letter to the Editor, *Christian Science Monitor*, WSHS, ADA, Series 3, Box 53, File: Taxes Correspondence, n.d.

89. Peter Lindert, "Median and Mean Money Income of Families Before Taxes, by Type of Family: 1947–1998," table Be67–84, in *Historical Statistics of the United States, Earliest Time to the Present: Millennial Edition*, ed. Susan B. Carter et al. (New York: Cambridge University Press, 2006); Joint Committee, *Constitutional Limitation*, 14.

90. Department of Commerce, Bureau of the Census, *Current Population Reports, Consumer Income: Family Income of the United States, 1952*, Series P-60, No. 14, 27 April 1954, table A: Number of Families, by Family Income for the United States, 1952, http://www2.census.gov/prod2/popscan/p60–015.pdf.

91. Joint Committee, *Constitutional Limitation*, 14.

92. Ibid., 11.

93. This was not the first time Dirksen had supported or sponsored efforts to amend the Constitution. In the 1930s, the Illinois Republican had spoken in favor of the isolationist Ludlow Amendment requiring voter approval of any declaration of war by means of a national referendum. In the late 1940s he lent his support to the Twenty-Second Amendment, which limited presidents to two consecutive terms. In the 1950s he signed on as a cosponsor to the Equal Rights Amendment, and in the 1960s he proposed constitutional amendments to allow for prayer in public schools, and to undermine the "one man-one vote" standard established by the U.S. Supreme Court in its rulings in *Baker v. Carr* and *Reynolds v. Simms*. For Dirksen's attempts to manipulate the "Constitution to serve his political interests," see David Kyvig, "Everett Dirksen's Constitutional Crusades," *Journal of the Illinois State Historical Society* 95, 1 (Spring 2002): 68–85. For representative arguments in favor of the tax limitation amendment, see Robert Dresser, "The Case for the Income Tax Amendment: A Reply to Dean Griswold," *American Bar Association Journal* 39 (January 1953): 25–28, 84–87, www.heinonline.com; Frank Packard, "Put a Ceiling on Taxes!" *Kipplinger Magazine* (August 1951): 43–44, available online from Google Books.

See also House Committee on Government Operations, *Limitation of Federal Expenditures: Hearing on H.R. 2 and H.J. Res 22*, 83rd Cong., 1st sess., 13 April 1953 (Washington, D.C.: GPO, 1953); and Senate Judiciary Committee Subcommittee, *Taxation and Borrowing Powers of Congress: Hearing on S.J. Res. 61*, 83rd Cong., 2nd sess., 13 May 1954 (Washington D.C.: GPO, 1954). Taxpayer groups cited House Committee on Government Operations, 40.

94. Testimony of Rep. Ralph Gwinn (R-N.Y), Senate Judiciary Committee Subcommittee, 12.

95. Samuel Pettingill, "The History of a Prophecy: Class War and the Income Tax," *American Bar Association Journal* 39 (June 1953): 474–75.

96. Abraham Lefkowitz, "The UDA and the NAM," Draft Remarks to the UDA Tax Conference in WSHS, ADA, Series 1, Box 33, File: Taxation Conference 1942.

97. ADA, 1953 Platform, cited in Edward D. Hollander, "Memorandum: Taxes—Some Questions to Be Considered in Determining ADA Position," 5 November 1953, in WSHS, ADA, Series 3, Box 52, File: Taxes, Correspondence, 1953–1957.

98. Dresser, 28.

99. Erwin Griswold, "Can We Limit Taxes to 25 Percent?" *Atlantic Monthly*, August 1952, 78.

100. Allen Otten, "Tax Overhaul: Universal Sales Levy? Income Tax Ceiling? No More Excises?" *Wall Street Journal*, 21 April 1953, 1.

101. These special provisions often had unanticipated consequences. For example, the accelerated depreciation provision, which was designed as an incentive to businesses to invest in new equipment, ultimately and inadvertently fueled the growth of suburban shopping centers, and may have contributed to postwar suburban sprawl and urban disinvestment. For more, see Thomas Hanchett, "U.S. Tax Policy and the Shopping-Center Boom of the 1950s and 1960s," *American Historical Review* 101, 4 (October 1996): 1082–1100. For the consequences of this "private welfare state" on its public counterpart, see Nelson Lichtenstein, "From Corporatism to Collective Bargaining: Organized Labor and the Eclipse of Social Democracy in the Postwar Era," in *The Rise and Fall of the New Deal Order, 1930–1981*, ed. Gary Gerstle and Steve Fraser (Princeton, N.J.: Princeton University Press, 1988): 122–53; Beth Stevens, "Blurring the Boundaries: How the Federal Government Has Influenced Benefits in the Private Sector," in Weir et al., 123–48. The decision to exempt employer contributions to employee health funds ultimately cost the Treasury enormous sums in lost revenue and provided an indirect government subsidy for the private health insurance enjoyed by a certain, favored, segment of the working population. For more, see Hacker, *Divided Welfare State*.

102. Ronald F. King, *Money, Time, and Politics: Investment Tax Subsidies and American Democracy* (New Haven, Conn.: Yale University Press, 1993), 140.

103. Cross-national scholarship has shown that governments that rely more heavily on invisible—albeit regressive—forms of taxation (e.g., national sales taxes, value added taxes) have faced less resistance from taxpayers and been able to build more secure and

generous welfare states. Revenue systems which rely on property or income taxation have traded progressivity for visibility—a trade-off that has ultimately limited the ability of these governments to extract tax revenues from their citizens, and so acted as a check on welfare spending. More visible forms of revenue extraction often require taxpayers to submit substantial lump-sum payments, or entail regular withholding of earned income. Tax consciousness has tended to act as a check on *visible* forms of state spending. See Sven Steinmo, *Taxation and Democracy: Swedish, British, and American Approaches to Financing the Modern State* (New Haven, Conn.: Yale University Press, 1993), esp. chap. 7; Monica Prasad, *The Politics of Free Markets: The Rise of Neoliberal Economic Policies in Britain, France, Germany, and the United States* (Chicago: University of Chicago Press, 2006).

104. Committee 4 of the Republican National Advisory Committee, "Report on Taxation and Finance," 18 May 1944, in Taft Papers, Box 164, File: Taxation.

105. See W. Elliot Brownlee, "Tax Regimes, National Crisis, and State-Building in America," in *Funding the Modern American State, 1941–1995: The Rise and Fall of the Era of Easy Finance*, ed. W. Elliot Brownlee (Washington, D.C.: Woodrow Wilson Center Press, 1996), 85.

106. Franklin D. Roosevelt, "Message to Congress on Tax Revision," 19 June 1935; "Acceptance Speech for the Renomination for the Presidency," Philadelphia, 27 June 1936, in Woolley and Peters, 15088.

107. On tax expenditures, see Stanley Surrey, *Pathways to Reform: The Concept of Tax Expenditures* (Cambridge, Mass.: Harvard University Press, 1973).

108. Cohen, *A Consumers' Republic*.

109. Frederic A. Delano et al. to Franklin Roosevelt, 24 August 1943, quoted in Collins, *More*, 14.

110. Harry Truman, "Annual Message to Congress: The President's Economic Report," 6 January 1950, *Public Papers of the Presidents of the United States: Harry S. Truman: 1950* (Washington D.C.: GPO, 1965), 19; Truman, "Special Message to Congress on Tax Policy," 23 January 1950, ibid., 121.

111. Walter Reuther, "Reuther Challenges of 'Fear of Abundance,'" *NYT*, 16 September 1945, SM5.

112. Alfred Sloan, *The Challenge: Address at Annual Dinner of Second War Congress of American Industry and the National Association of Manufacturers*, 10 December 1943, in Taft Papers, Box 752, No File.

113. General Electric Advertisement: "People's Capitalism," *U.S. News and World Report*, 15 June 1956.

114. Sloan, *Challenge*

115. On business leaders' fears of big government and its effect on private industry, see Collins, *Business Response*; Beardsley Ruml, "A Look Ahead: Address to the American Retail Federation," 29 February 1944," in Taft Papers, Box 752, File: Postwar Economic Planning, George Committee.

116. Employment Act of 1946, quoted in Collins, *More*, 16.

117. Harry Truman, "Radio Report to the American People on the Status of the Reconversion Program," 3 January 1946, in Woolley and Peters, 12489.

118. Arthur M. Schlesinger, Jr., *The Vital Center: The Politics of Freedom* (Boston: Houghton Mifflin, 1949).

119. All these advertisements appeared in *U.S. News and World Report* in 1950–1960. See, e.g., Republic Steel, "Last Will and Testament" *U.S. News*, 27 October 1950; Warner and Swasey, "Federal Aid Is as Childish as Santa Claus or Easter Rabbits," 28 September 1959; "Robin Hood in Chin Whiskers," 11 May 1959; "You and a Guy Named Ivan," 2 March 1951; "Security Is No Manly Word," 11 May 1951; Timken Roller Bearing Company, "We Shall Force the United States to Spend Itself to Destruction," 8 February 1952; Electric Light and Power Companies, "The Song the Sirens Sing," 28 July 1950 and "How 'Big' Should Government Be?" 29 February 1952.

120. "Wagner Plan Seen as a Bid to Idleness," *NYT*, 13 January 1944, 38.

121. "Proposed Statement of Policy and Program (Strictly Confidential and Not for Publication in Any Form), Supplement to GOP platform proposed by Republican Members of Congress, Taft Papers, Box 786, File: Republican Policy and Propaganda.

122. Dresser, 25–28 and 84–87.

123. *Senator Robert A. Taft on Taxing and Spending*, issued by the National Taft-for-President Committee, Washington, D.C., 1948, in Taft Papers, box 240, file: Taxing and Spending (1948).

124. Rep. Leon H. Gavin (R-Pa.), quoted in ADA, "Quotes Against Co-Op Housing, House Debate, Mar. 1950," in WSHS, ADA, Series 3, Box 56, File: Welfare 1958.

125. A. H. Raskin, "35% Limit on Taxes Is Urged by N.A.M.," *NYT*, 2 December 1954, 1.

126. "Reds Linked to Relief!" *New York Journal-American*, 22 May 1947, 1, 1; "Oust Reds in City Jobs!" *New York Journal-American*, 23 May 1947, 1, 1; "Accused Red Passport Violator Holds Relief Post!" *New York Journal-American*, 1, 1.

127. Burris Jenkins, Jr., "What? No Caviar?" *New York Journal-American*, 22 May 1947, 1, 20.

128. For more, see Julian Zelizer, *Arsenal of Democracy: The Politics of National Security from World War II to the War on Terrorism* (New York: Basic Books, 2010).

129. Cohen, 118. On the effect of Cold War spending on the rise of the Sunbelt and the transformation of the economic geography of the United States, see Bruce Schulman, *From Cotton Belt to Sunbelt: Federal Policy, Economic Development and the Transformation of the South, 1938–1980* (Durham, N.C.: Duke University Press, 1991).

130. For more on the FHA and the role it and other federal housing programs played in transforming the metropolitan landscape in postwar United States, see Kenneth Jackson, *Crabgrass Frontier: The Suburbanization of the United States* (New York: Oxford University Press, 1985), chaps. 11, 12.

131. National Economic Council, *Tax Dollars Are Your Tax Dollars*, Pamphlet, in Taft Papers, Box 316, File: 1950 Campaign Miscellany, 1949–50.

132. See Alan Brinkley, *The End of Reform: New Deal Liberalism in Recession and War* (New York: Knopf, 1995).

133. Jeffries, 416.

134. Council of Economic Advisors, *Annual Economic Review* (1950): 75, cited in King, 134.

135. Walter Heller, "Economic Growth, Challenge, and Opportunity: Address to the Loeb Awards Annual Presentation Luncheon," New York, 18 May 1961, in JFK Library, Heller Papers, Events File, Box 26, quoted in King, 227.

136. Harry Truman, "Special Message to Congress on Tax Policy," 23 January 1950, Woolley and Peters, 13545.

137. See Stein, chaps. 10–11.

138. "U.S. Tax Ceiling at 25% Is Urged, Senate Committee Considers Constitutional Amendment—Humphrey Is Opposed," *NYT*, 28 April 1954, 25.

139. Robert A. Taft, "Are We Heading for Financial Disaster? Address to American Retail Federation," 4 April 1950, Taft Papers, Box 316, File: 1950 Campaign Miscellany.

Chapter 2. Market Failure

1. Mitchell proposed a thirteen-point plan to reduce the city's welfare rolls. The plan would have (1) converted cash aid into vouchers or in-kind payments; (2) required all able-bodied relief recipients to perform work relief for forty hours a week; (3) denied cash assistance to anyone who refused work relief; (4) denied aid to any mother who had an additional "illegitimate" child while on public assistance; (5) denied relief to anyone who had voluntarily left employment; (6) capped public assistance payments at the salary of the lowest paid municipal employee; (7) required a monthly review of all public assistance cases by the corporation council; (8) required all "migrants" to the city to provide a "concrete offer of employment" and limit aid to such "newcomers" to two weeks; (9) limited all aid payments to three months/year; (10) required all recipients to report monthly to the Public Welfare Department to reassess the status of their case; (11) provided for closed, rather than open-ended, appropriations for the city's public welfare department; (12) provided for a monthly expenditure limit on all categories of public aid; and (13) provided any child deemed to be living in an "unsuitable home environment" be immediately removed and placed in foster care. See "Newburgh Welfare Rules," *NYT*, 16 July 1961, 48 and "Newburgh Welfare Rules in Effect," *NYT*, 16 July 1961, 48.

2. John Averill, "Newburgh Center for GOP Joust," *Los Angeles Times*, 13 August 1961, B13, quoted in Lisa Levenstein, "From Innocent Children to Unwanted Migrants and Unwed Moms: Two Chapters in the Public Discourse on Welfare in the United States, 1960–1961," *Journal of Women's History* 11, 4 (Winter 1999): 25.

3. NBC White Paper, "The Battle of Newburgh" (New York: NBC News, 28 January 1962).

4. Joseph Loftus, "Newburgh Code Stirs Welfare Review," *NYT*, 16 August 1961, IV10.

5. Levenstein, 17. An August 1961 Gallup Poll found overwhelming support for most of Mitchell's program. The survey did not mention Newburgh by name but gauged public support for the various elements of the Newburgh "13-Point Plan." According to the survey, 85 percent of respondents supported proposals to substitute work relief for cash assistance; 84 percent approved of proposals to require all "able men on relief" to take any "job offered that pays the going rate"; 75 percent approved of Mitchell's proposal to require all new residents to prove that they had had a "definite job offer" before moving as a condition of relief. Gallup also polled the public's attitude toward assistance to women with more than one "illegitimate child," and found that only about 10 percent of those polled favored "continuing to increase the relief aid for each new child born." See Gallup Poll, Survey 648K, 13 August 1961, Questions 50, 32, 51; Survey 648K, 16 August 1961, Question 53a, reprinted in George Gallup, ed., *The Gallup Poll: Public Opinion, 1935–1971* (New York: Random House, 1971), 3: 1730–31.

6. "Newburgh Welfare Rules."

7. George McKennally quoted in Joseph P. Ritz, *The Despised Poor: Newburgh's War on Welfare* (Boston: Beacon Press, 1966), 48.

8. Joseph Mitchell, quoted in "Opinion of the Week: At Home and Abroad: Problem of Relief," *NYT*, 16 July 1961, IV9; "Battle of Newburgh."

9. "Relief: Soapbox Derby," *Newsweek*, 31 July 1961, 27.

10. Department of the Treasury, *The Tax Program: Some Questions and Answers*, Pamphlet, Lyndon B. Johnson Library (hereafter LBJL), LE/FI, Box 51, File: 22 November–20 December 1963.

11. John. F. Kennedy, "Text of a Letter from the President to the Honorable Wilbur Mills, Chairman of the House Ways and Means Committee," 19 August 1963, NARA, Senate Finance Committee Files, RG 46, Box 16, File: Revenue Tax Cut/Presidential Message, 2 of 2; Secretary Douglas Dillon Testimony, House Ways and Means Committee, *President's 1963 Tax Message: Hearing Before the Committee on Ways and Means*, 88th Cong., 1st sess., 13–15, 19 March 1963 (Washington, D.C.: GPO, 1963), 543; Secretary Willard Wirtz, Testimony, Ways and Means, ibid., 725.

12. Secretary Luther Hodges, Testimony, ibid., 545.

13. Kennedy to Mills.

14. Bruce Jansson, *The Sixteen-Trillion-Dollar Mistake: How the U.S. Bungled Its National Priorities from the New Deal to the Present* (New York: Columbia University Press, 2001), chap. 8.

15. Arthur Okun, quoted in Robert M. Collins, *More: The Politics of Economic Growth in Postwar America* (New York: Oxford University Press, 2000), 59.

16. Bertram Harding, *A Narrative History of the War on Poverty*, 18, LBJL, White House Central Files (hereafter WHCF), Administrative History, OEO, Box 1 (Crisis of 1967), File: Vol. 1, Part 2, Narrative History 3 of 3.

17. Sven Steinmo, *Taxation and Democracy: Swedish, British, and American Approaches to Financing the Modern State* (New Haven, Conn.: Yale University Press, 1993), 11.

18. Herbert Stein, *The Fiscal Revolution in America* (Lanham, Md.: AEI Press, 1990), 373.

19. Walter Heller, *New Dimensions of Political Economy* (New York: Harper and Row, 1965), 117, quoted in Stein, 380.

20. Democratic National Committee, "The 1960 Democratic Fact Book: The Democrat's Case, People, Peace, Principles," Smithsonian Institution (hereafter SI), National Museum of American History (herafter NMAH), Political Archives; Democratic National Convention, Platform Writing Committee, "Democratic Platform: The Rights of Man," SI, NMAH, Political Archives. Economic growth had figured prominently in the 1960 campaign. Republican nominee, Vice President Richard Nixon, ran largely on the Eisenhower administration's record of peace and prosperity, touting the "wondrous benefits of the free enterprise system" in the face of the communist threat. Campaign materials often made this point none too subtly, reminding voters that the "Seven Most Prosperous Years in American History Have Been Under a Republican Administration Without War," and claiming that "Republican Times are Good Times." Indeed, throughout the campaign the GOP relentlessly pushed this feel-good economic message, going so far as to commission a song celebrating the economic fruits of Republican leadership. Called the "Good Time Train," the song promised both "good times now and always, and peace among free men" as the result of a GOP win in November. Kansas Republican National State Committee Flier, RNC, *Republican Times are Good Times*, pamphlet, RNC Press Release, July 1960, "Republicans Sing in '60," all in SI, NMAH, Political History Archives. See also Carl Brauer, "Kennedy, Johnson, and the War on Poverty," *Journal of American History* 69, 1 (June 1982): 98–119.

21. John F. Kennedy, "Special Message to the Congress: Program for Economic Recovery and Growth," 2 February 1961, Woolley and Peters, http://www.presidency.ucsb.edu/ws/?pid=8111.

22. John F. Kennedy, "The New Frontier: Acceptance Speech of John F. Kennedy," Democratic National Convention, 15 July 1960, SI, NMAH, Political Archives.

23. Kennedy, "Program for Economic Recovery and Growth."

24. See John F. Kennedy, "Special Message to Congress on Budget and Fiscal Policy," 24 March 1961," in Woolley and Peters, 8549

25. Stein, 391.

26. Council of Economic Advisors Oral History Memoir, 34, 39, in John F. Kennedy Presidential Library, quoted in Collins, *More*, 51.

27. John F. Kennedy, "The President's News Conference," 7 June 1962, Woolley and Peters, 8698.

28. "President Outlines Tax Cut in State of the Union Message," *CQ*, 18 January 1963, 45.

29. Cited in "Tax Issue Looms Large in 88th Congress's Agenda," *CQ*, 4 January 1963, 14.

30. All quoted in "Budget, State of the Union Message Debate," *CQ*, 18 January 1963, 52.

31. "Key Lobby Groups Flay President's Tax Proposals," *CQ*, 22 February 1963, 224.

32. AFL-CIO Department of Research, "Needed: Tax Cuts to Create Jobs," *AFL-CIO American Federationist*, July 1963, NARA, SFC, Subject Files, Taxes, Box 15, No File.

33. George Meany, Testimony, Ways and Means, *President's 1963 Tax Message*, 1981.

34. Rep. James Byrnes (R-Wisc.), ibid., 534.

35. Text of Rep. Byrnes Reply to President's Tax Cut Speech, *CQ*, 27 September 1963, 1695.

36. Byrnes, *President's 1963 Tax Message*, 534.

37. Joint Senate-House Republican Leadership, quoted in "Administration Tax Proposal Hearings Open," *CQ*, 15 February 1963, 198.

38. "Joint Economic Committee Issues Annual Report," *CQ*, 15 March 1963, 322.

39. Dillon, Ways and Means, *President's 1963 Tax Message*, 452.

40. Ibid., 629.

41. Kermit Gordon, Ways and Means, *President's 1963 Tax Message*, 757.

42. Dillon, ibid.

43. Eileen Shanahan, "Dillon Musters Business Backing for Cut in Taxes," *NYT*, 21 October 1963, 1.

44. Secretary Luther Hodges, Ways and Means, *President's 1963 Tax Message*, 545.

45. Rep. Hale Boggs (D-La.), ibid., 540.

46. The White House early on decided not to push too hard for the revenue-raising structural reforms it had initially proposed. The administration's first priority, Dillon had assured the Ways and Means Committee, was to "remove the burden of unemployment" and stimulate economic growth. See Dillon, ibid., 614.

47. Kennedy to Mills.

48. President John F. Kennedy, "Remarks to National Conference of the Business Committee for Tax Reduction in 1963," 10 September 1963, reprinted in *CQ*, 13 September 1963, 1575.

49. Robert D. Novak, "Tax Cut Climate," *Wall Street Journal*, 7 January 1963, 1.

50. "Tax Bill Winning General Lobby Support," *CQ*, 13 September 1963, 1564.

51. Novak, 1.

52. "Joint Economic Committee," 327.

53. Tom Wicker, "White House Presses Tax Bill: A Major Effort Is Being Made to Garner Strong Public Support," *NYT*, 8 September 1963, E8.

54. Quoted in Julian Zelizer, *Taxing America: Wilbur D. Mills, Congress, and the State, 1945–1975* (Cambridge: Cambridge University Press, 1998), 200.

55. Department of the Treasury, *The Tax Program*.

56. Walter Heller to Clark Kerr, 16 February 1963, reprinted in William Leuchtenburg, ed., *The Council of Economic Advisors Under President Johnson*, Research Collections in American Politics: Microfilms from Major Archival and Manuscript Collections (Bethesda, Md.: Lexis-Nexis Academic and Library Solutions, 2004).

57. "Business Leaders to Urge Tax Cut Without Reforms," *Wall Street Journal*, 26

April 1963, 3; "Random Notes from All Over: How to Be Put on a Committee," *NYT*, 13 May 1963, 16.

58. Cathie Jo Martin, "American Business and the Taxing State: Alliances for Growth in the Postwar Period," in *Funding the Modern American State, 1941–1995: The Rise and Fall of the Era of Easy Finance*, ed. W. Elliot Brownlee (Washington, D.C.: Woodrow Wilson Center Press, 1996), 368, 374. According to *Congressional Quarterly*, the Business Committee could claim a great deal of credit for moving Congress and the country closer to the administration's position on tax reduction because it was the "only organization" that had "stimulated much sentiment throughout the country for or against the bill." See "Tax Bill Winning General Lobby Support," 1565.

59. Business Committee for Tax Reduction in 1963, "Statement of Principles," 25 April 1963, WSHS, ADA, Series 3, Box 53, File: Taxes Correspondence 1963.

60. Citizens' Committee for Tax Reduction and Revision in 1933, Press Release, 7 July 1963, in Leuchtenberg, ed., *Council of Economic Advisors*.

61. Edward Hollander, Leon Keyserling, Robert Nathan, John P. Roche, and Marvin Rosenberg, on behalf of Americans for Democratic Action, Letter, 24 April 1963, in WSHS, ADA, series 3, box 53, file: Taxes, Correspondence, 1963.

62. Industrial Union Department, AFL-CIO, Press Release, 8 Wednesday 1963, WSHS, ADA, Series 3, Box 53, File: Taxes Correspondence, 1963.

63. Henry Fowler, Memorandum for the President, "Briefing Memorandum for Meeting with Citizens' Committee for Tax Reduction and Revision on Thursday (January 9) at 4:00 p.m., LBJL, LE/FI, Box 52, File: LE/FI, 4 January–14 February 1964.

64. See Heller to Herman Wells, Fred Harrington, and Clark Kerr, 4 May 1963, in Leuchtenburg, ed.

65. Memorandum to Walter Heller, from Rashi Fein, "Citizens' Committee on the Tax Bill, Current Status," 6 May 1963, in Leuchtenberg, ed.

66. Citizens' Committee for Tax Reduction and Revision in 1963, "Statement of Principles," No Date, in WSHS, ADA, Series 3, Box 53, File: Tax Correspondence, No Date.

67. Citizens' Committee for Tax Reduction and Revision in 1963, Letter, 12 August 1963, NARA, SFC, Subject Files, Taxes, Box 15, No File.

68. Citizens Committee for Tax Reduction and Revision in 1963, Bulletin No. 5, 5 September 1963, in Leuchtenberg, ed.

69. "House Tax Report Filed; GOP Members Urge Defeat," *CQ*, 20 September 1963, 1637.

70. Ibid.

71. Rep. Mills (D-Ark.), "Address on H.R. 8363," 16 September 1963, *CQ*, 20 September 1963, 1668.

72. Ibid.

73. "House Votes $11.1 Billion Tax Cut, 271–155," *CQ*, 27 September 1963, 1673.

74. Henry Fowler, Memorandum to the Secretary, "Tax Bill: Strategy and Tactics," LBJL, WHCF, LE/FI Box 51, File: LE/FI 11, 22 November–20 December 1963.

75. Ibid.

76. Sen. Gore (D-Tenn.) to President Kennedy, 28 June 1962, reprinted in Finance Committee, *Revenue Act of 1934: Hearings*, 88th Cong., 1st sess., 15 October 1963, (Washington D.C.: GPO, 1963), 343.

77. Gore to Kennedy, 15 November, 1962, reprinted in ibid., 344.

78. Johnson, "Annual Message to the Congress on the State of the Union," 8 January 1964, in Woolley and Peters, 26787.

79. "Transcript of Johnson's Remarks on the Tax-Reduction Measure at Its Signing," *NYT*, 27 February 1964, 18.

80. Secretary Dillon, quoted in Lawrence Lindsey, *The Growth Experiment: How Tax Policy is Transforming the U.S. Economy* (New York, Basic Books, 1990), 34.

81. Walter Heller, Memorandum for the President, "Economic Welfare and the Pace of Expansion," 11 December 1964, LBJL, EX BE 5, Box 23, File BE 5 1 November 1964–29 January 1965.

82. Gardner Ackley, Memorandum for the Honorable Joseph A. Califano, "Tax Cuts Since 1962," 31 December 1966, Gen FI 9, Box 56, File: FI 11, 29 August 1966–2 January 1967.

83. Office of the White House Press Secretary, "Gains from Effective Policies for an Expanding Economy," 30 October 1964, LBJL, EX BE 5, Box 23, File: BE, 12 January–31 October 1964.

84. Gardner Ackley, "Economic Welfare and the Pace of Expansion," 11 December 1964, LBJL, EX BE 5, Box 23, File BE 5, 1 November 1964–29 January 1965.

85. Walter Reuther, "An Economy of Opportunity," 8 January 1965, LBJL, EX WE 9 Box 25, File: WE 9, 26 December 1964–31 January 1965.

86. Johnson, "Annual Message."

87. Harding, 15; Michael Harrington, *The Other America: Poverty in the United States* (New York: Macmillan, 1962); Dwight MacDonald, "Books: Our Invisible Poor," *New Yorker* 28, 48 (19 January 1963): 82–132. See also Dona Hamilton and Charles Hamilton, *The Dual Agenda: Race and the Social Welfare Policies of Civil Rights Organizations* (New York: Columbia University Press, 1997), 123–26.

88. Walter Heller, Memorandum for the President, "Progress and Poverty," 1 May 1963, LBJL, WHCF, LEG BKG, EOA, Box 1, File: CEA Draft History of the War on Poverty (1 of 3).

89. Robert Lampman, Memorandum to Walter Heller, "An Offensive Against Poverty," 10 June 1963, 4, ibid.

90. Walter Heller, Memorandum for the Cabinet, "1964 Legislative Programs for 'Widening Participation in Prosperity': An Attack on Poverty," 5 November 1963, ibid.

91. Quoted in Harding, 19.

92. Lampman to Heller.

93. Adam Yarmolinsky, Memorandum for Mr. Shriver, 6 February 1964, LJBL, WHCF, ADM HIST OEO, Box 2, File: Vol. II—Documentary Supplement, chap. 1 (2 of 2).

94. William Capron, Memorandum to Walter Heller, "Johnsonian Talking Points on Poverty—in Johnsonian Style," 5 December 1963, LBJL WHCF, LEG BKG EOA, Box 1, File: CEA Draft of the History of the War on Poverty.

95. House Committee on Education and Labor, Subcommittee on War on Poverty Program, *HR 10440: Economic Opportunity Act of 1964, Hearings,* 88th Cong., 2nd sess., March–April 1964 (Washington, D.C.: GPO, 1964), 22.

96. Lyndon B. Johnson, cited in Kermit Gordon, Memorandum for Agency Heads, 23 November 1964, LBJL, WHCF, EX WE 9, Box 25, File: WE 9, Poverty Program (The Great Society), 1 October–10 December 1964; William Capron, Memorandum to Walter Heller, "Johnsonian Talking Points on Poverty—in Johnsonian Style."

97. Quoted in Harding, 21.

98. Though they rejected the popular press's indictment of ADC, welfare experts in the late 1940s and 1950s were nonetheless troubled by the apparent immorality of recipients. As social worker and author of one of the first comprehensive analyses of ADC policy and ADC recipients Winifred Bell later noted, welfare workers too felt "affronted by the broken and besieged families who reflected the ways and values of poverty." Winifred Bell, quoted in Jennifer Mittelstadt, *From Welfare to Workfare: The Unintended Consequences of Liberal Reform* (Chapel Hill: University of North Carolina Press, 2005), 47.

99. Phyllis Osborn, "Aid to Dependent Children: Realities and Possibilities," *Social Service Review* 28 (1954): 162; Hilda Arndt, "An Appraisal of What the Critics Are Saying About Public Assistance," *Social Service Review* 26 (1952): 475.

100. "Text of the President's February 1 Public Welfare Message," *CQ,* 2 February 1962, 140. The Public Welfare Amendments of 1962 built on a series of smaller changes to the ADC program that began in the 1950s, beginning with the Social Security Amendments of 1956. Although this law fell short of requiring states to provide ADC clients with "meaningful" social services—as the 1962 law did—it nevertheless represented a first step toward toward incorporating more services into ADC. For a comprehensive history of the 1962 law and its antecedents, see Charles Gilbert, "Policy-Making in Public Welfare: The 1962 Amendments," *Political Science Quarterly* 81, 2 (June 1966): 196–224.

101. *CQ,* 17 August 1962, 1368.

102. Bureau of Public Assistance (BPA), *Services in the Aid to Dependent Children Program: Implications for Federal and State Administration,*(Washingotn D.C.: GPO, 1959), 1; Arndt, 475.

103. Sargent Shriver, Memorandum for the President, "National Anti-Poverty Plan," 10 October 1965, LBJL, WHCF, EX WE 9, File: WE 9, 14 October–17 December 1965.

104. Advisory Commission on Intergovernmental Relations, *Welfare: The Growth of a Federal Function* (Washington, D.C.: GPO, 1980), 49.

105. Brauer, "Kennedy, Johnson," 108.

106. Johnson, quoted in Harding, iii.

107. Walter Heller, Draft, "Message on Poverty," 3 March 1964, LBJL, WHCF, Leg-

islative Background Economic Opportunity Act, Box 2, File: Message on Poverty. As the next chapter will argue, these promises eventually came back to haunt the Johnson administration when congressional conservatives used rising AFDC rolls to claim that the War on Poverty had failed.

108. Lyndon B. Johnson, OEO Public Affairs, Memorandum to all OEO Staff Members, "Remarks of the President at Swearing-In-Ceremony of Hon. Sargent Shriver as Director, Office of Economic Opportunity, East Room of the White House," 16 October 1964, LBJL, WHCF, Administrative History OEO, Box 2, File: "Vol. II—, Documentary Supplement, chap. 1 (2 of 2).

109. "Why Should Conservatives Support the War on Poverty?" LBJL, WHCF, Legislative Background, Economic Opportunity Act, Box 2, File: Legislative History of the Poverty Program.

110. Johnson, "Remarks of the President "

111. Johnson, "Annual Message."

112. Harding, 9.

113. See Hamilton and Hamilton; Thomas F. Jackson, "The State, the Movement, and the Urban Poor: The War on Poverty and Political Mobilization in the 1960s," in *The "Underclass" Debate: Views from History*, ed. Michael Katz (Princeton, N.J.: Princeton University Press, 1993), 403–39.

114. Nancy MacLean, *Freedom Is Not Enough: The Opening of the American Workplace* (New York: Sage, 2006), 104.

115. A. Phillip Randolph, Opening Remarks, White House Conference on Civil Rights, 17 November 1965, in *Civil Rights During the Johnson Administration: A Collection from the Holdings of the Lyndon B. Johnson Administration, Part IV: The White House Conference on Civil Rights (Microform)* (Frederick, Md.: University Publications of America, 1984), Reel 16, Frame 0530–37; Carl Holman, Berl Bernhard, and Harold Fleming, Memorandum to Lee. C. White, "Health and Welfare," 3 December 1965, in *Civil Rights During the Johnson Administration*, Part IV, Reel 6, Frame 087. Historians have tended to view black claims for equal economic rights as a late 1960s phenomenon, the product of black nationalism and a substantial departure from the movement's more "legitimate" Southern phase. Robert O. Self has pointed out, however, these narratives misunderstand the claims made by the "black nationalist" movement, treat the Southern experience as normative, and ignore a fundamental component of postwar African American politics in both the North and the South—the political confrontation with power structures that sustained and created legal, civil, social, and economic inequality. Charles and Dona Hamilton have likewise recovered the history of the "dual agenda" of national Civil Rights organizations' simultaneous pursuit of social and Civil Rights for all Americans. See Robert O. Self, *American Babylon: Race and the Struggle for Postwar Oakland* (Princeton, N.J.: Princeton University Press, 2003); Hamilton and Hamilton.

116. Martin Luther King, Jr., "Annual Report of Martin Luther King, Jr., President SCLC, Annual Convention, Savannah," 28 September–2 October 1964, 14, A. Phillip Randolph Papers (hereafter APRP), LoC, Reel 2, Frame 0567.

117. Ibid., Frame 0568–69; For a similar critique of mainstream liberal policy, see Bayard Rustin, Address to Democratic National Convention, Atlantic City, N.J., August 1964, quoted in William Forbath, "Caste, Class, and Equal Citizenship," *Michigan Law Review* 98, 1 (October 1999), 86.

118. Whitney M. Young, Jr., "The Urban League and Its Strategy," *Annals of the American Academy of Political and Social Science* 357 (January 1965): 107.

119. Whitney M. Young, Jr., "Domestic Marshall Plan," *NYT*, 6 October 1963, 240.

120. Ibid.

121. "Freedom Budget: Third Draft," APRP, Reel 18, Frame 0771–0774, 0778.

122. Ibid., 0778, 0777.

123. President Johnson announced the White House Conference on Civil Rights in June 1965, during his commencement address to the graduating class of Howard University. Intended to promote the next and more profound stage in the battle for Civil Rights," the Conference fell victim to both the backlash to the so-called Watts riots in August 1965 and to the political fallout from the release of Daniel Patrick Moynihan's controversial *Report on the Negro Family*. Hoping to defuse the Moynihan controversy, and contain the growing rift between the Civil Rights community and the administration, the White House scaled back its plan for the conference, inviting only 240 "experts" to a preliminary "planning conference" in November 1965. The press generally deemed the conference a "flat failure" and blamed the "civil rights disaster" on the "shrill cries of Negro militants." For the reports of the planning sessions, and the recommendations forwarded to the White House, see *Civil Rights During the Johnson Administration*. For a narrative account of the conference, see Kevin Yuill, "The 1966 White House Conference on Civil Rights," *Historical Journal* 41, 1 (March 1998): 259–82. For a documentary history of the Moynihan controversy, see Lee Rainwater and William Yancy, eds., *The Moynihan Report and the Politics of Controversy* (Cambridge, Mass.: MIT Press, 1967); Daryl Michael Scott, *Contempt and Pity: Social Policy and the Image of the Damaged Black Psyche, 1880–1996* (Chapel Hill: University of North Carolina Press, 1997), chap. 8.

124. "Freedom Budget: Third Draft," Frame 0778, 0776–0781.

125. A. Phillip Randolph, Letter to AFL-CIO Executive Council, 3 November 1966, APRP, Reel 18, Frame 0758.

126. "Freedom Budget, Third Draft," Frame 0772.

127. King, "Annual Report," 18, APRP Reel 2, Frame 0571.

128. A. Phillip Randolph, Letter to John Lewis, 11 July 1966, APRP, Reel 18, Frame 0756.

129. "Freedom Budget, Third Draft," Frame 0771.

130. Dorothy DiMascio, Testimony, Senate Finance Committee, *HR 12080: Social Security Amendments of 1967; Hearings*, 90th Cong., 1st sess., August–September (Washington, D.C.: GPO), 1470.

131. Whitney Young Testimony, Ways and Means, *President's 1963 Tax Message*, 1304.

132. Ibid., 1305.

133. White House Task Force on Income Maintenance (IMTF), Report, 21 November 1966, LBJL, WHCF, Legislative Background on the Social Security Amendments of 1967, Box 1, Report of Income Maintenance Task Force, File: Report of Income Maintenance Task Force, 9.

134. Finance Committee, *H.R. 12080: Social Security Amendments*, 1467.

135. Edward Sparer, "The Right to Welfare," in *The Rights of Americans: What They Are and What They Should Be*, ed. Norman Dorsen (New York: Random House, 1971), 87.

136. Charles A. Reich, "The New Property," *Yale Law Journal* 73, 5 (April 1964): 735, 746. Reich worried that the "new property" of government largesse would jeopardize the fundamental rights of individuals unless citizens' rights to government subsidy were protected by law. Without such legal and constitutional protections, Reich feared the emergence of a "new feudal state" in which citizens were forced to choose between subsistence and exercising their rights.

137. Charles A. Reich, "Individual Rights and Social Welfare: The Emerging Legal Issues," *Yale Law Journal* 74, 7 (June 1965): 1255. Reich's theory of the "new property" received some validation from the Supreme Court. Although the Court ultimately declined to declare a constitutional right to welfare, it did admit that it might be "more realistic to regard welfare entitlements as more like 'property' than a 'gratuity.'" In a decision authored by Justice William Brennan, the Court acknowledged that "forces not within the control of the poor" had contributed to their "poverty" and suggested that welfare might "help to bring within the reach of the poor the same opportunities that are available to others to participate meaningfully in the life of the community." Supreme Court, *Goldberg v. Kelley*, 397 U.S. 254, 90 S. Ct. 1011, 23 March 1970, 264-65 n8. For an analysis of welfare rights advocates' claims to a constitutional right to welfare, see Elizabeth Bussiere, *(Dis)Entitling the Poor: The Warren Court, Welfare Rights, and the American Political Tradition* (University Park: Pennsylvania State University Press, 1997); Martha Davis, *Brutal Need: Lawyers and the Welfare Rights Movement* (New Haven, Conn.: Yale University Press, 1993).

138. Michael K. Brown, *Race, Money and the American Welfare State* (Ithaca, N.Y.: Cornell University Press, 1999), 267.

139. On the transformation of the federal income tax, see Carolyn C. Jones, "Mass-Based Income Taxation: Creating a Taxpaying Culture, 1940-1952," in Brownlee, 107-47.

140. Andrea Louise Campbell, *How Policies Make Citizens: Senior Political Activism and the American Welfare State* (Princeton, N.J.: Princeton University Press, 2003), 2.

141. Poll: "The Blacks: Too Much, Too Soon?" in "The Troubled American: A Special Report on the White Majority," *Newsweek*, 6 October 1969, 45.

Chapter 3. Things Fall Apart

1. Ben Wattenberg, Memorandum to Douglas Cater, "Talking Points for Monday Speech to AFL-CIO Policy Committee," 4 February 1967, Lyndon B. Johnson Library (hereafter LBJL), Welfare (EX WE 9), Box 28, File: WE 9, January–8 February 1967.

2. "The Troubled America: A Special Report on the White Majority," *Newsweek*, 6 October 1969, 29. See also "Man and Woman of the Year: The Middle Americans," *Time*, 5 January 1970, 10.

3. Pemburt Heights Association, Letter to Rep. Martha Griffiths (D-Mich.), 1967, Martha W. Griffiths Papers (hereafter MGP), Bentley Historical Library, University of Michigan, Ann Arbor, Box 21.

4. Letter to Rep. Griffiths, 15 September 1966, MGP, Box 21.

5. Pete Hamill, "The Revolt of the White Lower Middle Class," *New York Magazine*, 13 April 1969, reprinted in *The White Majority: Between Poverty and Affluence*, ed. Louise Kapp Howe (New York: Random House, 1970), 10–22; Peter Schrag, "The Forgotten American," *Harpers*, August 1969, 27. According to Schrag, by the end of the 1960s, the "forgotten American" of the working and middle classes had become the "most alienated person in America," defined most by his "omission and semi-invisibility."

6. Letter to Rep. Griffiths, 2 November 1969, MGP, Box 21.

7. Letter from F. J. Halik of Detroit to Sen. Philip Hart (D-Mich.), 2 November 1969, MGP, Box 37, File: Inflation.

8. Letter from Martha Seligman of Detroit to Rep. Griffiths, 15 February 1966, MGP, Box 26, File: President's Poverty Program.

9. Ben Wattenberg, Memorandum to Douglas Cater, "Talking Points for Monday Speech to AFL-CIO Policy Committee," 4 February 1967, LBJL, Welfare (EX WE 9), Box 28, File: WE 9, January–8 February 1967; Christopher Howard, *The Hidden Welfare State: Tax Expenditures and Social Policy in the United States* (Princeton, N.J.: Princeton University Press, 1997). See also Jacob Hacker, *The Divided Welfare State: The Battle over Public and Private Social Benefits in the United States* (New York: Cambridge University Press, 2002).

10. June L. Alexander to Rep. Griffiths, 20 June 1968, MGP, Box 28.

11. Critics did more than question the effectiveness of War on Poverty programs; they indicted poverty workers and their government sponsors for "contributing" to the outbreak of violence in cities like Newark and Detroit. Newark mayor Hugh Addonzio, for example, accused poverty workers of "fueling the rash of wild and extremist behavior and actions that led up to the riot." Iowa Republican Sen. William Prouty publicized a letter from Newark police commissioner Dominick Spina warning that "riots and anarchy" would be the direct consequence of OEO-funded community action programs in Newark. See Bertram Harding, *A Narrative History of the War on Poverty*, 579, LBJL, White House Central Files (hereafter WHCF), Administrative History OEO, Box 1 (Crisis of 1967), File: Vol. 1, Pt. 2, Narrative History (3 of 3); Republican Coordinating Committee, Task Force on Job Opportunities and Welfare, Improving Social Welfare, 11 December 1967, NARA, SFC, Subject Files: Medicaid—Suggested Amendments, File: President's 1967 Welfare Program.

12. Harding, 544.

13. Charles Schultze, Memorandum to the President, "Great Expectations vs. Dis-

appointments," 7 November 1966, LBJL, Welfare (EX WE9), Box 28, File: WE 9, 15 October–31 December 1966.

14. President Lyndon B. Johnson, "Annual Message to Congress on the State of the Union: 1967," 10 January 1967, in John Woolley and Peters, www.presidency.ucsb.edu/ws/?pid=28338.

15. Schultze, Memorandum to the President.

16. For Johnson's "guns and margarine" speech, see James Reston, "A Midterm Report: Guns and Margarine Speech Is Found Lacking in Old Rhetoric and Promises," *NYT*, 11 January 1967, 17.

17. See Advisory Council on Intergovernmental Relations, *Public Assistance: The Growth of the Federal Function* (Washington, D.C.: GPO, 1980).

18. Wilbur J. Cohen, Memorandum to the President, "Re: Social Security Bill," 14 July 1967, LBJL, WHCF, LE/WE, Box 158, File: LE/WE 6, 22 November 1963–31 August 1967.

19. Margaret Malone, "Major Provisions of HR 12080 . . . As Reported Favorably by the Committee on Ways and Means and Major Provisions of HR 5710 (Administration Bill) Not Included in HR 12080," LoC, Legislative Reference Service, Education and Public Welfare Division, 11 August 1967, NARA, WM, RG 233, Leg. Files: HR 5710, Box 10A, No File.

20. Johnson, "Statement by President upon Signing the Social Security Amendments and upon Appointing a Commission to Study the Nation's Welfare Programs," 2 January 1968, *Public Papers of the Presidents of the United States: Lyndon B. Johnson, 1968–1969*, Book 1 (Washington, D.C.: GPO, 1970), 14–15.

21. Advisory Council on Public Welfare, Staff Paper, "Greater Adequacy of Income for Needy People: Recommendations Made to the Advisory Council on Public Welfare," 9 September 1965, NARA II, RG 363, Box 1, Advisory Council Files, File: Advisory Council Actions Taken or Deferred.

22. U.S. House, Ways, and Means Committee, *H.R. 12080: Social Security Amendments of 1967, Report*, 90th Cong., 1st sess., August 1967 (Washington, D.C.: GPO, 1967), 95–96.

23. Republican Coordinating Committee, "Improving Social Welfare."

24. Ronald Reagan, quoted in Edward Berkowitz, *Mr. Social Security: The Life of Wilbur J. Cohen* (Lawrence: University Press of Kansas, 1995), 252.

25. ACIR, *Public Assistance*, 55.

26. Ibid., 49.

27. Congress, House of Representatives, Committee on Ways and Means, *Section-by-Section Analysis and Explanation of the Provisions of HR 5710, the "Social Security Amendments of 1967," as Introduced on February 20, 167, Prepared and Furnished by the Department of Health, Education, and Welfare*, 90th Cong., 1st sess. (Washington, D.C.: GPO, 1967), 1; See also Wilbur J. Cohen, Memorandum to Evelyn Thompson, 20 February 1967, NARA, SFC, RG 46, Box 42, File: Presidential Social Security Proposal.

28. Wilbur J. Cohen, Memorandum to the President, Re: Social Security Bill, 14 July

1967, LBJL, WHCF, LE/WE, Box 158, File: LE/WE 6, 22 November 1963–31 August 1967.

29. James Lyday, Memorandum for Robert Levine, "Ways and Means Committee Social Security Proposals," 5 August 1967, LBJL, WHCF, LE/WE Box 158, No File.

30. See Harding, 579; Republican Coordinating Committee, "Improving Social Welfare."

31. "House Unit Prepares Welfare Aid Changes Forcing Many Able Bodied Adults Off Rolls," *Wall Street Journal*, 27 July 1967, 9, quoted in Berkowitz, *Mr. Social Security*, 255.

32. Jennifer Mittlestadt, *From Welfare to Workfare: The Unintended Consequences of Liberal Reform, 1945–1965* (Chapel Hill: University of North Carolina Press, 2005), 165–66. As Mittlestadt and others have pointed out, however, the War on Poverty, designed with the male breadwinner in mind, did little for most of an AFDC population comprised of poor women and their children. Indeed, the Office of Economic Opportunity explicitly discriminated against women in their work and manpower development programs, providing only 15 percent of War on Poverty jobs to them. See Diana Pearce, "Welfare Is Not for Women: Why the War on Poverty Cannot Conquer the Feminization of Poverty," in *Women, the State, and Welfare*, ed. Linda Gordon (Madison: University of Wisconsin Press, 1990), 265–80.

33. "Key LBJ Comments from Tax Message," *Washington Post*, 4 August 1967, A4.

34. House, "Rep. Wilbur D. Mills of Arkansas Speaking for HR 12080, Social Security Amendments of 1967," *Congressional Record*, 90th Cong., 1st sess., 17 August 1967, H 10668.

35. House Committee on Ways and Means, *Report on HR 12080, the Social Security Amendments of 1967*, 90th Cong., 1st sess., 7 August 1967, (Washington, D.C.: GPO, 1967), 96.

36. Ibid.

37. Ibid., 110.

38. Mills, speaking for HR 12080, H 10674.

39. House, "Rep. John Byrnes of Wisconsin Speaking for HR 12080," H10677–78.

40. Sen. Russell Long (D-La.), in Senate Committee on Finance, *Hearings, HR 12080, the Social Security Amendments of 1967, Part II*, 28–31 August, 11, 12, 18, 19 September 1967, 90th Cong., 1st sess. (Washington, D.C.: GPO, 1967), 789.

41. For the rhetorical appeal of this kind of welfare politics, see Michael Weiler, "The Reagan Attack on Welfare," in *Reagan and Public Discourse in America*, ed. Michael Weiler and W. Barnett Pearce (Tuscaloosa: University of Alabama Press, 1992), 248.

42. Mills, "Address on HR 12080," *Congressional Record*, 2598.

43. Ways and Means, *Report, HR 12080*, 97.

44. Senate Committee on Finance, *Social Security Amendments of 1967: Part VII – Work Incentive Program*, Confidential Committee Print, 90th C, 1st Sess., NARA, SFC, Bill Files, "HR 12080," Box 28.

45. On the evolution of "workfare" programs, see Nancy E. Rose, *Workfare or Fair*

Work: Women, Welfare, and Government Work Programs (New Brunswick, N.J.: Rutgers University Press, 1995).

46. For more, see Joanne Goodwin, "'Employable Mothers' and 'Suitable Work': A Re-Evaluation of Welfare and Wage-Earning for Women in the 20th Century United States," *Journal of Social History* 29, 2 (Winter 1995): 253–74.

47. Sen. Russell Long, Senate Finance Committee, *Hearings, HR 12080*, 1537; "Welfare Protesters Rebuked," *Washington Post*, 21 September 1967, A2. Long's outburst came after a group of welfare mothers representing the National Welfare Rights Organization (NWRO) staged a "wait-in" in the Finance Committee hearing room. For the welfare rights movement, see Felicia Kornbluh, *The Battle for Welfare Rights: Politics and Poverty in Modern America* (Philadelphia: University of Pennsylvania Press, 2007).

48. "A Proposal by the Southern Christian Leadership Conference for the Development of a Nonviolent Action Movement for the Greater Chicago Area," in *The Eyes on the Prize: Civil Rights Reader*, ed. Cyborne Carson (New York: Penguin, 1991), 296.

49. New Jersey Legislature, Welfare Investigating Committee, *The Aid to Dependent Children Program in New Jersey* (Trenton, N.J, 1963), 1, 41.

50. Daniel Patrick Moynihan, *The Negro Family: The Case for National Action*, U.S. Department of Labor, Office of Policy Planning and Research, March 1965, 14, reprinted in *The Moynihan Report and the Politics of Controversy*, ed. Lee Rainwater and William L. Yancey (Cambridge, Mass.: MIT Press, 1967).

51. Leo Irwin, Letter to Rep. Lloyd Meeds (D-Wash.), NARA, Ways and Means, 90th Cong., Leg. Files, Box 21, No File; "Welfare—Some Say 'Freeze' Will Be Heartless," *NYT*, 17 December 1967, NARA, SFC, Leg. Files, HR 12080, Box 33, File: Press Clippings

52. Peter Edelman, Memo to Sen. Robert Kennedy (D-N.Y.), "HR 12080: Conference Report," 8 December 1967, NARA Ways and Means, 90th Cong. Leg Files, HR 12080, Box 21A, No File.

53. Quoted in Sidney Schanberg, "Lindsay Sees Rise in City Relief Costs if U.S. Cuts Funds," *NYT*, 11 December 1967, NARA, Senate Finance Committee, Leg. Files, HR 12080, Box #33, File: Press Clippings.

54. U.S. Senate Committee on Finance, *HR 12080: Brief Summary of Major Provisions*, 90th Cong, 1st sess., 5 October 1967 (Washington, D.C.: GPO, 1967), 60; Congress, Ways and Means and Finance Committees (Joint Publication), *Summary of Social Security Amendments of 1967*, December 1967 (Washington D.C.: GPO, 1967), 20. For background on Long's "Runaway Poppas" amendment to HR 12080, see Finance Committee, "Runaway Parents Location and Liability: Memorandum," "Runaway Parents: Draft, 11/1/67," "Amendment Not Yet Formally Introduced, 'Run-Away Poppa' (Sen. Long)"; "Explanation of How 'Run-Away Poppa' Amendment of Senator Long's Would Work," 23 October 1967, NARA, Senate Finance Committee, Bill Files, "HR 12080," Box 35, File: Runaway Poppas.

55. A close reading of the legislative history of HR 12080 suggests that congressional architects intended that law to make AFDC eligibility contingent on a woman's ability or willingness to cooperate with state authorities in establishing paternity and collecting

support orders. However, the 1967 law did not explicitly direct states to condition AFDC receipt on such cooperation. As such, it was open to judicial challenge. Between 1969 and 1973, the Supreme Court upheld fifteen lower court decisions striking down state regulations that made cooperation in paternity establishment a condition of continued AFDC receipt. In *Doe v. Flowers*, for example, the Court cited an earlier decision in *Doe v. Shapiro*, to argue that "although the state argues with considerable force that the Social Security Act requires it to take affirmative steps to ascertain the paternity of illegitimate children receiving AFDC assistance, we do not think that [the 1967 provision] was ever intended to allow a state to disqualify an otherwise eligible child." Quoted in Gwendolyn Mink, *Welfare's End* (Ithaca, N.Y.: Cornell University Press, 1998), 59.

56. U.S. Senate Committee on Finance, *The Welfare Mess: A Scandal of Illegitimacy and Desertion*, address by Sen. Russell Long, 92nd Cong., 1st sess., 14 December 1971 (Washington, D.C.: GPO, 1971), 3.

57. Sen. Pete Dominici (R-N.M.), "Final Vote on H.R. 3153," Social Security Amendments of 1973, 93rd Cong., 1st sess. *Congressional Record* 119, pt. 30 (1 December 1973), 39055.

58. Ways and Means Staff, "Confidential Conference Committee Memorandum, Senate Amendment No. 198 (AFDC-Work Training)," NARA, Ways and Means, Leg. Files, HR 12080, box 21A, no file.

59. According to the Department of Health, Education, and Welfare, for example, "with such positive features . . . as the availability of work training, training incentive payments, day care and earned income exemptions," compelling "AFDC mothers" to "undergo training" would be "unnecessary. HEW Sec. John Gardner made a similar case to the Finance Committee, arguing that the positive work incentives in the bill would be enough to rehabilitate welfare recipients and allow them to "solve their family and social adjustment problems" and help them to "get a decent job." See John Gardner, Testimony, Senate Finance Committee, *Hearings, HR 12080*, 215; Department of Health, Education, and Welfare, "Proposed Public Welfare and Child Health Amendments to HR 12080," Social Security Amendments of 1967, NARA, SFC, Bill Files: HR 12080, Box 30, No File.

60. Quoted in Gareth Davies, *From Opportunity to Entitlement: The Transformation and Decline of Great Society Liberalism* (Lawrence: University Press of Kansas, 1996), 174. Mindful of Mills's power on the Hill, Cohen went out of his way to assure the chairman that the administration planned to work with him on meaningful welfare reform. When the *Washington Post* reported that the "two Wilburs" had clashed over the Social Security and welfare reform bill, Cohen promised the chairman that "nothing could be further from the truth." Wilbur Cohen to Wilbur Mills, 23 August 1967, NARA, WMC, Bill Files: HR 5710, Box 21C, No File.

60. Cohen, Memorandum to the President, "Social Security Bill," 28 August 1967, LBJL, WHCF, LE/WE Box 158, File: LE/WE 6, 23 November 1963–31 August 1967.

61. Finance Committee, *Hearings, HR 12080*, 215.

62. The NWRO pursued a dual political and legal strategy to secure the "rights" of welfare recipients. The legal strategy, pursued in concert with "poverty lawyers" funded

under the OEO's Legal Services Program, comprised a juridical attack on state-level welfare laws and administrative practices designed to culminate in the establishment of a constitutional right to welfare. Although the NWRO and the LSP lawyers success-fully challenged "suitable home," "substitute father," and state residency laws, the U.S. Supreme Court ultimately declined to create a constitutional right to welfare. For more information on LSP legal strategy, see Elizabeth Bussiere, *(Dis)Entitling the Poor: The Warren Court, Welfare Rights, and the American Political Tradition* (University Park: Pennsylvania State University Press, 1997); Martha Davis, *Brutal Need: Lawyers and the Welfare Rights Movement* (New Haven, Conn.: Yale University Press, 1993).

63. "Welfare Protesters Rebuked," *Washington Post*, 21 September 1967, A2.

64. Finance Committee, *Hearings, HR 12080*, 1537.

65. "Welfare Protesters Rebuked."

66. George A. Wiley, "Letter from the President," *NWROs in Action: Newsletter of the National Welfare Rights Organization* 21 (Washington, D.C.: National Poverty Rights Action Center, 1967).

67. Finance Committee, *Hearings, HR 12080*, 1465, 1466.

68. Ibid., 1465.

69. "Motherhood: A Full Time Job: A letter to Senator Steven Young," *Welfare Fighter* 1, 20 (Washington, D.C.: National Poverty Rights Action Center, 1970).

70. Lillian Baines, "Why Not a Subsidy for Mothers," *Welfare Fighter* 1, 19.

71. This citizen-mother claim had deep roots in the American welfare tradition. As Gwendolyn Mink, Linda Gordon, Theda Skocpol, and many others have pointed out, throughout the late nineteenth and early twentieth centuries, social welfare discourse and policy tied women's roles as mothers to the future of the nation itself. Despite their "political invisibility," Mink argues, this "maternalist" politics assigned women a "weighty political significance as the guardians of male virtue and the reproduc-ers of the republican order." Early twentieth-century social welfare policies provided women with special protections (protective labor legislation) or with minimal levels of economic security (mothers' pensions). For the importance of "maternalism" in early twentieth-century social welfare policy formation, see Sonya Michel and Seth Koven, eds., *Mothers of a New World: Maternalist Politics and the Origins of Welfare States* (New York: Routledge, 1993). See also Theda Skocpol, *Protecting Soldiers and Mothers: The Political Origins of Social Policy in the United States* (Cambridge, Mass.: Belknap Press of Harvard University, 1992); and Linda Gordon, *Pitied but Not Entitled: Single Mothers and the History of Welfare, 1890–1935* (Cambridge, Mass.: Harvard University Press, 1994).

72. For more on the relationship between the feminist movement of the late 1960s and 1970s and the maternalist claims of welfare mothers, see Johanna Brenner, *Women and the Politics of Class* (New York: Monthly Review Press, 2000). See also Pearce.

73. Sen. Russell Long, "Work Requirements, Draft Dear Colleague," NARA, SFC, Bill Files, HR 12080, Box #1, No File.

74. Kornbluh, 91.

75. This claim comes from a 1970 edition of the *Welfare Fighter*, official NWRO press organ. See Barnes, "Why Not a Subsidy for Mothers," 9.

76. John Gardner, Memorandum for the President, 11 December 1967, LBJL, WHCF, LE/WE Box 158, File: LE/WE 6, 9/1/67–12/31/67; Joe Califano, Memorandum for the President, 11 December 1967, 10:15 p.m., LBJL, WHCF, LE/WE Box 158, File: LE/WE 6, 9/1/67–12/31/67.

77. Gardner, Memorandum for the President.

78. Califano, Memorandum for the President, 11 December 1967, 4:40 p.m.

79. Mike Manatos, Memorandum for the President, 13 December 1967, 11:45 A.M., LBJL, WHCF, LE/WE Box 168, File: LE/WE 6, 9/1/67–12/31/67.

80. Califano, Memorandum for the President, 9 December 1967, with Johnson's note attached, dated 10 December 1967, LBJL, Confidential File, LE/WE 6, Box 64, quoted in Davies, 199.

81. See, e.g., Gardner Ackley, Memorandum for the President, "Scare Talk on the Tax Increase," 2 September 1965, LBJL, WHCF, Gen FI 9, Box 55, File: FI 11 Taxation, 29 June 1965–16 March 1966.

82. Walter Heller, Letter to the Editor of the *Minneapolis Sunday Tribune*, No Date, LBJL, GEN FI 19 Box 55, File: FI 11 Taxation, 29 June 1965–16 March 1966.

83. John J. Wallis, "Total Government Expenditure, by Function: 1902–1995," table Ea61–124, in *Historical Statistics of the United States, Earliest Times to the Present: Millennial Edition*, ed. Susan B. Carter, Scott Sigmund Gartner, Michael R. Haines, Alan L. Olmstead, Richard Sutch, and Gavin Wright (New York: Cambridge University Press, 2006), http://dx.doi.org.

84. Ackley, Memorandum for the President, "Policy Implications of the Budget," No Date, LBJL WHCF, Gen FI 9, Box 55, File: FI 11 Taxation, 29 June 1965–16 March 1966.

85. Lyndon Johnson, Handwritten note on Memorandum from Joe Califano, 17 December 1966, LBJL, WHCF, Gen FI 9, Box 55, File: FI 11 Taxation, 29 June 1965–16 March 1966. In late June, the president explicitly directed his "fiscal advisors to avoid speculation as to the future of the economy and specifically whether or not additional taxes are needed." See Joseph E. Kintner, Memorandum for Henry H. Fowler et al., "President's Desire for No Speculation Regarding Increased Taxes or Future Economic Problems," 29 June 1966, LBJL, GEN FI 11, Box 55, File: FI 11, 12 March–20 August 1966.

86. Johnson, "Annual Message to the Congress on the State of the Union," 12 January 1966, in Woolley and Peters, 28015.

87. George McGovern, *Congressional Record*, 19 September 1967, quoted in Davies, 189.

88. Walter Reuther, "Fiscal Policy for 1967," forwarded to President Lyndon Johnson, 22 December 1966, LBJL, EX BE 5, Box 25, File: BE 516 December 1966–15 March 1967.

89. Joseph Bowman, Memorandum to Henry Hall Wilson, Jr., "Subject: House Debate on the Tax Adjustment Act of 1966, February 23, 1966," 24 February 1966, LBJL, LE/FI Box 52, File: LE/FI 11, 15 February 1964–2 April 1966.

90. Quoted in Harding, 21.

91. "The Economy: Time to Touch the Brakes," *Time*, 18 March 1966.

92. Republican National Committee, *Great Society Funny Money* Campaign Flier, 1964, SI, NMAH, Political Archives.

93. Gardner Ackley, Memorandum for the President: The State of the Economy," 1 December 1966, LBJL, WHCF, EX BE 5, Box 24, File: "BE 5, 16 December 1966–15 March 1967. See also Willard Wirtz, Memorandum for Honorable Joseph Califano, "Tax Policy," 15 November 1966, LBJL, WHCF, EX FI 11–4, Box 60, File: F 11–4, 11 October–15 December 1966; Walter Heller, Memorandum for the President, "The Tax Increase Issue Today," 14 December 1966, LBJL, WHCF, Gen FI 9, Box 56, File: FI 11, 24 September 1966.

94. Bruce Jansson, *The Sixteen-Trillion-Dollar Mistake: How the U.S. Bungled Its National Priorities from the New Deal to the Present* (New York: Columbia University Press, 2001), 161.

95. Robert McNamara, Henry Fowler, Willard Wirtz, Connor, Charles Schultze, Gardner Ackley, Clark Clifford, and Joe Califano, Memorandum for the President, 9 January 1967, LBJL, WHCF, EX FI 11–4, Box 60, File: FI 11–4, 16 December 1966–15 January 1967.

96. William McChesney Martin, Memorandum for the President, 13 December 1966, LBJL, WHCF, EX FI 11–4, Box 60, File: FI 11–4, 11 October–15 December 1966.

97. Lyndon B. Johnson, "Annual Address to the Congress on the State of the Union," 10 January 1967.

98. Henry Fowler, Letter to Sen. John Williams (R-Del.), 22 November 1967, NARA, Senate Finance Committee, 90th Cong., Bill Files, Box #3, "HR 15414," Folder: Surtax Amendment to 15414.

99. Johnson, quoted in Gilbert Burck, "Capitol Hill's 'Show Me' Economist," *Fortune*, February 1968, 204, in NARA, Senate Finance Committee, 90th Cong., 90A-F8, Box 23, File: Economic Policy-Excess Profits Tax.

100. Gardner Ackley, Memorandum for the President, "The Case for Higher Taxes," 10 May 1966, LBJL, GEN FI 11, Box 55, File: FI 11, 17 March 1966–20 August 1968.

101. Walter Heller, Memorandum for the President, "Accelerator vs. Brakes," 11 July 1967, LBJL, EX FI 11–4, Box 60, File: 11 June–15 July 1967.

102. Henry Fowler, Memorandum for the President, 11 May 1966, LBJL, GEN FI 11, Box 55, File: FI 11, 17 March–20 August 1966.

103. Fowler to Williams, 22 November 1967..

104. Council of Economic Advisors, Quoted in Edwin Dale, No title, *NYT*, 2 February 1968, NARA, Senate Finance Committee, Subject Files, Box 23, "Revenue: Economic Policy—Excess Profits Tax, File: Revenue: Economic Policy.

105. Walter Heller, Memorandum for the President, "Conversation with Wilbur

Mills, August 19, 1966," 20 August 1966, LBJL, GEN FI 11, Box 55, File: FI 11, 17 March–20 August 1966.

106. Rep.Wilbur Mills, quoted in "Delay Hinted for Any Tax Rise Until Jan. 1," *Wall Street Journal*, 21 June 1967, NARA SFC, Subject Files, Box 23, Revenue: Economic Policy—Excess Profit Tax, File: Revenue: Economic Policy.

107. Wilbur Mills, Edward Fried Oral History Memoir, Tape 1, 38, quoted in Robert M. Collins, *More: The Politics of Economic Growth in Postwar America* (New York: Oxford University Press, 2000), 75.

108. "The New Congress," *Newsweek*, 21 November 1966, 38.

109. Fowler to Williams.

110. Mills, quoted in Burck, 206.

111. "Text of Mills Statement on Federal Spending and Growth of Government," *NYT*, 7 October 1967, quoted in Julian Zelizer, *Taxing America: Wilbur D. Mills, Congress, and the State, 1945–1975* (Cambridge: Cambridge University Press, 1998), 265.

112. "Now the Year of the Worried Bull," *Newsweek*, 8 January 1968, in NARA, Senate Finance Committee, Subject Files, Box 23, File: Economic Policy—Excess Profits Tax.

113. Burck, 207.

114. John Martin, "Confidential Memorandum to House Conferees on HR 15414: Section 1, 2, 3, 4 and 17 (Smathers-Williams Expenditure Cut and Tax Surcharge Amendment)," NARA, Ways and Means, 90th Cong., Leg. Files, Box 27, HR 15414, No File.

115. Mills, cited in "Committee Roundup: Administration Renews Plea for Tax Surcharge," *Congressional Quarterly,* 26 January 1968, 104, in NARA, SFC, 90th C, Bill Files, Box #1, "15114-15414," No folder.

116. Mills remarks, 75th Anniversary celebration of Security Trust Company of Rochester, New York, 22 May 1967, "Expenditure Control and Tax Policy," NARA, Senate Finance Committee, Subject Files, Box 23, File: Revenue: Economic Policy.

117. For more, see Collins, *More*, 69–85.

118. Quoted in Edwin Dale, No title, *NYT*, 2 February 1968, NARA, Senate Finance Committee, Subject Files, Box 23, File: Revenue: Economic Policy. As Robert Collins points out, the international crisis of 1968 "did not lack for drama." To many economists and policymakers the rush on gold that began in March signaled the "first act of a world depression." According to one member of the Johnson Treasury Department, "everybody was just petrified. It was a hair raising period in which we literally had to watch the gold markets day by day, hour by hour." See Collins, *More*, chap. 3, and "The Economic Crisis of 1968 and the Waning of the 'American Century,'" *American Historical Review* 101, 2 (April 1996): 396–422.

119. Marjorie Hunter, "Senate Prodding House to Break Tax Rise Impasse," *NYT*, 24 March 1968, NARA, Senate Finance Committee, 90th Cong., Bill Files, RG 46, Box 1, No File.

120. Senate Finance Committee, Press Release, "Finance Committee Reports Excise

Tax Extension Bill," 14 March 1968, NARA, Ways and Means Committee, 90th Cong., Bill File: HR 15414, No File. Observers noted that the White House mounted a disorganized attack on the tax and spending bill, with the president pushing actively for a smaller cut, and the Treasury taking a more hands-off approach. The Treasury Department worked with the Senate bill's Democratic cosponsor, George Smathers (D-Fl.), on the tax and spending bill. See Henry Fowler, Memorandum for the President, "Contingency Plan on Senate Amendment to Tax Adjustment Act," 27 March 1968, LBJL, WHCF, LE/FI Box 52, File: LE/FI, 3 April 1966.

121. U.S. Congress, Conference Committee, *Revenue and Expenditure Control Act of 1968: Explanation of Bill HR 15414 as Agreed to in Conference*, 90th Cong., 2nd sess., 10 June 1968, Committee Print (Washington, D.C.: GPO, 1968), 3.

122. Minutes of Special Cabinet Meeting, 14 May 1968, LBJL, Cabinet Papers, Box 13, quoted in Collins, *More*, 96

123. Lyndon Johnson, Message, *Aid for the Aged*, 23 January 1967 (Washington, D.C.: GPO, 1967), 1.

124. Ibid., 3.

125. Tom Vail, Memorandum to Frank McDermott, "Re: Proposed Financing for the President's Recommendations on Social Security, 12 January 1967, NARA, SFC, Bill Files, HR 12080, File: President's Social Security Proposals. The administration proposed to increase the joint employee/employer payroll tax in two steps, from its current level of 8.8 percent, to 9 percent in 1969 and 10 percent in 1972. The administration also recommended an incremental increase in the amount of income subject to the payroll tax—also known as the wage base—from its current level of $6,600 to $10,800 by 1973.

126. "Social Security: Drifting Off Course," *Fortune*, December 1967, 104.

127. President's Task Force on Income Maintenance, "Report of the Task Force on Income Maintenance, Administratively Confidential," LBJL, LEG BKG SSA 1967, Box 1, File: Report of the Income Maintenance Task Force, November 1966, table C, 33, 9.

128. Paul Samuelson quoted in "Social Security: Drifting Off Course," 104.

129. Julian Zelizer, "The Uneasy Relationship: Democracy, Taxation, and State Building Since the New Deal," in *The Democratic Experiment: New Directions in American Political History*, ed. Meg Jacobs, William J. Novak, and Julian Zelizer (Princeton, N.J.: Princeton University Press, 2003), 289.

130. "Social Security: Drifting Off Course," 104.

131. John Herbers, "Malaise in Congress: Members Found Edgy and Frustrated as They Sense Shift in Voters' Values," *NYT*, 20 March 1967, 15.

132. Norman C. Miller, "Revolt over Benefits: House Is Set to Cut Social Security Rise Proposed by Johnson," *Wall Street Journal*, 28 February 1967, 1, 16.

133. Jon Bajkia and Eugene Steuerle, "Individual Income Taxation Since 1948," *National Tax Journal* 44, 4 (December 1991), table A.1. By contrast, the federal income tax had grown by a relatively modest 15 percent over the same period—from 8.7 percent of personal income in 1948 to 10 percent in 1968.

134. "Social Security: Drifting off Course," 105.

135. Walter Reuther Testimony, U.S. House Committee on Ways and Means, *President's Proposals for Revision in the Social Security System: Hearings*, 90th Cong., 1st sess., 20–23 March, 4, 5 April 1967 (Washington, D.C.: GPO, 1967), 1466.

136. Ibid., 1425.

137. Margaret Malone, "The Social Security Amendments of 1967: Summary of Major Provisions" (Washington D.C.: Congressional Research Service, Education and Public Welfare Department, 18 December 1967), 1. The legislation included a number of other liberal, and costly, provisions, including a new program to extend benefits to "persons age 72 and over" who, for one reason or another, had not paid into the system and thus were not entitled to benefits, a liberalization of the "retirement test" that allowed seniors to more easily combine wage earning with OASDI receipt, and the expansion of new benefits to about 65,000 "widows and widowers" of "deceased workers."

138. For an account of this extraordinary period of expansion, see Martha Derthick, *Policymaking for Social Security* (Washington, D.C.: Brookings Institution Press, 1979), chap. 17.

139. CEA, "Draft History of the War on Poverty," 18, LBJL, WHCF, Legislative Background Economic Opportunity Act, Box 1, File: CEA Draft History of the War on Poverty.

140. President's Task Force on Income Maintenance (IMTF), "Report of the Task Force on Income Maintenance, Administratively Confidential," LBJL, Legislative Background Social Security Amendments of 1967, Box 1, File: Report of the Income Maintenance Task Force, November 1966, table C.

141. Ibid., 9.

142. Ibid., 9, 8.

143. Ibid., 46.

144. Ibid., 34.

145. Ibid., 34, 36.

146. Gardner Ackley, "Basic Issues in Income Maintenance," November 1966, LBJL, Welfare (GEN WE 4), Box 15, File: WE6, 1 April–30 November 1966. President Johnson read the memorandum in December 1966, and directed "tell Joe Califano to examine this . . . and come back to me."

Chapter 4. Fed Up with Taxes

1. St. Louis Tax Reform Group, Press Release, 15 February 1973, in Wisconsin Historical Society (hereafter WHS), MEJ Box 18F: 8TJP BKGR, St. Louis Tax Reform Group and Missouri Tax Reform Group (2).

2. ANTE UP, *Taxaction* 2, 6 (June 1975); 2, 8 (August 1975); in WHS, MEJ, Box 18, File 1: TJP, BKGR, State Organizations-Calif. Americans Nonpartisan for Tax Equity.

3. Isaac Martin, *The Permanent Tax Revolt: How the Property Tax Transformed American Politics* (Stanford, Calif.: Stanford University Press, 2008), 54.

4. For a study of the importance of tax policy to the Democratic and Republican

platforms after 1968, see Susan B. Hansen, *The Politics of Taxation: Revenue Without Representation* (New York: Praeger, 1983), 86–97 and table 3.2; U.S. Department of Commerce, Bureau of the Census, *Statistical Abstract of the United States: 1979* (Washington, D.C.: GPO, 1979), table 442.

5. See, e.g., "Man and Woman of the Year: The Middle Americans," *Time*, 5 January 1970, 13; "The Troubled American: A Special Report on the White Majority," *Newsweek*, 6 October 1969. For Nixon as "one of the most class aware presidents of the postwar era," see Jefferson Cowie, "Nixon's Class Struggle: Romancing the New Right Worker, 1969–1973," *Labor History* 43, 3 (Fall 2003): 257–83.

6. Murray Friedman, *Overcoming Middle Class Rage* (New York: Westminster Press, 1971), 13.

7. Kevin Phillips, *The Emerging Republican Majority* (New Rochelle, N.Y.: Arlington House, 1969), 463.

8. Richard M. Scammon, "Into the '70s: A GOP Decade?" *Newsweek*, 6 October 1969, 68.

9. Jefferson Cowie, "Vigorously Left, Right, and Center: The Crosscurrents of Working-Class America in the 1970s," in *America in the Seventies*, ed. Beth Bailey and David Farber (Lawrence: University Press of Kansas, 2004), 80–82.

10. Michael Harrington, "Two Cheers for Socialism," *Harpers*, October 1976, 78, quoted in Cowie, "Vigorously," 76.

11. Scammon, "Into the '70s: A GOP Decade?"

12. Richard M. Scammon and Ben Wattenberg, *The Real Majority* (New York: Coward-McCann, 1970); see also Elizabeth Brenner Drew, "Washington Report," *Atlantic Monthly*, April 1968.

13. Jack Newfield and Jeff Greenfield, *A Populist Manifesto: The Making of a New Majority* (New York: Praeger, 1972), 5.

14. George A. Wiley, Untitled Speech, 5 March 1973, WHS, GWP, Box 10, Folder 3, quoted in Isaac Martin, "The Origins of Populist Neoliberalism, or How the Tax Revolt Turned Right," paper presented at Annual Meetings of the Social Science History Association, Portland, Oregon, 3–5 November 2005.

15. Colson to Haldeman, 14 September 1970, quoted in Cowie, "Romancing," 269. As Cowie points out, while some in the White House, most notably Chuck Colson, Labor Secretary George Shultz, and Patrick Buchanan, were convinced the working class held the key to the "New American Majority," the president's more traditionally conservative advisors doubted the efficacy of the "blue-collar strategy." The idea that "labor would leave the Democrats to join us," Treasury official Charls Walker advised, was simply "wrong."

16. Martin, *Permanent Tax Revolt*.

17. Richard M. Nixon, "Address to the Nation on Domestic Programs," 8 August 1969, *Public Papers of the Presidents of the United States: Richard M. Nixon, 1969*, Book 1 (Washington, D.C.: GPO, 1971), 638–39.

18. For a reprint of Pete Hamill's article, see *The White Majority: Between Poverty and Affluence*, ed. Louise Kapp Howe (New York: Random House, 1970), chap. 1.

19. Andrew Hacker, "Is There a New Republican Majority?" in Howe, 277.

20. Quoted in Vincent Burke and Vee Burke, *Nixon's Good Deed: Welfare Reform* (New York: Columbia University Press, 1974), 45.

21. One of the staff members assigned to the welfare "problem" was Daniel Patrick Moynihan, a Department of Labor official during the Johnson years, author of the infamous 1965 *Report on the Negro Family*, and Nixon's "liberal-in-residence." Though Moynihan played a key part in the FAP, his role has been overstated, in part because he has written so voluminously on the subject. Moynihan was only one of a key group of advisors who urged the president to endorse the FAP for both political and policy reasons. See Daniel Patrick Moynihan, *The Politics of a Guaranteed Income* (New York: Random House, 1973). For his post-1965 views on "welfare" and the problem of dependency, see Moynihan, "The Crises in Welfare," *Public Interest* 10 (Winter 1968): 3–30.

22. Worth Bateman, quoted in Burke and Burke, *Nixon's Good Deed*, 53.

23. Arthur Burns, Memorandum for the President, "A Plan for Welfare Reform," 14 July 1969, Nixon Presidential Materials Project (hereafter NPMP), White House Special Files (hereafter WHSF), John D. Ehrlichman (hereafter JDE), SSF, Box 38, File: Welfare Book; Maurice Stans, Memorandum for the President, 7 May 1969, NPMP, WHSF, JDE, Box 40, File: Welfare Book, Reaction.

24. Burns, Memorandum to the President, "A Review of the "Revolt of the White Lower Middle Class" by Pete Hamill," 16 May 1969, NPMP, WHSF, Staff Member Office Files (hereafter SMOF), JDE, SSF, Box 39, File: Attitudes Toward Welfare.

25. Spiro Agnew, Memorandum to the President: FSS, 4 August 1969, NPMP, WHSF, JDE, SSF, Box 38, Welfare Book, 2 of 2.

26. Shultz and Burns borrowed this description from Hamill's study of the "rage of the white lower middle class." Nixon had read the *New York Magazine* article in May 1969; impressed and moved by Hamill's conclusions, he ordered his staff to summarize the article's salient points and "indicate what the government can do about it." Burns interpreted Hamill's findings as a "clear, and perhaps a not too early warning" that the president should drop the FAP. The white working class, he concluded, was angry with a government that ignored its needs and declining standard of living, while providing ever greater welfare benefits to "some fat welfare bitch." Nixon believed this point was "crucial" and directed presidential aide John Ehrlichman to tell "Shultz, Finch, Moynihan, et al." to "consider the implications and find an answer." Shultz responded to the president's request by ceding the validity of Hamill's observations—which largely mirrored Nixon's own—while rejecting Burns's policy conclusions. "The present situation," Hamill had warned, "is working its way to the point of no return. The working-class white man feels trapped, and even worse, in a society that purports to be democratic, ignored." See Burns, Memorandum to the President; Alexander Butterfield to JDE, Memorandum, 2 June 1969, NPMP, WHSF, SMOF, JDE, SSF, Box 39, File: Attitudes Toward Welfare; and

George Shultz, Memorandum for the President, 16 May 1969, quoted in Alan Matusow, *Nixon's Economy: Booms, Busts, Dollars, and Votes* (Lawrence; University Press of Kansas, 1998). See also Pete Hamill, "The Revolt of the White Lower Middle Class," *New York Magazine*, 13 April 1969, reprinted in Howe, 10–22.

27. George Shultz, Memorandum for the President, 16 May 1969, quoted in Matusow, 28.

28. Richard M. Nixon, "Address to the Nation on Domestic Problems," 8 August 1969, Woolley and Peters, http://www.presidency.ucsb.edu/.

29. The president explicitly directed his speechwriters and surrogates to tailor their defenses of the FAP to the needs of taxpayers, and to ignore entirely those "currently on welfare" or the "black unemployed." He also told his speechwriters to use "off the welfare rolls and onto the tax rolls" as often as possible in defending and defining the FAP. See JDE Notes, No Date, NPMP, WHSF, SMOF, JDE, SSF, Box 38, File: Welfare Book, Domestic Speech, 8 August 1969.

30. Department of Health, Education, and Welfare, Office of the Assistant Secretary for Planning and Evaluation, "Selected Characteristics of Families Eligible for the Family Assistance Plan, 1971 Projections," 2 February 1970, NARA, RG 46, SFC, Bill Files: HR 16311, Box 69A, File: Administration Material.

31. "Effects of the '70 Vote," *U.S. News and World Report*, 16 November 1970, 22.

32. JDE Notes, 2 April 1971, NPMP, WHSF, SMOF, JDE, Box 5, File 2.

33. Marisa Chappell, *The War on Welfare: Family, Poverty, and Politics in Modern America* (Philadelphia: University of Pennsylvania Press, 2009), 84.

34. Testimony to the Senate Finance Committee, Hearing on HR 16311, 10 September 1970, 2107; Richard Armstrong, "The Looming Money Revolution Down South," *Fortune*, June 1970, 152, both cited in Chappell, 83.

35. "Long Blasts 'Lazy' Women on Welfare," *Washington Evening Star*, No Date, NARA, SFC, Subject Files, Box 61, File: AFDC; Senate Finance Committee, Press Release, "Television Interview with Senator Russell B. Long, June 7, 1972," 9 June 1972, NARA, RG 233, WM, Fill Files: HR 1, Box 39, File: HR 1: Conti.

36. "Interview with Governor Reagan: Welfare, America's No. 1 Problem," *U.S. News and World Report*, 1 March 1971, 39.

37. Ronald Reagan, quoted in *National Review* 22, 27 (14 July 1970): 718.

38. "Interview with Governor Reagan," 39.

39. Journalist Nick Kotz points out that his story was one of Reagan's favorites. He told it in the *U.S. News* interview, which, according to the White House, became the source for the Nixon's retelling. Kotz notes that the governor's press secretary did not know where Reagan got the example. See Nick Kotz, "The Political Complexion of the Welfare Reform Issue: The President Borrows from Governor Reagan," *Washington Post*, 15 May 1971, A14.

40. Moynihan, *Politics of a Guaranteed Income*, 278.

41. For example, the American Conservative Union produced a pamphlet geared

Notes to Pages 105–107

specifically to working-class voters, *The Family Assistance Plan: A Guaranteed Annual Income—What It Means to YOU as a Taxpayer*, quoted in Chappell, 99.

42. "Ending Poverty," *New Republic*, 7 August 1971, 8–9, quoted in Chappell, 94.

43. George A. Wiley, Memo, 12 April 1972, Series 4, Box 581, Folder: Welfare Reform Analysis—NWRO, 71–72; LWV Detroit to Lucy Benson, 24 February 1972, Series 4, Box 598, Folder: Welfare Reform State and Local—Michigan-Wisconsin, 71–72, LWV Papers, both cited in Chappell 66; Rep. Charles Rangel (D-N.Y.), quoted in Warren Weaver, Jr., "20 in House Seek Welfare Plan giving $6500 to a Family of 4," *NYT*, 7 April 1971, 22.

44. For an analysis of the FAP, Nixon's success in dividing his liberal opposition, and his attempts to use federal policy to undermine and defund liberal political networks, see Bruce Schulman, *The Seventies: The Great Shift in American Culture, Society, and Politics* (New York: Free Press, 2001), chap. 1.

45. Quoted in Chappell, 105.

46. JDE Notes, 3 October 1972, NPMP, WHSF, SMOF, JDE, Box 6, File 5.

47. For more on SSI and the growth of the Social Security system, see Jill Quadagno, "From Old-Age Assistance to Supplemental Security Income: The Political Economy of Relief in the South, 1935–1972," and John Myles, "Postwar Capitalism and the Extension of Social Security into a Retirement Wage," in *The Politics of Social Policy in the United States*, ed. Margaret Weir, Ann Shola Orloff, and Theda Skocpol (Princeton, N.J.: Princeton University Press, 1988), 235–64, 264–92.

48. Although Congress failed to enact the FAP, it did make a number of smaller incremental changes to the AFDC system and the nation's social safety net, most notably the consolidation of existing adult programs—Old Age Assistance and Aid to the Blind—into the new program Supplemental Social Insurance (SSI). Congress also amended the "workfare" program created in 1967 and created a new system of federally enforced child support collection for AFDC children. For more, see R. Kent Weaver, *Ending Welfare as We Know It* (Washington, D.C.: Brookings Institution Press, 2000).

49. See Jon Margolis, "Survival in the Working Class," *Newsday*, 1969, cited in Chappell, 111.

50. Joint Economic Committee (JEC), Subcommittee on Consumer Economics, Staff Study: "Inflation and the Consumer in 1975," 10 February 1974, 1–5, in WHS, MEJ, Box 16, File 18: NCTJ-TJA-Congress. Inflation-driven wage increases often pushed taxpayers into higher tax brackets—a phenomenon known as bracket creep. Because brackets were smallest in the lower- and middle-income ranges, and larger toward the top, bracket creep largely affected lower- and middle-income taxpayers. See Alan Murray, "Income Tax Progression and Inflation," 26th National Conference of the Tax Foundation, December 1974, cited in JEC Staff Study, 25.

51. Chappell, 123.

52. Congress had directed the Treasury Department to undertake this audit as part of the Revenue and Expenditure Control Act of 1968.

53. House Ways and Means Committee, *Tax Reform, 1969, Part 1: Hearings*, 91st Cong., 1st sess., 4 September 1968, (Washington, D.C.: GPO, 1969), 4; John Witte, *The Politics and Development of the Federal Income Tax* (Madison: University of Wisconsin Press, 1985), 166; "House Committee Begins Major Tax Reform Proposals," *CQ*, 28 February 1969, 312; see also U.S. Congress, Joint Committee on Internal Revenue Taxation, *Summary of HR 13270, Tax Reform Act of 1969 as Reported by the Committee on Finance*, 91st Cong., 1st sess., 18 November 1969 (Washington, D.C.: GPO).

54. Eileen Shanahan, "Taxes: Why Reforms, at Last, May Be in Reach," *NYT*, 27 July 1960, E2; "House Committee Begins Major Tax Reform Proposals."

55. Anthony Lewis, "When Tax Justice Is Not Seen to Be Done," *NYT*, 3 August 1969, E11.

56. Eileen Shanahan, "Full Nixon Tax Reform Bill Seems Unlikely in '69," *NYT*, 20 March 1969, 23. For more on the "tax community" and its efforts to reform the Internal Revenue Code, see Julian Zelizer, *Taxing America: Wilbur D. Mills, Congress and the State, 1945–1975* (Cambridge: Cambridge University Press, 1998).

57. "Tax-Relief Bill with Some Reform Provisions Reported," *CQ*, 7 November 1969, 2186.

58. "Surtax in Danger," *NYT*, 27 June 1969, 36.

59. Eileen Shanahan, "House Is Warned by Mills on Taxes," *NYT*, 7 August 1969, 24.

60. John W. Finney, "Economy 1: A Lot of Politics in That Tax Bill," *NYT*, 14 December 1969, E1.

61. Senate Committee on Finance, *Tax Reform Act of 1969: Hearings*, 91st Cong., 1st sess., 4, 5 September 1969 (Washington, D.C.: GPO, 1969), 10, 513.

62. Jonathan Rose to Peter Flanigan, "Possible Veto of Tax Bill," 19 December 1969, NPMP, WHCF, Subject Files, FI, Box 58, File: EX FI 11 Taxation 5 of ?.

63. David Kennedy, Robert P. Mayo, and Paul McCracken, Memorandum to RMN, 19 December 1969, NPMP, WHCF, Subject Files, FI, Box 58, File: EX FI 11, Taxation, 5 of ?.

64. Andrew H. Malcolm, "Shift of Tax Burden Sought," *NYT*, 11 January 1971, 67.

65. Robert Bartell, Acting President, National Tax Action, quoted in "Measures to Finance Schools Are Being Defeated Across U.S.," *NYT*, 24 May 1970, 80.

66. Martin, *Permanent Tax Revolt*, 55.

67. "Phone Tax Protest Planned," *NYT*, 13 April 1970, 70.

68. Martin, *Permanent Tax Revolt*, 56.

69. Quoted in "Economic Issues: Views of Top Democratic Rivals," *CQ*, 10 June 1972, 1332. For the evolution of McGovern's economic policy, see Gordon Weil, *The Long Shot: George McGovern Runs for President* (New York: Norton, 1973); Theodore White, *The Making of the President, 1972* (New York: Atheneum, 1973). McGovern proposed to redress the imbalance in the federal income tax system by raising the minimum tax, increasing corporate tax rates, and reforming existing estate and gift tax laws. In his "National Fair Share Program," centrist Senator Ed Muskie (D-Me.) promised to

eliminate $14 billion in unfair loopholes. After he had declared his candidacy for the presidential nomination, the conservative Mills introduced legislation in the Ways and Means Committee that promised to "repeal virtually all tax preferences over the period 1974–1976." "Economic Issues: Views of Top Democratic Rivals," 1332–1336; Democratic National Convention, "Majority Report of the Platform Committee," *CQ*, 1 July 1972, 1728–29

70. Majority Report of the Platform Committee, 1728–29.

71. Ibid., 1730.

72. Jerry Berman, Memorandum to CHNBP Steering Committee, "Counter or Alternative Budget," Draft, 14 February 1973, WHS, GWP, Box 4, File: CHNBP.

73. Ibid.

74. Paul Clancy, "Ex-Senator Stumps for Tax Reform," *Charlotte Observer*, 15 February 1973, WHS, MEJ, Box 17, File 4: Background, National Organizations, Tax Action, Harris.

75. Carl P. Leubsdorf, "Harris Launching 'Tax Justice Campaign,'" *Montgomery Journal*, 12 February 1973, WHS, MEJ, Box 17, File 4: Background, National Organizations, Tax Action, Harris.

76. The advisory board of the Tax Action Campaign included representatives from the Communications Workers of America, Textiles Workers Union of America, Retail Clerks International Association, International Union of Electrical Workers, Brotherhood of Electrical Workers, International Brotherhood of Painters and Allied Trades, American Federation of Government Employees, United Mine Workers, and AFL-CIO of Florida, North Carolina, and West Virginia. Liberal economists John Kenneth Galbraith, Paul Douglas, and Mary Dublin Keyserling, and Civil Rights leaders Andrew Young, George Wiley, and Bayard Rustin also sat on the new organization's advisory board. See Advisory Board, Tax Action Campaign, WHS, MEJ, Box 17, File 4: Background, National Organizations, Tax Action, Harris.

77. Tax Action Campaign, "Tax Action Day—April 16, 1973," Summary of Activities, in WHS, MEJ, Box 17, File 4: National Organizations, Tax Action, Fred Harris.

78. Wiley, "The Need for a Taxpayers' Uprising," Speech to National Council of the Church of Christ Conference on Taxes and Redistribution of Wealth, 5 March 1973, in WHS, MEJ, MS 766, Box 11, File: Tax Reform Conference.

79. Movement for Economic Justice, News Release, "Former Welfare Head to Organize Taxpayers," 5 March 1973, in WHS, MEJ, Box 22, File: Tax Justice Project, Mailings, Flyers, Newsletters.

80. At the national level, the movement for welfare rights petered out after 1972 and the NWRO officially closed its doors in 1975. Welfare activism continued at the local level, as small groups of welfare recipients came together to challenge state and local welfare laws and regulations. See Anelisse Orleck, *Storming Caesar's Palace: How Black Mothers Fought Their Own War on Poverty* (Boston: Beacon Press, 2005); Kathryn L. Nasstrom, *Everybody's Grandmother and Nobody's Fool: Frances Freeborn Pauley and the*

Struggle for Social Justice (Ithaca, N.Y.: Cornell University Press, 2000); Felicia Kornbluh, *The Battle for Welfare Rights: Politics and Poverty in Modern America* (Philadelphia: University of Pennsylvania Press, 2007).

81. Movement for Economic Justice, Flier, *About the Movement for Economic Justice*, WHS, MEJ, MS 766, Box 11, File: Tax Reform Conference; Movement for Economic Justice, Letter, 6 February 1973, in WHS, MEJ, Box 22.

82. Wiley, "Need for a Taxpayer's Uprising"; Discussion Draft on Organization, 29 August 1974, WHS, MEJ, File 4: TJP BKGR—State Organizations, California Tax Reform Association.

83. Community Tax Aid for the Tax Justice Project and the Movement for Economic Justice, *Tax Clinic Handbook: A Guide for Volunteers*, 1973, WHS, MEJ, Box 22, File 15: Tax Clinics, Tax Clinic Handbook.

84. Movement for Economic Justice, Letter, 6 February 1973.

85. Barry [No Last Name] to Tom and Ralph [Nader], Memorandum, "Organizing in Ways and Means Districts," 5 May 1973, WHS, MEJ, Box 17, File 6: TJP, BKGR—Tax Reform and Research Group (Nader).

86. Movement for Economic Justice, Flier, *Welfare for Wall Street*, in Tax Organizing Kit Prepared by the MEJ for Unions, WHS, MEJ, Box 16, File 21: NCTJ, TJA, Unions.

87. Movement for Economic Justice, Flier, *The Political Pickpockets*, in Tax Organizing Kit.

88. Movement for Economic Justice, Flier, *America—Why Business Loves to Leave It*, in Tax Organizing Kit.

89. Tax Justice Project, Flier, *How to Write Your Congressman*, in Tax Organizing Kit.

90. Tax Justice Project, Flier, *Tax Reform—Crucial in the Fight Against Recession and Inflation*, in Tax Organizing Kit.

91. National Committee for Tax Justice, Draft, "Dear Colleague Letter," 18 November 1975, WHS, MEJ, Box 16, File 20: NCTJ TJA Mailings.

92. Dave Aylward, Memorandum, "Setting Up an Organization—Some Caveats," 7 February 1973, WHS, MEJ, Box 22, File 13: TJP Tax Clinics, Misc.

93. California Action League (CAL), Flier, *Cut the Waste, Not the Services or the Employees*, 1977, WHS, MEJ, Box 18, File 3: TJA Background State Organizations CAL (2).

94. Mike Barnes, "What Is Cal?" 23 July 1975, WHS, MEJ, Box 18, File 2: TJP, BKGR, State Organizations CAL (1).

95. "Welfare and Our Taxes," *Beyond Just Gripes: St Louis Tax Reform Group Newsletter* 2, 1 December 1972, in WHS, MEJ, box 18, file 11: TJP BKGR, St. Louis Tax Reform Group and Missouri Tax Reform Group (3).

96. Wiley, "Need for a Taxpayers' Uprising."

97. Worth Bateman and Jodie Allen, "Income Maintenance: Who Gains and Who Pays," in *Blue Collar Workers: A Symposium on Middle America*, ed. Sar Levitan (New York: McGraw-Hill, 1971), quoted in Chappell, 118.

98. Wiley, Draft Testimony, Ways and Means Committee, WHS, MEJ, Box 16, File 18: TJA-Congress.

99. Testimony of Robert Loitz, Chairman, NCTJ, Draft/prepared, 15 July 1975, WHS, MEJ, Box 16, File 18: TJA-Congress.

100. Stanley Surrey and Paul McDaniel, *Tax Expenditures* (Cambridge, Mass.: Harvard University Press, 1985), quoted in Christopher Howard, "The Hidden Side of the American Welfare State," *Political Science Quarterly* 108, 3 (Fall 1993): 407.

101. For a thorough history of the emergence of the "tax reform faction" of the "tax community" and the significance of its contribution to the discourses of tax reform, see Zelizer, chap. 9.

102. Wilbur Mills, "The Prospects for Tax Reform in the 93rd Congress," *National Public Accountant*, February 1973, quoted in Zelizer, 309–10.

103. The volume and value of this tax spending was, indeed, impressive. Although lawmakers had used tax code to support certain groups or activities since the beginning of the federal income tax in 1913, the value of these tax expenditures, as they were known, increased exponentially with the growth of the U.S. taxing state after World War II. These special tax rates, exemptions, deductions, deferrals did not provide tax breaks only to well-connected companies and individuals; they also underwrote such social welfare goals as income security, home ownership, and access to child care. By spending through the tax code, lawmakers had managed to achieve certain social goals without creating new programs or appropriating additional funds. Usually attached to a massive tax bill, tax expenditures generated little political conflict and often escaped the public's notice. Tax spending became increasingly popular with both Democratic and Republican lawmakers in the 1950s and 1960s, as the political costs associated with new or expanded direct spending increased. See Christopher Howard, *The Welfare State Nobody Knows: Debunking Myths About U.S. Social Policy* (Princeton, N.J.: Princeton University Press, 2007), chap.1; also W. Elliot Brownlee, "Tax Regimes, National Crisis and State-Building in America," in *Funding the Modern American State, 1941–1995: The Rise and Fall of the Era of Easy Finance*, ed. W. Elliott Brownlee (Washington, D.C.: Woodrow Wilson Center Press, 1996), 98–99.

104. Economic Affairs Committee, Democratic Policy Council, 1972, "Issues and Alternatives in Economic Policy," NPMP, WHCF, SMOF, Herbert Stein, Box 49, File: Memoranda.

105. George McGovern, "A Balanced Full Employment Economy," Remarks to New York Society of Social Security Analysts, 29 August 1972, WHS, GWP, Box 32, File 9: Politics, U.S. Presidential Campaign, 1972.

106. Joseph Pechman and Benjamin Okner, *Individual Income Tax Erosion by Income Class*, in Joint Economic Committee, *Economics of Federal Subsidy Programs: Part I, General Study Papers*, 92nd Cong., 2nd sess., 8 May 1972 (Washington, D.C.: U.S. GPO, 1972), 26.

107. Benjamin Okner, in Joint Economic Committee, Subcommittee on Priorities and Economy in Government, *Economics of Federal Subsidy: Hearings*, 92nd Cong., 1st sess., 13, 14, 17 January 1972 (Washington D.C.: GPO, 1972), 66.

108. Surrey quoted in Tony Bennett, Memorandum to George A. Wiley, 15 March

1973, "3/13/73: The Tax Reform Dinner—Some Skimby Notes," in WHS, GWP, Box 42, File 8: Tax Justice Project '73.

109. Musgrave quoted in ibid.

110. George A. Wiley, "notes on Trip to Milwaukee, Wisconsin," 8 May 1973, WHS, GWP, Box 42, File 4, also cited in Chappell, 124.

111. Mike Barnes, Letter to CAL Supporters, "What Is CAL?" 23 July 1975, WHS, MEJ, Box 18, File 2: TJP, BKGR, State Organizations, CAL.

112. "Mauled by Federal Programs, Steps Urged to Ease Middle-Class Tax Burdens," *CQ*, 8 April 1978, 828–33.

113. Michael K. Brown, "The Segmented Welfare State: Distributive Conflict and Retrenchment in the United States, 1968–1984," in *Remaking the Welfare State: Retrenchment and Social Policy in America and Europe*, ed. Michael K. Brown (Philadelphia: Temple University Press, 1988), 198.

114. The national media description of the middle and working classes shifted in the mid-1970s. Where the late 1960s and early 1970s had seen a proliferation of almost hysterical warnings about the potentially violent frustration and anger of the Silent Majority, by 1974 these narratives had been supplanted by stories about a broad middle class squeezed by high taxes and a rising cost of living. The Middle American of the mid-1970s was not the blue-collar worker featured in the first wave of stories, but a "young magazine editor in the Midwest," a "Pittsburgh stockbroker," or a "Philadelphia public relations executive." *U.S. News and World Report* called the "middle class" an "Everyman's—or Everywoman's—Club, open to almost anyone who wants to join, whether secretary, teacher, lawyer, welder, cab driver or store keeper." *Business Week* likewise concluded that the "middle class now includes everyone from plumbers, truck drivers, and mechanics to engineers and middle managers." See "Squeeze on America's Middle Class: A Special Report," *U.S. News and World Report*, 14 October 1974, 42; "Middle Class Squeeze," *Business Week*, 10 March 1975, 54.

115. "Nixon Proves It's Time for Tax Justice," *Memo from* COPE, 4 February 1974, in WHS, MEJ, Box 20, File 5: TJP BKGR Taxes, Loopholes, Who Gets Them and What They Cost.

116. Russell Barta, "Are the Rules Changing," *America*, 20 October 1971, 345, quoted in Chappell, 114.

117. Tax Action Project, Working Group Discussion Paper (Confidential) 7 June 1973, WHS, MEJ, Box 17, File: 4: TJP BKGR Nat'l Organizations—Tax Action Campaign—Fred Harris.

118. "Nixon Proves It's Time for Tax Justice."

119. Chappell, 141.

120. Patrick Buchanan to H. R. Haldeman, "Dividing the Democrats," 5 October 1971, NPMP, WHSF, SMOF, Patrick Buchanan (hereafter PB), Box 1, File: June, 1971.

121. Patrick Buchanan, Memorandum to the President, 3 April 1972, NPMP, WHSF, SMOF, PB, Box 2, File: April 1972.

122. Ed Harper to JDE, Confidential Memorandum re Taxes and Analysis of Poll Data, 23 November 1971, NPMP, WHCF, SMOF, Herbert Stein, Box 49, File: Memoranda.

123. Louis Harris, "President Trailing on Issue of Taxes," *Chicago Tribune*, 9 October 1972, in WHS, MEJ, Box 17, File 4: BKG, National Organizations, Tax Action, Harris.

124. U.S. House Committee on Ways and Means, *Message from the President on Tax Reform*, 91st Cong., 1st sess., 21 April 1969 (Washington, D.C.: GPO, 1969), 4.

125. The VAT then under consideration by the administration would provide an income tax credit for taxpayers earning up to $8,000 a year or a refund to about 25 million taxpayers in order to make it roughly proportional. It would net about $5.1 billion for each percentage point of tax—meaning that a 5 percent VAT would net about $25.5 billion. The proposal specified certain reforms to the existing tax structure, reducing the net gain from the new tax to about $9 billion for new expenditures. The proposed reforms included $5 billion in revenue sharing, $4 billion for depreciation reform, a $3 billion proposal for tax credits to defray tuition costs, about $500 million for child care allowances and $3.5 billion for the integration of personal and corporate taxes. Memorandum for the President, 3 December 1970, Information, Value Added Tax, NPMP, WHCF, Subject Files, FI, Box 58, File: EX FI 1, Taxation, October–December 1970.

126. John Huntsman to JDE, Memorandum, "Re: HR 1," 30 October 1971, NPMP, WHSF, SMOF, JDE, Alphabetical Subject Files, Box 18, File: Scrapbook 1 of 1.

127. John Connally, Memorandum to the Honorable John D. Ehrlichman, Re: Tax Reform Issue, 12 May 1972, NPMP, WHCF, Subject Files, FI, Box 60, File: EX VI, 11, Taxation, March–May 1972.

128. Harris, "President Trailing on Issue of Taxes."

129. Herb Stein to President Nixon, "Re: The Economy at Early June," 8 June 1972, NPMP, WHCF, SMOF, Herbert Stein, Box 45, File: Memoranda for the President, 2 of 4.

130. Patrick Buchanan and Kenneth Khachigian, "Assault Strategy," June 8, 1972, NPMP, WHSF, SMOF, PB, Box #2, File: June 1972.

131. Patrick Buchanan to Julie Eisenhower, 17 July 1972, NPMP, WHSF, SMOF, PB, Box 2, File: July 1972.

132. Telephone conversation between Ehrlichman and George Shultz relating to conversation between Shultz and George Meany, NPMP, WHSF, SMOF, JDE, Box 28, File: August 1972. Meany's refusal to offer his endorsement to McGovern reflected and exacerbated the class fissures in the Democratic Party. Having lost the battle to get hawkish Sen. Henry "Scoop" Jackson (D-Wash.) or even moderate Edmund Muskie (D-Me.) to head the Democratic ticket; outraged by the diminution of organized labor power to influence the party's nomination process, Meany complained volubly that the party had abandoned economic liberalism for social liberalism. "The presidential campaign," he asserted a week before the election, "has confirmed and strengthened my deep conviction that the best interests of the working people of the Democratic Party

and of the United States call for the repudiation of George McGovern." Meany, "Statement," 25 October 1972, NPMP, WHSF, SMOF, PB, Box 2, File: October 1972.

133. Buchanan and Khachigian.

Chapter 5. Game Over

1. "Game Satirizing Life on Welfare Draws Criticism, but Sells Well," *NYT*, 30 November 1980, 60; Nicholas Lemann, "Cheat Thrills and 'Public Assistance,'" *Washington Post*, 11 November 1980, B1; U.S. Court of Appeals, 2nd Ct., *Hammerhead Enterprises Inc. v. Brezenoff*, 28 April 1983, http://openjurist.org/707/f2d/33.

2. Hammerhead Enterprises, *Public Assistance: Why Work for a Living When You Can Play This Great Welfare Game*, 1980, author's personal collection.

3. Lemann, B3.

4. *Hammerhead Enterprises v. Brezenoff*, 6. The racial and gender politics in *Public Assistance* were hard to miss. Many of the chance situations—"pitch pennies all day," "Lincoln needs a new paint job," "Finance company repossesses your Cadillac," not to mention repeated references to illegitimacy—drew on racial stereotypes about African Americans. Not surprisingly, the NAACP urged members to boycott stores that sold the game. NOW condemned the game for "perpetuat[ing] myths and totally misrepresent[ing] the role of women on welfare." Chief of the New York City Human Resources Agency, Stanley Brezenoff, attacked the game as an "ugly and damaging slam at . . . society's poorest citizens" that did a "grave injustice to taxpayers and welfare clients alike." Carter administration Health and Human Services secretary Patricia Harris criticized its racism and sexism and dismissed it as a "vicious brand of stereotyping." See *Hammerhead Enterprises, Inc. v. Brezenoff*, 9 and Footnote n2.

5. Lemann. B3.

6. "Game Satirizing."

7. Republican National Committee, Research Division, *Fact Book 1978*, August 1978, in Paul L. Kesaris, ed., *Papers of the Republican Party* (Frederick, Md.: University Publications of America, 1987), Reel 14, Frame: 0252–0254.

8. John Palmer and Isabel Sawhill, "Overview," in *The Reagan Record: An Assessment of America's Changing Domestic Priorities*, Urban Institute Study (Cambridge, Mass.: Ballinger, 1984), 4.

9. Carol Horton, *Race and the Making of American Liberalism* (New York: Oxford University Press, 2005), 193.

10. For more on this "democratic dilemma," see Julian Zelizer, "The Uneasy Relationship: Democracy, Taxes, and State Building Since the New Deal," in *The Democratic Experiment: New Directions in American Political History*, ed. Meg Jacobs, William J. Novak, and Julian Zelizer (Princeton, N.J.: Princeton University Press, 2003), 276–300.

11. As numerous historians have recently pointed out, this "victimization narrative" developed first at the grass roots, in local battles over neighborhood and school inte-

gration, as well as in local tax politics. See, e.g., Kevin Kruse, *White Flight: Atlanta and Modern Conservatism* (New York: Oxford University Press, 2000); Matthew D. Lassiter, *The Silent Majority: Suburban Politics in the Sunbelt South* (Princeton N.J.: Princeton University Press, 2006); Thomas Sugrue, *The Origins of the Urban Crisis: Race and Inequality in Postwar Detroit* (Princeton, N.J.: Princeton University Press, 1996).

12. Leonard Silk, "The Battle over Taxes," *NYT*, 23 September 1976, 72. Carter's political misstep was compounded by a transmission error in the AP dispatch that omitted Carter's promise to lower taxes on "middle-income taxpayers," and his apparent confusion over the difference between "mean" and "median" income.

13. Ronald Reagan, "Remarks at the Annual Meeting of the United States Chamber of Commerce," 22 April 1982, *Public Papers of the Presidents*, 516, quoted in Marissa Chappell, "From Welfare Rights to Welfare Reform: The Politics of AFDC, 1964–1984" (Ph.D. dissertation, Northwestern University, 2002), 244.

14. Ronald Reagan, First Inaugural Address, Washington, D.C., 20 January 1981, in Gerhard and Peters, 43130.

15. In general, wage inflation lags price inflation. In 1973, for example, the Consumer Price Index increased by 8.7 percent; hourly wages for the same period increased by only 6.2 percent.

16. Robert J. Samuelson, *The Great Inflation and Its Aftermath: The Past and Future of American Affluence* (New York: Random House, 2008), 22–23.

17. Theodore White, *America in Search of Itself: The Making of the President, 1956–1980* (New York: Harper and Row, 1982), 155.

18. Carl Everett Ladd and Seymour Martin Lipset, "Public Opinion and Public Policy," in *The United States in the 1980s*, ed. Peter Duignan and Alvin Rabushka (Stanford, Calif.: Hoover Institution, 1980), 77.

19. A 1976 study of 2,000 families found that although middle- and upper-income Americans had "little difficulty keeping up with rising prices," inflation and economic insecurity threatened their "plans for the future." See David Caplovitz, "Making Ends Meet: How Families Cope with Inflation and Recession," *Annals of the American Academy of Political and Social Science* 456, (July 1981): 88–98. On meat boycotts and consumer politics, see Meg Jacobs, *Pocketbook Politics: Economic Citizenship in the Twentieth Century* (Princeton, N.J.: Princeton University Press, 2005); Lizabeth Cohen, *A Consumers' Republic: The Politics of Mass Consumption in Postwar America* (New York: Knopf, 2003).

20. Stuart Eizenstadt quoted in John Herbers, "Deep Government Disunity Alarms Many U.S. Leaders," *NYT*, 12 November 1978, 1, 78.

21. Quoted in Ladd and Lipset, 77.

22. Caplovitz, 97.

23. American National Election Studies (ANES), Title, table 5A.3, http://www.electionstudies.org/. ANES asked respondents: "Do you think that people in the government waste a lot of money we pay in taxes, waste some of it, or don't waste very much of it?" Over the entire survey period (1958–2004), the vast majority of respondents an-

swered, "a lot" or "some." Between 1964 and 1980, however, the number of people who thought the government wasted only "some" of the tax money dropped from 44 to 18 percent.

24. Postwar liberal dominance had been sustained in part by economic growth and widespread faith in Keynesian macroeconomic management. With "stagflation" in the 1970s, the "expert consensus" that had developed around a modified Keynesian fiscal management agenda dissolved in the face of intractable inflation and unemployment. As Nixon economic advisor Herbert Stein later pointed out, a host of "respectable options" became available to politicians concerned both to address the weaknesses in the economy and to sustain their electoral base. Herbert Stein, "The Fiscal Revolution in America, Part II," in *Funding the Modern American State, 1941–1995: The Rise and Fall of the Era of Easy Finance*, ed. W. Elliot Brownlee (Washington, D.C.: Woodrow Wilson Center Press, 1996), 266.

25. Thomas B. Edsall, *The New Politics of Inequality* (New York: Norton, 1984), 17.

26. Jimmy Carter, quoted in Edward Cowan, "President Submits Tax-Cut Plan for 'Fairer and Simpler' System," *NYT*, 22 January 1978, 1.

27. David Rosenbaum, "Tax Cut Urged on Incomes Below $100,000," *NYT*, 22 January 1978, 32.

28. Robert Reinhold, "Urban League Fights $25 billion Tax Cuts," *NYT*, 18 January 1978, A15.

29. Edward Cowan, "Ullman Opposes Plans to Tighten Business Expense Account Taxes," *NYT* 19 January 1978, A1.

30. In March, Sen. Edmund Muskie (D-Me.), chairman of the Senate Budget Committee, leaked a new Congressional Budget Office report on tax expenditures. Taxpayers with annual incomes over $50,000, the CBO found, had received almost one-third of the money "spent" through the federal tax code in 1977. Like Secretary Barr's testimony in 1969 about the coming "tax revolt," Muskie's release of the CBO report was designed in large part to arouse the anger of the middle-class taxpayer against the unfair tax advantages of those at the upper end of the income scale. This time, however, the report went largely unnoticed.

31. "Carter Aides Plead Case for Economic Plan," *CQ*, 4 February 1978, 273–74.

32. "Edward Cowan, "President and House Democrats Discuss Tax Cut Without Reform," *NYT*, 22 April 1978, 1.

33. Robert Brandon, quoted in "Congress Approves $18.7 Billion," 3027; Public Citizen, Letter, 5 October 1979, NARA, SFC, 95th Congress, House Bills Referred to Senate Committee, Box 9 of 9, No File.

34. "The Year in Review: Foreign Policy, Economics, Defense, Top 1978 Key Votes," *CQ*, 25 November 1978, 3335.

35. Steiger died of a heart attack less than six months after the passage of the 1978 Revenue Act. See Richard Haloran, "Rep. William A. Steiger, Hailed as New GOP Hope, Dies at 40," *NYT*, 5 December 1978, B19.

36. Treasury Secretary Michael Blumenthal described the Steiger Amendment as the "fat-cat amendment" in a May letter to the thirty-seven members of the House Ways and Means Committee, cited in Thomas Mullaney, "Economic Scene: Standing Ground on Capital Gains," *NYT*, 19 May 1978, D2; he used the term "Millionaires' Relief Act" in late June, cited in Edward Cowan, "Plan to Cut Gains Tax Draws Fire," *NYT*, 29 June 1978, D1. See also Clyde Farnsworth, "Momentum for Tax Cut: A Lower Ceiling on Capital Gains Levies Wins Paradoxical Level of Political Support," *NYT*, 17 July 1978, D3.

37. See Robert M. Collins, *More: The Politics of Growth in the Postwar United States* (New York: Oxford University Press, 2000), 179–82.

38. Jude Wanniski, "The Mundell-Laffer Hypothesis—A New View of the World Economy?" *Public Interest* 39 (Spring 1975): 31.

39. In 1827, Say wrote, "Taxation pushed to the extreme has the lamentable effect of impoverishing the individual without enriching the state . . . taxes paid to the government by the subject are not refunded by its expenditures—[government] never can replace the value [taken] because it produces no value whatever." Jean Baptiste Say, *A Treatise on Political Economy*, trans. C. R. Prinsep, from 4th ed. (London: Grigg Elliot, 1827), 412, 378. See also Paul Craig Roberts, *The Supply-Side Revolution: An Insider's Account of Policymaking in Washington* (Cambridge, Mass.: Harvard University Press, 1984), 20; Norman B. Ture, "The Department of the Treasury," in *Mandate for Leadership: Policy Management in a Conservative Administration*, ed. Charles Heatherly (Washington, D.C.: Heritage Foundation, 1981), 648.

40. Ture, 648. Ture pulled no punches in his dismissal of Keynesian demand management: "Supply-side economics rejects the whole demand-side approach. No real increase in income can occur unless there is a change in the real output. No change in real output can occur unless there is a change in the supply of labor and/or capital. Tax cuts alone cannot increase real disposable income and spending. Any such increase will occur only if the tax cuts first affect the incentives to supply labor and capital, resulting in an increase in the use of these production inputs, more real output and hence more real income" (650).

41. Collins, 182.

42. For more on the growth of this conservative counterestablishment, see Alice O'Connor, "Financing the Counterrevolution," in *Rightward Bound: Making America Conservative in the 1970s*, ed. Bruce Schulman and Julian Zelizer (Cambridge, Mass.: Harvard University Press, 2008); Steven Teles, "Conservative Mobilization Against Entrenched Liberalism," in *The Transformation of American Politics: Activist Government and the Rise of Conservatism*, ed. Paul Pierson and Theda Skocpol (Princeton, N.J.: Princeton University Press, 2007), 160–88.

43. John Brooks, "Annals of Finance: The Supply Side," *New Yorker*, 18 April 1982, 100. Wanniski is the only one who remembers this meeting or the drawing on the napkin.

44. Wanniski, quoted in ibid., 104.

45. Norman Miller, "Tax Cut Plan Gives GOP a New Issue—And a New Face, *Wall Street Journal*, 9 September, 1978 1.

46. Brooks, 106.

47. Rep. William Steiger (R.-Wisc.), quoted in Edward Cowan: "Issue and Debate: Capital Gains Tax: Wealth, Egalitarianism, the Economy, *NYT*, 9 June 1978, D3; Cowan, "Blumenthal Assails Bill Designed to Cut Capital Gains Tax, *NYT*, 16 May 1978, 47; Cowan, "Plan to Cut Gains Tax Draws Fire," *NYT*, 29 July 1978, D1.

48. Prepared Statement of National Association of Manufacturers, Senate Committee on Finance, *Hearings: HR 13270: To Reform the Income Tax Laws*, 4, 5 September 1978, 91st Cong., 1st sess. (Washington, D.C.: GPO, 1978), 229.

49. Prepared Statement of Jack Carlson, Chief Economist, National Chamber of Commerce in Senate Committee on Finance, *Hearings: HR 13270*, 246.

50. Cowan, "Blumenthal Assails Bill."

51. Eugene McCarthy, "Capital Gains and Carter's Economics," *Washington Evening Star*, 13 August 1978, reprinted in *Hearings: H.R. 13270*, 203–4.

52. "Rich, Poor, and Taxes," *Washington Post*, 2 June 1978, A16.

53. "How to Unsoak the Rich," *NYT*, 19 May 1978, A26.

54. Prepared Testimony of Andrew Biemiller, Legislative Director, AFL, CIO, *Hearings: H.R. 13270*, 427–28.

55. Statement of Leon Shull, on Behalf of Americans for Democratic Action, *Hearings: H.R. 13270*, 500–501.

56. Mullaney; Blumenthal quoted in Cowan, "Issue and Debate."

57. President Jimmy Carter, News Conference, 26 June 1978, "Transcript of President's News Conference on Foreign and Domestic Matters," *NYT*, 27 June 1978, A12.

58. Farnsworth.

59. Text of S. 125, Sunset Tax Act, Library of Congress, http://thomas.loc.gov.

60. For a history of "tax expenditures," as well as an analysis of their share of the federal budget, see Senate Committee on the Budget, *Tax Expenditures: Relationship to Spending Programs, Background Material on Individual Provisions*, 95th Cong., 2nd sess., September 1978, Committee Print. See also Christopher Howard, "The Hidden Side of the American Welfare State," *Political Science Quarterly* 108, 3 (1993): 403–36.

61. This provision was part of the 1974 Budget Act. For more, see Howard.

62. Sen. Edward Kennedy (D-Mass.) speaking on behalf of the "Glenn Amendment" to the Tax Reform Act of 1978, *Congressional Record*, 95th Cong., 2nd sess., 7 October 1978, 34510–12.

63. Sen. John Glenn (D-Ohio) on behalf of "Glenn Amendment," 34520.

64. Sen. Lloyd Bentsen (D-Tex.) against "Glenn Amendment," 34524.

65. Sen. Ted Stevens (R-Alaska) against "Glenn Amendment," 34529.

66. Ibid, 34530.

67. Sen. Clifford Hansen (R-Wyo.) against "Glenn Amendment," 34530.

68. Milton Friedman, "What Belongs to Whom," *Newsweek*, 13 March 1978, 71.

The phrase "Do Not Fold, Spindle or Mutilate," a warning on IBM "punch cards," became in the 1960s a rallying cry against alienation, abstraction, oversimplification, and dehumanization. The first overtly political use of the phrase came in the early 1960s by members of the Free Speech Movement on the University of California Berkeley campus. See Steven Lubar, "'Do Not Fold, Spindle, or Mutilate: A Cultural History of the Punch Card," *Journal of American Culture* 15, 4 (Winter 1992): 43–55.

69. Ladd and Lipset, 65.

70. Farnsworth.

71. Recent research has demonstrated that a high degree of political trust is necessary to sustain redistributive programs that require a majority to make financial sacrifices to pay for programs—like welfare or food stamps—that provide visible benefits to only a small minority. Trust is even more important when programs are perceived to assist "undeserving" groups "likely to waste whatever government money they receive." Low levels of trust are likely to make citizens less supportive of redistributive policies. See Marc J. Hetherington, *Why Trust Matters: Declining Political Trust and the Demise of American Liberalism* (Princeton, N.J.: Princeton University Press, 2005), 83; John T. Scholz and Mark Lubell, "Adaptive Political Attitudes: Duty, Trust, and Fear as Monitors of Tax Policy," *American Journal of Political Science* 42, 3 (1998): 903–20; Monica Prasad, *The Politics of Free Markets: The Rise of Neoliberal Economic Policies in Britain, France, Germany, and the United States* (Chicago: University of Chicago Press, 2006).

72. Proposition 13 accomplished this in several ways. It required local California governments to limit property tax rates to 1 percent of assessed value. It returned assessments to 1975 levels and restricted future assessment increase to 2 percent per year (until the event of a sale). Finally, it required a legislative supermajority of two-thirds for any future tax increases. In recent years, some scholars have claimed that Proposition 13 and its success were responsible for "turning" the "tax revolt" to the right. Although Proposition 13 was important, it was not decisive and did not by itself transform the politics of taxation in the United States. The "right turn" was already apparent in Congress's rejection of the modestly redistributive reform proposals suggested by President Carter. What is more, as the previous chapter argued, GOP legislators and conservative political entrepreneurs had begun developing a tax cut agenda to woo the "Silent Majority" into the Republican fold in the early 1970s. Proposition 13 did, however, serve as a "focusing event" for legislators that "tax cuts could be a political winner." As Everett Carl Ladd pointed out in 1979, the fact that "more than a few political leaders" were then "*acting* as though public resistance to taxation has stiffened markedly" was "in itself enormously consequential to the tax revolt—quite apart from what mass public opinion politics are." Perhaps most important, as Elliot Brownlee and Gene Steurle have argued, Proposition 13's success convinced Reagan that "the time had . . . come to focus the movement to limit government around middle-class protests over taxes." See Everett Carl Ladd, Jr., with Marilyn Potter, Linda Basilick, Sally Daniels, and Dana Suszkiw, "The Polls: Taxing and Spending," *Public Opinion Quarterly* 43, 1 (Spring 1979): 178; Isaac Martin, *The Permanent Tax Revolt: How the Property Tax Transformed American Politics* (Stanford,

Calif.: Stanford University Press, 2008); Brownlee and Steuerle, "Taxation," in *The Reagan Presidency: Pragmatic Conservatism and Its Legacies*, ed. W. Elliot Brownlee and Hugh Davis Graham (Lawrence: University Press of Kansas, 2003), 157.

73. Jimmy Breslin, "Prop. 13: The Shot Heard Round America," *Los Angeles Times*, 5 June 1978, C7; Roscoe Drummond, "Tax Revolt: The Political Impact," *Christian Science Monitor*, 28 June 1978, 23.

74. Bill Peterson, "GOP Plans 'Blitz' to Push Tax Cut Bill," *Washington Post*, 7 July 1978, A4.

75. According to *Washington Post* columnist Art Pine, Proposition 13 signaled a "fundamental shift in the national outlook . . . the end of the share the wealth philosophy of the late 1960s and its willingness to enact new social programs that redistribute income to the poor." Proposition 13 supporters, like Jude Wanniski, routinely lauded the tax limitation movement as an "exhilarating adventure in democracy" that signaled the citizenry's rebuke of a "political class" that had "failed to do its job." See Art Pine, "Revolt Against Taxes . . . And Performance," *Washington Post*, 11 June 1978, H1; Jude Wanniski, "The California Tax Revolt," *Wall Street Journal*, 24 May 1978, 22.

76. Ladd et al., 127.

77. Jack Citrin, "Do People Want Something for Nothing? Public Opinion on Taxes and Government Spending," *National Tax Journal: Proceedings of a Conference on Tax and Expenditure Limitations* 32, 2 (June 1979): 127, 117. For more on voters' attitudes toward taxing and spending, as well as the relative popularity of federal, state, and local governments and taxes, see ACIR, *1980: Changing Public Attitudes on Governments and Taxes, a Commission Survey* (Washington, D.C.: GPO, 1980).

78. Cited in Ladd et al., 130.

79. "'Welfare Queen' Becomes Issue in Reagan Campaign," *NYT*, 15 January 1976, 51. The woman in question, Linda Taylor, was ultimately found guilty of welfare fraud and perjury. But the Circuit Court determined only that she had used two aliases to collect 23 public assistance checks worth $8,000. See "Chicago Relief 'Queen' Guilty," *NYT*, 19 March 1977, 8; Hetherington, 76–78.

80. Quoted in Sally Quinn, "Proposition Man: Howard Jarvis, the Tax Fighter, Is Riding High on Number 13," *Washington Post*, 29 June 1978, B1.

81. This belief was somewhat warranted, at least in the short term, in California, where the state had amassed a $5 billion surplus due largely to inflation. Voters believed the state could use this money to offset the revenues lost due to Proposition 13. See William Oakland, "Proposition 13—Genesis and Consequences," *National Tax Journal* 32, 2, supplement: Proceedings of a Conference on Tax and Expenditure Limitations, Held at the University of California, Santa Barbara, 14–15 December 1978 (June 1979): 387.

82. Mervin Field, "Sending a Message: Californians Strike Back," *Public Opinion* 1, 1 (July–August 1978): 5.

83. Yard signs pictured in "Revolt over Taxes," *Time*, 5 June 1978, 12.

84. Republican National Committee, Public Affairs Division, *The Carter Record*, August 1979, in *Papers of the Republican Party*, Reel 15, Frame 01165.

85. Proposition 13 placards pictured in *Newsweek*, 19 June 1978.

86. See Robert O. Self, *American Babylon: Race and the Struggle for Postwar Oakland* (Princeton, N.J.: Princeton University Press, 2003).

87. Conservative tax politics had decided racial implications. Eager to expand its electoral base among white working- and middle-class voters turned off by the "excesses" of both the Civil Rights revolution and the racist defenders of the Jim Crow status quo, the GOP perfected a putatively color-blind but deeply race-laden politics that pitted the legitimate rights of the implicitly white nonpoor majority against the illegitimate rights claims of the implicitly nonwhite poor minority. Where Democrats wanted to target federal dollars on "special groups," Republicans wanted to use federal funds to "help all Americans." Where Democrats relied on "expanded welfare, government jobs and racial preferences" to assure African Americans' social and economic advancement, Republicans promised to "remove barriers . . . to give low-income people, including blacks, and all Americans, more choice." Mobility for all Americans, the GOP promised, could best be provided not through government handouts but through the miracle of the market. Ronald Reagan told the NAACP early in his first term, the "well-being of blacks, like the well-being of every American is linked directly to the health of the economy." Though first advanced by racial liberals concerned to increase the nation's commitment to urban African Americans, conservatives easily captured this cultural discourse and turned it to quite a different purpose: containment of the welfare state and delegitimation of racial liberalism. For a contemporary example of the GOP "race-neutral" embrace of the market see RNC, *Fact Book 1978*. Reel 15, Frame 0295–0298; Ronald Reagan, "Remarks in Denver, Colorado, at the Annual Convention of the National Association for the Advancement of Colored People," 29 June 1981, *Public Papers of the President*, 575–76, quoted in Chappell, 247. For a critique of the racial politics of both left and right, see Daryl Michael Scott, *Contempt and Pity: Social Policy and the Image of the Damaged Black Psyche, 1880–1996* (Chapel Hill: University of North Carolina Press, 1997). See also essays in Michael K. Brown, ed., *Whitewashing Race: The Myth of a Colorblind Society* (Berkeley: University of California Press, 2003).

88. See Charles Murray, *Losing Ground: American Social Policy, 1950–1980* (New York: Basic Books, 1984).

89. George Gilder, *Wealth and Poverty* (New York: Basic Books, 1981), xii, 128, 135. Gilder and Murray were hardly alone. In the mid-1970s, a group of conservative intellectuals—housed in the new "counterestablishment" of conservative think tanks— reinterpreted the meaning of race in a way linked to the basic premises and promises of American liberalism. This new paradigm melded the race and class divisions of the 1970s by reversing Gunnar Myrdal's analysis of the "American dilemma." Neoconservative intellectuals, many of them disaffected leftists, developed a race- and class-laden analysis that defined affirmative action policies—including welfare programs designed to mitigate socioeconomic inequalities—as the moral equivalent of Jim Crow. Because these programs—whether they endorsed "quotas" in hiring or college admissions, or entailed redistribution of wealth from "haves" to "have-nots"—sacrificed the legitimate

rights of individuals in the name of the suspect rights claims of groups, they represented an unacceptable violation of the basic principles of American liberalism. This new conservative position accepted the Civil Rights and Voting Rights Acts' promise of political and civil citizenship for African Americans, but insisted that the elimination of de jure discrimination had fulfilled the mandates of the American Creed. With formal structures of racial discrimination putatively eliminated, the continued disadvantage of the African American poor could be attributed best to cultural deficiency or to the natural and normal—albeit regrettable—consequences of a free-market economic order. See Gunnar Myrdal, *An American Dilemma: The Negro Problem and Modern Democracy* (New York: HarperCollins, 1944). For the conservative "counterestablishment," see Edsall; Joel Rodgers and Thomas Ferguson, *Right Turn: The Decline of the Democrats and the Future of American Politics* (New York: Hill and Wang, 1986); Carol Horton, *Race and the Making of American Liberalism* (New York: Oxford University Press, 2005). For the "color-blind" ethos, see Matthew Lassiter, "Suburban Strategies: The Volatile Center in Postwar American Politics," in *The Democratic Experiment.*

90. For the development of the Sunbelt, see Bruce Schulman, *From Cotton Belt to Sunbelt: Federal Policy, Economic Development, and the Transformation of the South, 1938–1980* (Durham, N.C.: Duke University Press, 1994); on the grassroots development of Sunbelt conservatism, see Lisa McGirr, *Suburban Warriors: The Origins of the New American Right* (Princeton, N.J.: Princeton University Press, 2001).

91. See Schulman and Zelizer, "Introduction," in *Rightward Bound.*

92. White House, Office of the Press Secretary, "Fact Sheet: Fall Budget Program," 24 September 1981, Ronald Reagan Presidential Library (hereafter RRPL), Staff Member Office Files (hereafter SMOF), David Gergen Files, Box 3, File: Economy (June 1981–October 1982).

93. Sen. Bob Dole (R –Kans.), "Memorandum: Summary of the Principal Provisions of the Economic Recovery and Tax Act of 1981, as Agreed to by the Conferees," 1 August 1981, in RRPL, SMOF: Oglesby (Office of Legislative Affairs), Box 3 of 12, File: Misc: Members of Congress.

94. Richard Darman, *Who's in Control? Polar Politics and the Sensible Center* (New York: Simon and Schuster, 1996), 7, quoted in Gareth Davies, "The Welfare State," in *Reagan Presidency,* 211.

95. "Transcript of the President's News Conference on Foreign and Domestic Matters," *NYT,* 14 August 1981, A10.

96. ACIR, *1983: Changing Public Attitudes.*

97. "Transcript of the President's News Conference."

98. Quoted in Robert Mason, *Richard Nixon and the Quest for a New Majority* (Chapel Hill, N.C.: University of North Carolina Press, 2003), 27.

99. For most of the postwar period, the Democratic party had held a distinct advantage as the party best able to keep "the country prosperous"; by May 1981, the Democrats had ceded this advantage to the GOP, when 41 percent of those polled believed the GOP would do a "better job of keeping the country prosperous," as compared to the 28

percent who gave that advantage to the Democratic Party. According to the Gallup Poll, if the GOP could sustain and extend its "margin over the Democratic Party as the party of prosperity," it could look forward to a "major political realignment." Gallup Poll, "May 3: Party Best for Peace and Prosperity," *The Gallup Poll: Public Opinion, 1981* (Wilmington, Del.: Scholarly Resources, 1982), 95–96.

100. ACIR, *1980: Changing Attitudes*, 2.

101. The Kemp-Roth proposal cut marginal income tax rates by 10 percent a year for three years, with the cuts concentrated in the highest income brackets. The proposal also promised to link tax rates to the inflation rate. Program supporters believed that lower tax rates would stimulate productive investment currently discouraged by "confiscatory" tax rates.

102. Susan Hansen, *The Politics of Taxation: Revenue Without Representation* (New York: Praeger, 1983), 86–97, table 3–2.

103. David Gergen, "Briefing Book on the Economic Package," RRPL, SMOF, David Gergen, Box I, File: Briefing Material—Economic Package, 14 April 1981. The "mandate" was critical to the success of the Reagan program. According to historian Gil Troy, the president's advisors understood that mandates were usually more apparent than real—important constructs that "generated both their form" and their "force from expectations." Although most analysts have interpreted the 1980 election as the rejection of an unpopular president, rather than an enthusiastic endorsement of the Reagan program, the White House acted as if the "public" had "sanctioned the search for a new public philosophy to govern America." See Gil Troy, *Morning in America: How Ronald Reagan Invented the 1980s* (Princeton, N.J.: Princeton University Press, 2005), 53–60.

104. In a controversial interview with the *Atlantic*'s William Greider, David Stockman admitted that the "across-the-board" cuts called for by Kemp-Roth and by the ERTA were necessary for political rather than economic reasons. "The hard part of the supply-side tax cut," Stockman confided, "is dropping the top rate from 70 to 50 percent—the rest of it is a secondary matter." According to the OMB director, the "original argument was that the top bracket was too high, and that's having the most devastating effect on the economy. Then, the general argument was that, in order to make this palatable as a political matter, you had to bring down all the brackets. But, I mean, Kemp-Roth was always a Trojan horse to bring down the top rate." See William Greider, "The Education of David Stockman," *Atlantic Monthly*, December 1981.

105. Brownlee and Steuerle, 160.

106. Public Affairs Office, "Some Questions Answered," RLPL, Public Affairs, WHO, Box 2, File: Reagan Program for Economic Recovery.

107. "Draft Budget Speech, 27 April 1982, 8:00 p.m., RRPL, Craig Fuller Files, Series II, Subject Files, 1981–1985, OA 10972, Box 2, File: Economic/Budget Policy, April–May 1982.

108. "Draft: Budget Cutting Principles," 11 February 1981, RRPL, Speechwriting WHOO, Speech Drafts, 1981–1984, Box 2, File: "Address to Joint Session/Economy, 18

February 1981; Thomas M. Humbert, Memorandum, 3, 16–17, 1981, RRPL, SMOF: Edwin Meese, Box 5, File: Tax Bill Materials (5).

109. Reagan, Address to Joint Session; Reagan, "Address of the President to the Nation on the Economy," 5 February 1981, in Gerhard and Peters, 43132. The day after the speech, the Treasury Department sent the White House a list of concerns regarding the economic statistics and theories referenced in the speech. According to the Department analysis, many of the statistics were wrong, misleading, or unverifiable. See David Chew to Ken Khachigian, Memorandum, "Notes on the President's Speech," 6 February 1981, in RLPL, Speechwriting, WHOO, Speech Drafts, 1981–1989, Box 1, File: Address to the Nation (Economy).

110. Gallup Poll, 1981 "March 17: President Reagan," *Gallup Poll*, 59.

111. Andrew Kohut, "April 13: The Fragile Mandate," *Gallup Poll, 1981*, 79–80.

112. Quoted in David Stockman, *The Triumph of Politics: Why the Reagan Revolution Failed* (New York: Harper and Row, 1986), 232.

113. Adam Clymer, "Public Prefers a Balanced Budget to Large Cut in Taxes, Poll Shows," *NYT*, 3 February 1981, A1, B9.

114. Steven V. Roberts, "Congress Chiefs Predict Big Changes in Tax Plan," *NYT*, 10 March 1981, D1.

115. Rep. Ken Holland (D-S.C.) quoted in Steven W. Roberts, "3 Conservative Democrats Wary on Tax Cut," *NYT*, 17 May 1981, 32.

116. Citizens for Tax Justice, "The Reagan Tax Shift: A Report on the Economic Recovery Act of 1981, Part III, Why Did it Happen?" March 1982, 5, RRPL, CEA Records, Box 1 of 5, File: Economic Recovery Act of 1981: Effects (1).

117. Thomas P. O'Neill, *Man of the House: The Life and Political Memoirs of Speaker Tip O'Neill* (London: Bodley Head, 1987), 338, quoted in Davies, 211.

118. Office of the Press Secretary, "Fact Sheet"; Speech Draft on White House Stationery, 1981? (No Date). RRPL, Speechwriting, WHOO, Speech Drafts, 1981–1984, Box 2, File: Address to Joint Session, 18 February 1981.

119. Office of the Press Secretary, "Fact Sheet"; "Memorandum: Key Points on RR's Budget Cuts," RRPL, Public Affairs, WHO, Box 1, File: Reagan Tax Cut Plan (1 of 8).

120. Ronald Reagan, First News Conference on Foreign and Domestic Topics, 29 January 1981, "Transcript of President's First News Conference," *NYT*, 30 January 1981, A10.

121. Quoted in Greider, "The Education of David Stockman." A February 11 draft memorandum on "budget cutting principles" for example, listed eight principles for determining which programs to cut: (1) removing the non-needy; (2) "eliminating middle/high-income subsidies; (3) "eliminating subsidies to business"; (4) "eliminating regional subsidies"; 5) "ending needless duplication"; (6) "converting categorical aid programs into block grants"; (7) "improving cost-effectiveness"; and (8) "terminating counterproductive policies." See "Draft: Budget Cutting Principles."

122. Gergen, "Briefing Book on the Economic Package."

123. Martin Anderson, "The Objectives of the Reagan Administration's Social Welfare Policy," in *The Social Contract Revisited: Aims and Outcomes of President Reagan's Social Welfare Policy*, ed. D. Lee Bawden (Washington, D.C.: Urban Institute Press, 1984), 113.

124. Troy, 71.

125. Palmer and Sawhill, 3.

126. Only about 11 percent of the White House proposals would have affected Social Security, Medicare, or Unemployment Insurance.

127. The thirty-and-a-third provision had been created in 1967 as part of that year's Social Security Amendments. The law, which allowed AFDC recipients to retain the first $30 of any earned income plus one-third of additional earned income without a corresponding decrease in AFDC benefits was intended to provide beneficiaries with a financial incentive to work outside the home. For more, see Nancy E. Rose, *Workfare or Fair Work: Women, Welfare, and Government Work Programs* (New Brunswick, N.J.: Rutgers University Press, 1995), chaps. 4, 5.

128. Palmer and Sawhill, 13; D. Lee Bawden and John L. Palmer, "Social Policy: Challenging the Welfare State," in Palmer and Sawhill, 92.

129. Chappell, 248.

130. Speech Draft on White House Stationery.

131. Bob Carleson, Memorandum for Ed Gray, 19 March 1981, RRPL, Martin Anderson Files, CFOA 88–91, Box 4, File: "Welfare, 2 of 3."

132. Chappell, 260.

133. Palmer and Sawhill, 14.

134. R. Kent Weaver, *Ending Welfare as We Know It* (Washington, D.C.: Brookings Institution Press, 2000), 68.

135. Morton C. Blackwell, Memorandum to Elizabeth Dole re "Outside Support for the President's Economic Package," RLPL, SMOF: Elizabeth Dole, Series I, Box 18, File: Economic Recovery.

136. See Weaver. See also Tom Joe, *By the Few, for the Few: The Reagan Welfare Legacy* (Lexington, Mass.: Lexington Books, 1985).

137. "Draft Issue Alert: General Observations on the Urban Institute Report on *The Reagan Experiment*," 14 September 1982, RRPL, Edwin Meese Files, OA, 9456–9458, Box 25, File: Urban Institute Study: The Reagan Experiment.

138. Congress, House of Representatives, Office of the Majority Leader, "Some Questions and Answers for Democrats," 5 March 1981," RRPL, SMOF Oglesby, Box 4 of 12, File: Democratic Strategy.

139. Tip O'Neill, "Speaker's Statement: Press Conference," 8 April 1981, RRPL, Oglesby, Office of Legislative Affairs, Box 4 of 12, File: Democratic Strategy.

140. Steven V. Roberts, "Tax Pressures Illuminate Splits Among Democrats," *NYT*, 2 June 1981, B11.

141. Chamber of Commerce economist Richard Hahn, quoted in Citizens for Tax Justice, "Reagan Tax Shift."

142. Office of the Majority Leader, "Some Questions and Answers for Democrats"; O'Neill, "Speaker's Statement: Press Conference."

143. Edward Cowan, "Democrats Confronting Their Own Tax Dispute," NYT, 15 June 1981, D1–D5; Howell Raines, "On Tax Cuts The President Gives While the Getting Is Good," NYT, 7 June 1981, E1. See also Leonard Silk, "Economic Scene: Tax Writers' Christmas Tree," NYT, 26 January 1981, D2.

144. Gallup Poll, "June 7: Reagan's Economic Plan," Gallup Poll, 1981, 119–23.

145. On 23 July, a group of twelve corporate CEOs visited wavering Democrats to lobby on the tax bill. All twelve agreed "the president must go on TV" to combat the "perception that ours was a rich-man's tax bill." See Elizabeth Dole, Memorandum to Ed Meese, Jim Baker, Michael Deaver, and Max Friedersdorf, "Re Intelligence on the Tax Bill, 23 July 1982, 1:30 p.m., RRPL, SMOF, Oglesby, Office of Legislative Affairs, Box 2 of 12, File: Letters/Presidential, 1 of 2.

146. Ronald Reagan, Address to the Nation, 27 July 1981, in RLPL, SMOF: Edwin Meese, Box 5, File: Tax Bill Materials (#3).

147. Rep. Tip O'Neill (D-Mass.) to reporters, from AP report, in RRPL, Oglesby, Office of Legislative Affairs, Box 3 of 12, File: O'Neill's Strategy.

148. C. Eugene Steuerle, The Tax Decade: How Taxes Came to Dominate the Public Agenda (Washington, D.C.: Urban Institute Press, 1991), 42.

149. Grover Norquist, cited in Paul Krugman, "The Tax Cut Con," NYT, 14 September 2003.

150. Jonathan Weisman, "Reagan Policies Gave Green Light to Red Ink," Washington Post, 9 June 2004, A 11.

151. Palmer and Sawhill, 8.

152. Davies, 222.

153. Brownlee and Steuerle, 162, 168; See also Jacob Hacker and Paul Pierson, "Tax Politics and the Struggle over Activist Government," in Pierson and Skocpol, 262–63.

154. Palmer and Sawhill, 16.

155. W. Elliot Brownlee, "Tax Regimes, National Crisis, and State-Building in America" in Brownlee, Funding the Modern American State, 101.

156. Palmer and Sawhill, 9.

157. Paul Pierson, Dismantling the Welfare State? Reagan, Thatcher, and the Politics of Retrenchment (Cambridge: Cambridge University Press, 1994), 169.

158. James Stimson, Public Opinion in America: Moods, Cycles, and Swings, 2nd. ed. (Boulder, Colo.: Westview, 1998), cited in Paul Pierson and Jacob Hacker, Off Center: The Republican Revolution and the Erosion of American Democracy (New Haven, Conn.: Yale University Press, 2006), 38–39.

Epilogue: Stalemate

1. Carl Campanile, "Bam on Guard vs. 'Screw-Up': Warns NY Dems as McCain Zings 'Welfare' Tax Plan," New York Post, 18 October 2008.

2. Glenn Johnson, "McCain Criticizes Obama Tax Plan by Telling Florida Crowds to 'Hold onto Your Wallets," *Associated Press Newswire*, 17 October 2008.

3. Joseph Curl, "McCain Calls Obama's Tax Plan Socialist: Democrat Hits Back, Says Republicans Cuts 'Welfare,' " *Washington Times*, 19 October 2008, A1.

4. Julian Zelizer, "The Uneasy Relationship: Democracy, Taxation, and State Building Since the New Deal," in *The Democratic Experiment: New Directions in American Political History*, ed. Meg Jacobs, William J. Novak, and Julian Zelizer (Princeton, N.J.: Princeton University Press, 2003), 293.

5. Suzanne Mettler, "The Transformed Welfare State and the Redistribution of Political Voice," in *The Transformation of American Politics: Activist Government and the Rise of Conservatism*, ed. Paul Pierson and Theda Skocpol (Princeton, N.J.: Princeton University Press, 2007), 191.

6. C. Eugene Steuerle, *Contemporary U.S. Tax Policy* (Washington, D.C.: Urban Institute Press, 2004), 228.

7. Mettler, 191.

8. For the Tea Party movement and the 2010 Tea Party Convention, see Jonathan Raban, "At the Tea Party," *New York Review of Books* 57, 6 (10 March 2010. On the importance of political trust, see Marc J. Hetherington, *Why Trust Matters: Declining Political Trust and the Demise of American Liberalism* (Princeton, N.J.: Princeton University Press, 2005).

9. ANES, *The ANES Guide to Public Opinion and Political Behavior*, table 5A.5, "Trust in Government Index," http://www.electionstudies.org/nesguide/. The Trust in Government Index combines survey responses to four questions designed to measure the public's trust in government, tables 5A.1–5A.4.

10. ANES, table 5B.2, "People Don't Have a Say in What Government Does." On declining civic participation, see Robert Putnam, *Bowling Alone: The Collapse and Revival of the American Social Community* (New York, Simon and Schuster, 2000).

11. Withdrawal from public life has not been equally distributed. Wealthier and better-educated citizens are for more likely to vote and participate in other political activities than poorer, less-educated citizens. See Suzanne Mettler and Richard B. Freeman, "What, Me Vote?" in *Social Inequality*, ed. Kathryn Neckerman (New York, Sage, 2004), 703–28.

12. On tax expenditures, see Christopher Howard, *The Hidden Welfare State: Tax Expenditures and Social Welfare in the United States* (Princeton, N.J.: Princeton University Press, 1997), and *The Welfare State Nobody Knows: Debunking Myths About U.S. Social Policy* (Princeton, N.J.: Princeton University Press, 2007). On the consequences of the private welfare state, see Jacob Hacker, *The Divided Welfare State: The Battle over Public and Private Social Benefits in the United States* (Cambridge: Cambridge University Press, 2002)

13. For more on ERISA, see Jennifer Klein, *For All These Rights: Business, Labor, and the Shaping of America's Public-Private Welfare State* (Princeton, N.J.: Princeton University Press, 2003). On Title 7 of the Civil Rights Act, see Nancy MacLean, *Freedom Is Not Enough: The Opening of the American Work Place* (New York: Sage, 2006).

14. Hacker, 16.

15. Brian Balogh, "Keep Your Government Hands Off of My Medicare: A Prescription Progressives Should Fill," *Forum* 7, 4 (2009): 1. Of course, Americans are hardly alone in their dislike of new taxes. As Sven Steinmo's cross-national study of the politics of taxation in the U.S., Great Britain, and Sweden suggests, "no one, anywhere, likes the idea of new taxes." See Sven Steinmo, *Taxation and Democracy: Swedish, British, and American Approaches to Financing the Modern State* (New Haven, Conn.: Yale University Press, 1993), chap. 7.

16. On union decisions to pursue fringe benefits in lieu of industrial democracy, see Nelson Lichtenstein, "From Corporatism to Collective Bargaining: Organized Labor and the Eclipse of Social Democracy in the Postwar Era," in *The Rise and Fall of the New Deal Order, 1930–1980*, ed. Gary Gerstle and Steven Fraser (Princeton, N.J.: Princeton University Press, 1989), 144–45.

17. Walter Klodrubetz, Office of Research and Statistics, Department of Health, Education and Welfare, *Growth in Employee Benefit Plans, 1950–1965*, reprinted in House Committee on Ways and Means, *Hearings: President's Proposals for Revision in the Social Security System*, 90th Cong., 1st sess., 20–23 March, 4, 5 April 1967 (Washington, D.C.: GPO, 1967), 403–4.

18. White House Task Force on Income Maintenance (IMTF), Report, 21 November 1966, Lyndon B. Johnson Library, WHCF, Legislative Background on the Social Security Amendments of 1967, Box 1, Report of Income Maintenance Task Force, File: Report of Income Maintenance Task Force.

19. Center for Budget and Policy Priorities, "Strengths of the Safety Net: How the EITC, Social Security, and Other Government Programs Affect Poverty," 9 March 1998, http://www.cbpp.org/archiveSite/snd98–rep., accessed 30 January 2011.

20. Mettler, 212–13. For an analysis of the ways in which social welfare programs can engender political citizenship, see Andrea Louise Campbell, *How Policies Make Citizens: Senior Political Activism and the American Welfare State* (Princeton, N.J.: Princeton University Press, 2003). As studies of the National Welfare Rights Organization have shown, even unpopular, stigmatized, and stingy programs can help to politicize their recipients. Although the NWRO was short-lived and the larger battle for welfare rights has usually been "treated as one of the great errors of postwar history," Felicia Kornbluh's study of the movement suggests the ways in which AFDC, in combination with the black freedom movement, provided welfare recipients with the material and rhetorical resources to exercise their political rights. See Felicia Kornbluh, *The Battle for Welfare Rights: Politics and Poverty in Modern America* (Philadelphia: University of Pennsylvania Press, 2007).

21. Paul Krugman, "Health Care Realities," *NYT*, 31 July 2009, 23.

22. For an example of the "conventional wisdom" that assumes the Democratic Party "wins" on economic issues, see Thomas Frank, *What's the Matter with Kansas: How Conservatives Won the Heart of America* (New York: Metropolitan Books, 2004).

23. Mark A. Smith, "Economic Insecurity, Party Reputations, and the Republican Ascendance," in Pierson and Skocpol, 143, 146–50.

24. Jacob Hacker, *The Great Risk Shift: The Assault on American Jobs, Families, Health Care, and Retirement, and How You Can Fight Back* (New York: Oxford University Press, 2006), 27, 24.

25. Klein, 263.

26. Ben Wattenberg, Memorandum to Douglas Cater, "Talking Points for Monday Speech to AFL-CIO Policy Committee," 4 February 1967, LBJL, Welfare (EX WE 9), Box 28, File: WE 9, 1 January–8 February 1967.

27. On the fiscalization of American politics, see Paul Pierson, *Dismantling the Welfare State? Reagan, Thatcher and the Politics of Retrenchment* (Cambridge: Cambridge University Press, 1994); C. Eugene Steuerle, *The Tax Decade: How Taxes Came to Dominate the Public Agenda* (Washington, D.C.: Urban Institute Press, 1991).

28. Pew Research Center for the People and the Press, *Deconstructing Distrust: How Americans View Government* (1998), http://people-press.org/reports/display .php3?ReportID=95, cited in Howard, *Welfare State Nobody Knows*, 118.

29. Howard, *Welfare State Nobody Knows*, 119.

30. See Advisory Commission on Intergovernmental Relations (ACIR), *1981: Changing Public Attitudes on Governments and Taxes: A Commission Survey* (Washington, D.C.: GPO, 1981), 1.

31. For an overview of the 1996 Welfare Reform Bill, See R. Kent Weaver, *Ending Welfare as We Know It* (Washington, D.C.: Brookings Institution Press, 2000). For a critical analysis of the racial and gender biases in the U.S. state and their relationship to "welfare reform," see Gwendolyn Mink, *Welfare's End* (Ithaca, N.Y.: Cornell University Press, 1998).

32. Steuerle, *Contemporary Tax Policy*, table 3.4, 45.

33. Howard, *Welfare State Nobody Knows*, 99.

34. Christine Smith, *The Earned Income Tax Credit (EITC): An Overview* (Washington, D.C.: Congressional Research Service, 9 May 2009), 8.

35. Terry Neal, "Bush Faults GOP Spending Plan: 'I Don't Think They Ought to Balance Their Budget on the Backs of the Poor,'" *Washington Post*, 1 October 1999, A1.

36. Mettler, 213.

37. Steinmo, 195.

38. On the PAYGO rules adopted in the 1991 Budget Resolution, see Zelizer, 292; Steuerle, *Contemporary Tax Policy*, 162–64.

39. Hacker, *Divided Welfare State*, 315.

40. See Jacob Hacker and Paul Pierson, "Tax Politics and the Struggle over Activist Government," in Pierson and Skocpol, eds., 257–80; Hacker and Pierson, *Off Center: The Republican Revolution and the Erosion of American Democracy* (New Haven, Conn.: Yale University Press, 2005).

41. Quoted in Katrina Van Den Heuvel, "Books of the Times: Cabinet Member Picks His Loyalty and Pays the Price," *NYT*, 4 February 2004, E10.

42. As direct assaults on the welfare state have failed to bear fruit, conservatives have refined their techniques. The budget-busting tax cuts of 2001 and 2003, in com-

bination with a series of prolonged recessions, may have stacked the deck in favor of welfare state retrenchment by so severely "de-funding" the state that any new social spending programs will be out of the question, and even existing systems of social provision may come under threat. The "privatization" agenda, once the province of the radical fringe of the conservative right, has made its way into the mainstream of the Republican Party. Although President George W. Bush's plan to create private retirement accounts as an alternative to Social Security failed as a policy and as a political gambit, the GOP *Roadmap for America's Future* authored by House Budget Committee Ranking Member Paul Ryan (R-Wis.) includes a plan to introduce "private" accounts into the Social Security system, and proposes to replace Medicare, Medicaid, and the Children's Health Insurance Program (CHIP) with a voucher system to enable low-income households, seniors, and people with disabilities to buy private health insurance. For more on the politics of privatization, see Jacob Hacker, "Privatizing Risk Without Privatizing the Welfare State: The Hidden Politics of Social Policy Retrenchment in the United States," *American Political Science Review* 92, 2 (2004): 243–60. For the CBPP analysis of the Ryan *Roadmap*, see Paul N. Van de Water, "The Ryan Budget's Radical Priorities," 10 March 2010, Center for Budget and Policy Priorities, http://www.cbpp.org/cms/index .cfm?fa=view&id=3116.

INDEX

Page references in *italics* refer to illustrations

ACKNOWLEDGMENTS

This book, the product of almost a decade of work, would not have been possible without the support, understanding and inspiration of my colleagues, friends, and family. I have been unbelievably lucky in finding a group of people who will stick around, and even listen attentively, after hearing, "Well . . . it's a book about taxes."

At the University of Michigan, I was fortunate to find in Matthew Lassiter both a friend and a mentor. Matt arrived in Ann Arbor the same year I did, and it was by sheer, dumb luck that I landed in his graduate seminar on suburban America in fall 2000. Matt provided indispensible advice and thoughtful critiques, pushing me down new avenues of research and analysis and toward big ideas. I am forever grateful for his help, and for his belief both in this project, and in me—even when my own faith in both wavered.

My thanks too to Maris Vinovskis, whose careful and often critical readings of early versions of this text forced me to reexamine some of my assumptions, and to clarify my thinking particularly on the relationship between policy and politics. Gina Morantz-Sanchez also provided invaluable assistance in her self-described role as "intelligent reader." Perhaps more important, Gina's and Geoff Eley's seminar introduced me to a whole world of ideas that changed the way that I thought about doing history. For that, I thank them. My thanks also to Tony Chen, who agreed to be a reader even though he hardly knew me, and has since become a friend, and a welcome face in the conference crowd.

I am also indebted to Sonya Rose and Carol Karlsen, and to Tom Guglielmo who got me through my first year of teaching. Friends and colleagues like Lily Geismer, Kathy Worboys, Tamar Carroll, Tamara Walker, Allen J. Ward, Rob MacLean and Todd Robinson, helped make Ann Arbor a better place to live, study, and teach. A special thanks to Kate Luongo, who offered her friendship, her pool, her love of all things *Alias*, and reminded me that it was possible to have a life and complete a project at the same time.

My interest in policy history grew out of both my undergraduate education and my professional experiences as a *very* low-level staffer on Capitol

Hill. A special thanks to Frank Couvares and Martha Saxton who guided my initial forays into historical inquiry at Amherst College. I am also grateful to the wonderful people I met in my all too brief time in Washington, D.C.—a place I still sometimes think of as home. Their commitment and dedication to the business of lawmaking helped to convince me that policy and politics still matter. I would particularly like to thank Marybeth Salomone Testa, Jason Park, and Alyssa Caroselli for their friendship, support and for opening their homes to me when I needed a place to crash during my frequent D.C.-area research trips.

This project would not have been possible without considerable institutional support. Generous financial support from the University of Michigan and the Rackham School of Graduate Studies allowed me to concentrate on my research and to complete it in a relatively short time. The Smithsonian Institution and the National Museum of American History not only underwrote a few months of living in D.C., but also provided me access to the museum's invaluable collection of political ephemera and gave me a desk within spitting distance of Julia Child's kitchen. A research grant from the Lyndon B. Johnson Library allowed me to spend a week in Austin doing the research for chapters two and three. Indeed, this book would not have been possible without the assistance of the librarians and archivists at the Library of Congress Reading Room; the National Archives and Records Administration; the Nixon Presidential Materials Project; the Lyndon B. Johnson Presidential Library; the Ronald Reagan Presidential Library; the Bentley Historical Library at the University of Michigan; and the Wisconsin Historical Society.

I am particularly indebted to the University of Virginia and to the Miller Center for Public Affairs. I was among the first Miller Center Fellows, and benefited immeasurably from the experience. Brian Balogh and Sidney Milkis have truly built something special and deserve much of the credit for a new generation of scholars who take policy and politics seriously. The Miller Center also introduced me to Julian Zelizer, whose work on House Ways and Means Chairman Wilbur Mills and the politics of taxation helped to inspire this book, and who graciously agreed to serve as my faculty mentor for the duration of my fellowship.

I would also like to thank my friends and colleagues at Washington and Lee University for helping to make this book a reality. Like so many others at W&L, I owe a great deal to Gerry Lenfest and his commitment to faculty research and development. The generous support provided by the Lenfest Summer grants allowed me to take research trips to Southern California,

Washington D.C., and Wisconsin and made it possible for me to complete this manuscript. I would also like to thank my colleagues in the W&L history department, especially my three chairs, Ted Delaney, Holt Merchant, and David Peterson, for their support over the last five years. A special thanks to Sarah Horowitz, David Bello, Mark Carey and Jon Eastwood, whose support and friendship has improved both the quality of my life in Lexington and the quality of my work as a teacher and a scholar. I owe a great debt of gratitude to everyone at the University of Pennsylvania Press, and especially to Bob Lockhart. Early on, Bob saw the potential in this study and pushed me, every step of the way, to realize that potential. Without Bob's critical eye, this book would be very much different and very much weaker. My thanks as well to Eileen Boris, Margot Canaday and to everyone, including my good friend Bradley Reichek, who commented on early drafts of this manuscript for their thoughtful suggestions and critiques.

I am incredibly lucky to be part of a supportive and loving family that I actually like. My grandmother, Nancy Williams is the very model of what a politically and socially-engaged citizen should look like. Her vitality, her intellectual curiosity and her commitment to social justice are a constant inspiration and a reminder that one can grow older without growing rigid or dull. My brother Dan is perhaps my favorite person in the world, and certainly one of the funniest people I know. Most people talk to their siblings once or twice a month. I talk to mine whenever something funny, outrageous, or significant happens.

My love and thanks to all of my friends outside of academia who have provided much needed distraction and emotional support throughout this process. I would like particularly to thank my Amherst girls – Tara Kole, Trina Lear Berk, Sloane Furniss, Cyd Stevens. Amanda Arnold Sansone, and Heather "Kess Doggy Dog" Green—who I still, and will likely always, refer to as my roommates.

To my Lexington family—Paul, Lilly and Oreo—thank you for making me laugh and for loving me so much and so well.

Most of all, I would like to thank my mother and father, Chris and David Michelmore, for their unflagging support. Both Mom and Dad read through countless drafts of this manuscript, and offered invaluable advice, concrete suggestions for revision as well much-needed encouragement. Without their help and guidance, I would never have finished this project. I love you both very much. This book is for you.

CPSIA information can be obtained
at www.ICGtesting.com
Printed in the USA
LVHW051558030719
623119LV00016B/710